P9-DFR-434

DECEPTIONS
of WORLD WAR II

DECEPTIONS
of WORLD
WAR II

William B. Breuer

CHARTWELL
BOOKS

3780

Brimming with creative inspiration, how-to projects, and useful information to enrich your everyday life, Quarto Knows is a favorite destination for those pursuing their interests and passions. Visit our site and dig deeper with our books into your area of interest: Quarto Creates, Quarto Cooks, Quarto Homes, Quarto Lives, Quarto Drives, Quarto Explores, Quarto Gifts, or Quarto Kids.

© 2001 by William B. Breuer

This edition published in 2018 by Chartwell Books, an imprint of The Quarto Group, 142 West 36th Street, 4th Floor, New York, NY 10018, USA
T (212) 779-4972 F (212) 779-6058 **www.QuartoKnows.com**

This edition published with permission of and by agreement with Turner Publishing Company, LLC, 4507 Charlotte Ave, Suite 100, Nashville, TN 37209

All rights reserved. No part of this book may be reproduced in any form without written permission of the copyright owners. All images in this book have been reproduced with the knowledge and prior consent of the artists concerned, and no responsibility is accepted by producer, publisher, or printer for any infringement of copyright or otherwise, arising from the contents of this publication. Every effort has been made to ensure that credits accurately comply with information supplied. We apologize for any inaccuracies that may have occurred and will resolve inaccurate or missing information in a subsequent reprinting of the book.

Chartwell Books titles are also available at discount for retail, wholesale, promotional, and bulk purchase. For details, contact the Special Sales Manager by email at specialsales@quarto.com or by mail at The Quarto Group, Attn: Special Sales Manager, 401 Second Avenue North, Suite 310, Minneapolis, MN 55401, USA.

10 9 8 7 6 5 4 3 2 1

ISBN: 978-0-7858-3652-0

Printed in the United States of America

SUSTAINABLE FORESTRY INITIATIVE

Certified Sourcing

www.sfiprogram.org

SFI-01681

Label applied to text stock.

Dedicated to
DESMOND THOMAS DOSS
(1919–   )
A conscientious objector
who refused to carry a weapon
but volunteered for combat
as a medic in World War II.
Seriously wounded on Okinawa,
he was awarded the
Congressional Medal of Honor
for exceptional valor.

Without some dissimulation
No business can be carried on at all.

— Philip Dormer Stanhope,
Earl of Chesterfield
1749

Contents

Introduction

FORCE AND FRAUD have been the two cardinal principles of warfare since Sun Tzu, the Chinese warlord who conquered huge expanses of Asia, recorded his military theories in 550 B.C.: "Undermine the enemy, bewilder and confuse him, strike at his morale, then his army will fall to you."

Many centuries later, both sides in World War II sought to gain military, economic, political, or psychological advantage by an ongoing series of masquerades, intrigue, deceit, and fakery—the fraud equation about which Sun Tzu had written.

The Western Allies (especially the British, later the Americans) and the Germans skillfully blended Sun Tzu's ancient precepts with modern technology to gain even a slight advantage that could mean the difference between victory or defeat.

Cloak-and-dagger agencies in both camps, as well as military commanders, constantly considered schemes and ruses for misleading the enemy, for playing upon his fears, and for disturbing his mental balance. The idea of these masquerades and intrigue was to attract the enemy's attention to what the perpetrator wished him to see and to distract his attention from what he did not wish the enemy to see.

When successful, these ingenious machinations could coerce the enemy to move his forces to the wrong place or to refrain from shifting them to the right place, wasting his effort, time, and manpower.

Countless books have been written about the great battles, strategic designs, high-level decisions, and episodes of courage and boldness in the conventional fighting in World War II. Largely absent has been a comprehensive focus on how masquerades, intrigue, deceit, and fakery were often decisive factors. This book helps fill that reportorial void.

Part One

Heading toward
the Brink

A British Mole in
German Spy School

EARLY IN 1937, Adolf Hitler, four years after he had seized total power in Germany, ordered the Abwehr, the military intelligence branch of the Oberkommando der Wehrmacht (High Command) to create an espionage apparatus in Great Britain. Implementing the project was Colonel Karl Busch, a veteran intelligence officer and head of the Abwehr's Anglo-American Section.

Reacting with typical Teutonic efficiency, Busch set up two separate spy rings in Britain. One was composed of relatively petty agents, including scores of German *mädchen* (young women) who were planted as domestic servants in the homes of important Britons, including two Royal Navy admirals.

Like other spies, these female sleuths had been trained at Klopstock Pension, the Abwehr's secret espionage school in a multistory building near police headquarters in Hamburg. There they learned such diverse things as how to prepare English roast beef, how to operate a radio transmitter, and how to snap photos with a tiny camera that could be concealed in a pocket.

Not only young women who would serve as domestics received their baptism into the espionage game at Klopstock. Hundreds of would-be male agents also had been enrolled. Learning the tricks of the spy business was done much the same as in a college classroom. The instructors, many of whom had cut their espionage teeth spying on Great Britain and France in World War I, used aliases. They sat at desks on raised platforms, and there were blackboards behind them.

The Klopstock students studied how to use codes and sophisticated techniques for planting explosives and deadly poisons. They learned all about operating a special radio transmitter-receiver, the Agenten-Funk (Afu, for short), which weighed only thirty pounds and fit snugly in a small suitcase.

Along with learning how to operate the Leica camera, the students were taught how to make microfilm, a piece of celluloid about half the size of a postage stamp and used in a camera equipped with a special lens. The process was a technological marvel at the time.

Unbeknownst to the German *mädchen* serving in British homes and others in this insignificant Ring 1, they were regarded as expendable. Although some of the information gathered was helpful to the Abwehr officers at Hamburg,

Colonel Busch regarded the ring members collectively as sort of a gigantic decoy. If and when Germany and Britain were to go to war, Ring 1 was expected to absorb much of the attention of the vastly undermanned British counterespionage agency, MI-5, and the venerable Scotland Yard.

While the British sleuths theoretically would be chasing about in search of these petty spies all over the United Kingdom, Ring 2 would go into action, hopefully undetected. Many months, even years earlier, members of Ring 2 had established themselves into the fabric of British life: as farmers, jewelers, shopkeepers, laborers, even attorneys and a few doctors. They were to remain dormant, spending their time as good citizens of the Crown. Then, if Germany and Great Britain went to war, they were to uncover their long-hidden Afu radios and begin sending high-grade intelligence to their controllers in Hamburg.

In early 1938, Colonel Hinchley Cooke, a ponderous, no-nonsense man in MI-5 in London, became aware that the Abwehr had penetrated deeply into Great Britain. A British subject, Joseph Kelly, was caught red-handed by Cooke's undercover agents stealing blueprints from a new defense installation project where he was working as a bricklayer.

Kelly had sold a few of the top-secret documents to a Nazi agent—or at least, the Briton thought he was a German. Actually, the "buyer" was one of Cooke's men. After his arrest, facing a prison term, Kelly became quite talkative. He "fingered" several of his associates and his controller in England, Walther Reinhardt, an Abwehr agent who was masquerading as a German legation consul in Liverpool.

As time passed and war thunderheads began to gather over Europe, Colonel Cooke's file of cards on suspected German agents in Great Britain had grown steadily. A decision had been made not to arrest these suspects, however, because they would merely be sent back to Germany and new ones not known to MI-5 would take their places.

At about this same time in 1938, Cooke learned that the Abwehr was training its spies at Klopstock, so he decided to try to smuggle a mole into the school. It would seem to be an almost impossible task, but the man Cooke had chosen, a young British linguist, somehow managed to get a job in the Hamburg school, teaching colloquial English to spy recruits scheduled to slip into England.

From this point on, MI-5 agents in London were tipped off by their mole and were on hand to "greet" each new German "tourist" arriving in England. They were not arrested, but all were placed under surveillance. Soon each Nazi spy had a thick dossier on his activities and personal background—home, job, recreations, hobbies.

This bold young British mole had several schemes for alerting MI-5 to incoming Germans. Agents going on an espionage job had to take a course from him on English habits and customs. He suggested that when they arrived in England the spies should take the money the Abwehr had given them to a post office and open a postal savings account. This way, the agents wouldn't lose their money and perhaps have a difficult time getting a new supply from Hamburg, or so said the mole.

Next, the mole urged, it was necessary to demonstrate one's respectability before merging into British life. So it was important that the spy impress on the police that he was a man of means. This should be accomplished by contacting a police station and making a phony report about the loss of the postal savings passbook.

All of this hocus-pocus would have seemed bizarre to Britons, but the would-be German spies, few of whom were overburdened with brains, eagerly followed the advice when they reached England. The scheme had been the British plant's means for alerting MI-5 to the Abwehr spy's arrival. Strangers with "lost passbooks" were promptly placed on the select suspect list of MI-5.

From the scam by the Klopstock mole and other sources, in late August 1939, on the eve of war in Europe, MI-5 and Scotland Yard's Special Branch (dealing with espionage) had a good grasp of the spy picture of the two German rings. Some four hundred agents belonged to Ring 1, and thirty-five key spies to Ring 2.

Meanwhile, in Hamburg, Captain Herbert Wichmann, chief of the British desk at the Abwehr branch, knew that Adolf Hitler had set the time for invading Poland: dawn on September 1, 1939. So Wichmann flashed word to his legion of agents in the British Isles to prepare for covert action.

Wichmann, industrious, loyal, but not too cerebral, looked like Hollywood's version of a sinister Nazi officer: closely cropped hair, dueling scar, even a monocle on occasion. Actually, the widespread German espionage network in England had been built painstakingly over the years by Wichmann's predecessor, Captain Joachim Burghardt. Burly, unkempt, seemingly lethargic, Burghardt had been bounced from his key post in mid-1939, when he came out on the short end of a power struggle with an Abwehr bigwig in Berlin.

Precisely on schedule, Adolf Hitler's powerful war juggernaut struck neighboring Poland, and began converging on Warsaw from three sides. In speed, power, and finesse, the German offensive was unprecedented, and it created a new word in the languages of many nations: blitzkrieg (lightning war).

When Hitler curtly rejected a British ultimatum to withdraw, England and France, on September 3, declared war on the Third Reich. Within hours, agents of MI-5 and Scotland Yard, armed with information collected in recent years, fanned out in a mammoth spy hunt.

At the same time, Captain Wichmann in Hamburg was sitting in a tightly guarded communications post and breathing down the necks of his radio operators, who were repeatedly flashing a code word to Ring 1 and Ring 2: Go into action.

Wichmann had no way of knowing, nor did he have reason to suspect, that virtually his entire legion of spies in England was ensconced in Wormwood Scrubs, the prison that MI-5 had taken over for the anti-espionage activities.[1]

An Elderly German Casanova

RUDOLF VON SCHELIHA, an aging German aristocrat with impeccable manners, was on the staff of the German Embassy in Warsaw in 1938. A striped-pants career diplomat, he was suave and had expensive tastes. Although married to a woman of considerable means and himself drawing a respectable salary, he was almost constantly in debt, mainly because of his involvement in extramarital affairs with far younger women and an addiction to gambling, at which he usually piled up heavy losses.

One night Scheliha poured out his financial woes to a German journalist, and a few days later, the diplomat received a visit from a Soviet agent who dangled a large sum of money before the German's eyes. The bait was snatched off the hook: Scheliha became a spy for Soviet intelligence.

Because of his connections in the German Embassy, Scheliha was privy to most state secrets, and he dutifully passed these along to his Soviet contact. His financial payoff each time was relatively modest, but the money did permit him to continue his gambling and amorous liaisons.

One of Scheliha's torrid affairs was with an attractive, much younger lady high in Warsaw's society. It was costly: she had exquisite tastes and the diplomat had projected himself as a wealthy man, which may have been why she had been associating with him.

One night Scheliha was engaged in an all-night card party at the Polonia Hotel in Warsaw. He badly needed more money. Instead, he lost some fifty thousand zlotys (equivalent to about 10,000 American dollars in 2001). He was given only two weeks to pay his debt.

Hatching some reason to go to Berlin, Scheliha launched a frantic search of secret files for information that would bring a hefty payoff from the Soviets. He uncovered evidence that Adolf Hitler was planning to send his armed forces to conquer Austria and Czechoslovakia, then turn his focus onto Poland.

Returning to Warsaw with his hidden documents, the diplomat contacted his Soviet go-between and requested ten thousand dollars in American currency. The Soviet offered one thousand. The horse-trading resulted in an impasse.

Then, a week later, Scheliha was advised that his Soviet contact was prepared to make a far more substantial offer, and the German was to go to Zakopane, a fashionable winter resort, on a specified date. There he was to travel on skis to an abandoned hunting lodge high in the Tatra Mountains.

Reaching the lodge (despite his advanced years, he had kept himself in excellent physical condition), Scheliha was surprised to find a stranger, a courier who had been sent from Moscow. The German had expected to meet his regular Warsaw contact.

Wasting no time on chitchat, the courier displayed $6,500 in American money and said Moscow had offered this sum on a take-it-or-leave-it basis. It was suggested that the diplomat could sell the money on the black market and realize in excess of the ten thousand dollars he had sought.

Then the Soviet agent bluntly stated his instructions: If Scheliha refused this final offer, he was to be killed immediately at the lodge. The German was through dickering. He handed over the secret documents from the Berlin file and took the payoff. As suggested, Scheliha sold the dollars on the black market and received far more than he needed to pay off his current gambling debt.[2]

Return of a "Conquering Hero"

A BRIGHT SUN WAS BEAMING in the heavens as the German ocean liner *Europa* sailed majestically out of New York harbor, bound for Bremerhaven, Germany. Standing at the rail and watching the Manhattan skyline fade into the distance were Dr. Ignatz Griebl and his "traveling companion," a tall, statuesque blond beauty in her late twenties who was known in high society circles as Mrs. Katherine Moog Busch. It was June 1, 1937.

Pudgy, bespectacled Griebl was a prominent surgeon and obstetrician who enjoyed a lucrative practice in Yorkville, Manhattan's German community, often called Little Berlin.

Griebl had served as an officer in the German army in what was then called the Great War, and later he studied medicine at the University of Munich. In 1925, the young physician and his wife, Maria, who had been an Austrian army nurse in the European conflict, came to the United States and became naturalized citizens.

After setting up his practice in Yorkville, Griebl took a deep interest in what was going on in the "new Germany" of Adolf Hitler. While making many speeches, he had the Nazi swastika flag prominently displayed.

Although Griebl was a first lieutenant in the U.S. Army Medical Corps Reserve and displayed his commission on the wall of his office, in late 1935, he had written a letter to Josef Goebbels, the diminutive Nazi propaganda genius in Berlin, offering his services as an undercover agent. Goebbels sent back word through a courier that his request was granted.

In Berlin, the Abwehr (military intelligence) gave Griebl the code name Ilberg, and he was listed as A.2339 (the "A" indicated that he was an active spy).

Inhibited not one iota by the fact that he was married, and despite a heavy schedule of medical duties, Griebl found time to engage in a string of amorous adventures. "Ignatz feels that he is God's gift to women," a male friend once remarked. His current girlfriend, Katherine Moog Busch, who preferred to be called Kate Moog, was obsessed with the physician.

Moog lived in a luxurious fourteen-room apartment at 276 Riverside Drive, New York City, and had a stable of six servants. She had been born in Germany to wealthy parents, who brought her to the United States as a young girl. Behind a facade of constant gaiety, she was a shrewd businesswoman who operated several commercial ventures in New York City.

Energetic and bright, Griebl built a widespread espionage network within two years. His task was made easier by the fact that the United States was a spies' paradise. No single federal agency was charged with fighting subversive activities, and military and industrial leaders ignored even minimal security precautions.

Griebl had agents in key defense installations as far away as Buffalo; Boston; Baltimore; and Norfolk, Virginia. These moles harvested a bountiful crop of top-secret or restricted American military information, including specifications for every airplane being built by the Seversky Aircraft plant on Long Island, blueprints for three modernized navy destroyers, plans for a new four-blade propeller, maps of defense facilities, and tables of personnel strength of army units.

Griebl and Kate Moog had hardly settled into plush Suite F-21 on the *Europa* when the ship's steward, Karl Schlueter, came calling. Actually, Schlueter was the liner's Orstruppenführer, the Nazi Party functionary who had total control of the *Europa*. He could even issue orders to the ship's captain—and they had better be obeyed. Griebl and Schlueter had much to discuss, and they conferred often during the voyage.

When the *Europa* docked at Bremerhaven, Griebl and Kate Moog were greeted by a beaming reception committee headed by Dr. Erich Pfeiffer, chief of the Abwehr's *Nebenstellen* (branch) at Bremen.

Pfeiffer was a shadowy figure, a man of mystery with many aliases. He was known variously to his agents in the field as "N. Spielman," "Herr Dokter," or "Dr. Endhoff." He was the Abwehr's control officer for Ignatz Griebl.

Griebl had come to Germany for a "vacation," but the Abwehr rolled out the red carpet for him, as befitting the triumphant return of a conquering hero. The wide-eyed Kate Moog was dazzled by the VIP reception; her boyfriend was an even more important person than she had thought him to be.

Griebl and Moog were whisked to Berlin on an express train in a specially reserved compartment complete with iced champagne. In the capital, the couple was ensconced in a huge luxury suite in the Adlon, one of Europe's most famous hotels.

Wealthy Kate Moog, girlfriend of spymaster in New York City. Never charged. (New York Post)

Less than an hour after the two Americans entered the Adlon suite, there was a sharp knock on the door. Everything had been choreographed with typical Teutonic efficiency. Two solemn-faced uniformed men entered. They were high-ranking Abwehr officers.

Wasting no time on small talk, the Abwehr men escorted Griebl across Berlin to 76-78 Tirpitzufer, the global headquarters of the espionage agency. Within minutes, the physician was in the office of the Big Chief, Admiral Wilhelm Canaris. Griebl felt a surge of awe in the presence of the white-haired Canaris, the inscrutable supreme spymaster, one whose very name long had conjured visions of mystery and intrigue.

"I have summoned you here, Dr. Griebl, because I wish to thank you personally for your valuable work in the United States," the small man with a slight speech impediment said. "You have served the führer [Adolf Hitler] and the Fatherland well. I am sure you will continue, and even increase, your efforts."

Canaris paused briefly, staring at Griebl. Resuming, the Abwehr chief said that the führer did not expect him to continue his risky duties in the United States without compensation. Therefore, Griebl would be given a beautiful home in the towering mountains of Bavaria, where the führer himself had a retreat. Presumably, this domicile was for Griebl when he returned to Germany to live—through desire or to escape the clutches of the American authorities. (A few weeks later, an Abwehr courier would deliver to Griebl in New York City the title to the mansion, whose Jewish owners had been evicted.)

Then the Nazi spymaster had one more gift for his highly productive spy. Beginning immediately, Griebl would hold a commission in the German Air Defense (soon to be known as the Luftwaffe), with the pay to be accumulated in Berlin until such time as the physician returned to make his home in Germany.

Consequently, Ignatz Griebl no doubt became the only person to hold simultaneously a commission in the U.S. Army Reserve and the rank of captain in the German Luftwaffe.[3]

The "Poor Little Rich Girl"

EARLY IN 1938, at a cocktail party at an ornate hotel in Washington, D.C., vivacious and gorgeous Merry Fahrney was sipping champagne and eyeing the crowd in search of Dr. Herbert Scholz, consul at the German Embassy on Massachusetts Avenue. Tall and handsome, married to the wealthy daughter of a top executive of I.G. Farben, the huge German chemical trust, Scholz was on the "must-invite" list of every society lioness in Washington.

Fahrney, playgirl heiress to a fortune that her father had amassed in the United States, cavorted in intellectual circles where it was considered chic to be eccentric and to espouse some far-out cause. So her outspoken admiration for Adolf Hitler and Nazism was dismissed by her friends as merely another whim of a poor jaded little rich girl. But to the thirty-year-old Merry, her Nazi beliefs were no whim.

Herbert Scholz was cloaked in mystery. It was whispered in the capital's social whirl that he was actually an espionage official, masquerading behind the facade of a cosmopolitan playboy of impeccable manners and style. His image as a cloak-and-dagger operative in the United States on some sinister mission only added to his desirability as a guest at upper-crust parties and dinners.

The evaluation of the German "diplomat" almost hit the mark. Scholz was the resident director in the United States of the Sicherheitsdienst (SD), the secret service of the Schutzstaffel (SS), Adolf Hitler's elite military order that combined the rites of romantic Teutonism with cold-blooded power politics—with bloody mayhem thrown in on occasion.

Leader of the SD—and Scholz's boss in Berlin—was SS Brigadeführer (Major General) Reinhard Heydrich, tall, blond, and a skilled athlete. The thirty-four-year-old officer was extremely ambitious, and he was conniving to get all German espionage services merged under one leader—himself. Because of his cruel nature, even his own subordinates privately called him the Blond Beast.

Merry Fahrney had always believed in the direct approach, so she introduced herself to Dr. Scholz and minutes later invited him to a luncheon date to hear "an interesting proposition." Dashing and debonair, the SD spy, whose wife was back in Berlin, had become accustomed to being accosted by beautiful young women with interesting propositions, so he agreed to the rendezvous.

Scholz was well acquainted with Merry's background, for she had been in the society pages and the news columns regularly for her offbeat antics and two highly publicized divorces. The couple had hardly finished ordering at Pierre's, a posh restaurant on Connecticut Avenue, when Merry launched into a lengthy spiel about her admiration for Adolf Hitler. She concluded the oratory by offering her services as a spy.

Recognizing the espionage potential of a knowledgeable and sharp-minded woman who circulated in the highest circles in Washington, Scholz promptly accepted.

Merry giggled in delight. Routine society gatherings had become such bores. Now there would be a purpose in her life. She plunged eagerly into her covert mission and would prove to be a dedicated and productive spy for Nazi Germany.

Not all of Merry's intelligence was obtained at cocktail parties from half- to fully-inebriated government and military bigwigs. Often she climbed into her car and drove to American army posts in the South. A business card she had printed identified her as Susan Wadsworth, a survey specialist with the Civil Service Commission.

Once inside the gates of the military facilities, an easy task to accomplish, she would approach army officers, dazzle them with her smile and flirtatious demeanor, and ply them with questions. How many men were on the post? What were their units? With what kind of weapons were they armed? Flattered by her attention and no doubt wishing to convey their own importance, they eagerly responded to the queries.

As a spy, Merry had one shortcoming: She could not stand anonymity, a must for an undercover agent. She insisted on making periodic visits to the German Embassy, and there she basked in the praise of Herbert Scholz and other top officials.

Agents of the Federal Bureau of Investigation had the German Embassy under surveillance, and they began to note the comely, fashionably dressed young woman coming and going. Like most Washingtonians, they recognized her from her newspaper publicity. The G-men, as FBI agents were called, tailed Merry and, as hoped, she led them to other Nazi spies, who in turn were put under surveillance.

After Adolf Hitler declared war on the United States on December 11, 1941, the FBI swooped down on the Nazi spies Merry had identified by her contacts with them. Most were under diplomatic cover and, therefore, immune to arrest and prosecution; these were sent packing back to Germany.

But the FBI could not locate Merry. Later, they would learn that the SD had ordered her to go to Argentina. There she spent the rest of the war spying for Germany in South America.[4]

A Scheme to "Nazify" Thirty Million Americans

AFTER BUILDING UP GERMANY'S ARMED FORCES for five years, Adolf Hitler was ready to strike. It would be the opening round of his intricate plan of conquest to gain Lebensraum (living space) by seizing territory belonging to others in Europe. On March 13, 1938, the führer sent his booted legions plunging into Austria, and that tiny nation was gobbled up without a shot being fired.

Hitler called his action Anschluss (annexation), and Austria became a part of Grossdeutschland (Greater Germany).

Across the Atlantic later that month, eighteen journalists who worked for newspapers and magazines throughout the United States received an invitation to an event at what was still called the Austrian Embassy in Washington, D.C.—all expenses paid.

None were told the true reason for the invitation. But pay for writing for newspapers and magazines, even the larger ones, was modest. So what better way to get a paid vacation than to accept the offer to travel to Washington and be entertained?

German propaganda officials gave wide circulation to this painting of Adolf Hitler as a knight leading a holy crusade. (U.S. Army)

A typical clandestine publication by the Nazis to keep the United States out of the war in Europe. (Author's collection)

When the red carpet was laid out for the journalists in the Austrian Embassy, they discovered that all of them were American citizens of German ancestry. None knew that he had been selected after a careful study of his background by Abwehr agents under cover as embassy attachés.

Soon the secret was out: Each was offered a high-paying job on a chain of Nazi newspapers that would be published in eleven major cities in the United States. Clearly, these would be propaganda sheets designed to influence American public opinion and to keep the U.S. government from injecting itself into Hitler's machinations in Europe.

The journalists were angry. They sensed, rightly, that the Third Reich's treasury, with the approval of Hitler, would pour millions of dollars into this project. Not a single newsman accepted the offer, which would more than triple his current salary. All left the Austrian Embassy in a huff.

Behind this grandiose Nazi scheme to launch a Nazi newspaper chain was Dr. Ernst Böhle, a young, widely traveled intellectual who had become a Hitler favorite because of his convoluted scheme to "Nazify" all persons of German descent living outside the Third Reich—mainly the thirty million Americans who fit into this category.

In early 1938, the mild-mannered, bespectacled Böhle had told a Stuttgart rally of the so-called Congress of Germans Living Abroad (an organization that Böhle had created): "The complete German who is a citizen [of another country] is always a German and nothing but a German!"

Böhle's global operation was directed by the Deutsches Ausland Institut (German Overseas Institute) in Berlin. Under his guidance were two organizations, Welt-Dienst (World Service), located in the city of Erfurt, and Deutscher Fichte-Bund (German Fighters Society), whose headquarters was in Hamburg. The function of these two heavily financed groups was to supply Nazi propaganda saboteurs in the United States with tons of anti-Jewish and other incendiary materials designed to incite racial clashes and even civil war. Shipped to New York in unmarked crates, the pamphlets, tracts, magazines, and flyers were distributed by scores of Nazi sympathizers around the nation.

A typical Nazi propaganda spear carrier in the United States was Swedish-born Olov E. Tietzow, who was head of the American Guard, a "White Man's Party." A naturalized American citizen, Tietzow was sort of a traveling medicine-show huckster, dispensing Nazi snake oil. A tireless missionary, he deluged the country with pamphlets, one of which thundered: "The coming struggle here in America will be fought, not with ballots, but with bullets."

Within two years, Tietzow established operating bases in Minneapolis, Chicago, New York, Boston, Buffalo, Pittsburgh, and other major cities. His task was made easier by the fact that the U.S. government, incredibly, had no single agency to combat subversion in the nation.[5]

A Seminary Student Stalks Hitler

A TWENTY-ONE-YEAR-OLD Swiss theology student, Maurice Bavaud, said goodbye to his close friend, Marcel Gerbohay, and walked out of the seminary in the province of Britanny, France, where the two young men had studied for the past three years. Bavaud told classmates that he was going home for the summer recess. But when he climbed aboard a train for his family's residence in Neuchâtel, Switzerland, he knew he was never coming back to the seminary. It was May 1938.

Bavaud had become obsessed with a calling that he considered to be higher than the priesthood: killing the German dictator, Adolf Hitler. The idea had been planted in his head by his roommate, twenty-four-year-old Gerbohay. Gerbohay declared that the führer was the devil incarnate, that the German leader was dedicated to destroying Mother Church, that he talked of peace and was preparing to launch a war.

Bavaud wrestled strenuously with his conscience before deciding to take on the job of wiping out the German menace. The theologian was a devout Catholic and staunchly opposed to murder. However, in this case, he convinced himself, God would forgive him for doing away with the antichrist.

After moving in with his parents and five brothers and sisters, Maurice began preparing himself for the daunting task ahead. He knew the odds were against him. Hitler never went anywhere without at least twenty heavily armed bodyguards. His armored Mercedes-Benz weighed ten thousand pounds, and when in public, he wore a billed cap lined with nearly four pounds of heavy metal.

On October 9, 1938, after the führer had taken over the Sudetenland, a border region of Czechoslovakia, Bavaud decided it was time to act, telling his family that he was going to Mannheim, Germany, to find work as a draftsman, a trade at which he had worked before entering the seminary.

Meanwhile, Maurice had spent most of his meager savings to purchase a small automatic pistol and ammunition. Instead of going to Mannheim, he took a train to Berlin, four hundred miles to the north of Neuchâtel. He assumed that Hitler would be in the German capital.

Soon after his arrival, the young Swiss learned that his long journey had been for nothing: Hitler was at his mountain retreat in Bavaria, three hundred miles to the south. The führer had been coming to the Obersalzberg since 1925.

Getting off the train at Berchtesgaden, the valley town below Obersalzberg, Bavaud checked into a cheap hotel. Then, in the guise of a hiking tourist, he got as close to the Berghof, Hitler's palatial residence 1,650 feet in the sky, as he could without arousing suspicions.

Surrounding the outer perimeter of the sprawling estate was a nine-foot-high barbed-wire fence. Closer to the Berghof was a similar fence, six feet high. Black-uniformed SS soldiers, members of Hitler's elite private army, patrolled the vast area. But Bavaud hatched a plan. He would dress as a workman, cut through the two barbed-wire fences at night, and get as close as he could to the Berghof. There he would conceal himself until Hitler came outside, at which time the Swiss would shoot him.

Again Bavaud was thwarted. At the same time his train had pulled into Berchtesgaden, the führer's private train, the *Amerika*, had chugged out of the valley to take the German leader to the newly occupied Sudetenland. Discrete inquiry disclosed to the would-be assassin that Hitler planned to return to the Berghof, so the young man decided to wait him out.

While waiting for the führer's return, Bavaud took long walks in the heights around the Berghof. Now he began to have nagging doubts. He knew little about firearms, but he experimented with practice shots when in desolate areas and concluded that he would have to be within twenty-five feet of Hitler to kill him with the small pistol.

One day, Bavaud was eating a skimpy meal at an inn when he struck up a conversation with a friendly local police officer, Captain Karl Deckert, who was seated at the next table. The Swiss gave the impression that he was an ardent Nazi and casually inquired if there was any way he could meet Hitler. The policeman said that his job was security, so he knew there was no way the young man could meet the führer at the Berghof. But he did have a suggestion: go through Nazi Party channels in Munich during the annual celebration of the 1923 *putsch* (uprising), Hitler's first attempt to seize power in Germany and one that had landed him in prison. The führer, his top leaders, and hundreds of the Old Guard would march through the streets of Munich, as they had done fifteen years earlier on November 9.

On October 31, the seminary student arrived by train in Munich. This would give him time to familiarize himself with the parade route to be followed on the day of the annual march. His job was made easy. A Munich newspaper published a large map that showed the streets to be taken before the marchers arrived at the spacious Odeonsplatz, where, a decade and a half before, Hitler and his followers had been fired on by German policemen and sixteen Nazis were killed.

Now Bavaud had to decide from what vantage point he would fire his weapon as the führer marched along. From conversations with Munich residents, he learned that wooden grandstands were erected at points along the march for influential citizens. The Swiss decided to try to bluff his way onto a seat.

Bavaud approached a civilian guard at the grandstand he picked and told him that he was a correspondent for a Swiss newspaper but that he had lost his credentials. Without question, the guard provided a ticket.

On the big day, November 9, Munich was gripped by cold and overcast skies. Bavaud was up early. He dressed, put a seven-round clip into his pistol and slipped it into his overcoat pocket. To make sure he would get a seat near the front of the grandstand, he arrived at the site when only a few spectators were present.

As the Swiss waited, the grandstand rapidly filled. There was a festive air. Suddenly, a booming voice in the rows of seats called out: *"The führer is coming!"*

Bavaud felt the cold steel of the pistol in his pocket. Like the others, he stood to get a better view of Hitler, who would be leading the procession. As Hitler, flanked by his top Nazis such as Hermann Göring and Heinrich Himmler, drew closer, the would-be assassin's heart plummeted: the führer was going to pass on the far side of the broad street, out of range of the small pistol.

Bavaud nearly panicked. Momentarily he thought about crashing through the cordon of SS troops lining both sides of the street, dashing up to Hitler, and shooting him. Just as quickly, he scuttled the idea: He would never get past the guards. Crestfallen, the Swiss watched helplessly as his target marched past.

Still frustrated the next day, Bavaud decided to take a train back to Berchtesgaden and try again to get within shooting range of the German leader. But when he arrived at his destination, he learned that Hitler had decided to remain in Munich for one more day to lecture a large group of Nazi Party officials.

Bavaud's frustration deepened, but his determination to succeed remained burning brightly. He took a train back to Munich. There he found that Hitler had boarded the *Amerika* only two hours earlier and was heading back to Berchtesgaden to spend the weekend on the Obersalzberg.

Bavaud was on the brink of giving up his assassination effort. He had been missing meals the past few days and had but the equivalent to three American dollars in his pocket. He vowed to make one final try. However, on reaching Berchtesgaden, he discovered that his target had left by train that morning for Berlin.

Bavaud had decided that his task was hopeless and that he was going home to Neuchâtel. He bought a train ticket that would take him only about twenty miles of the one hundred and fifty miles to the Swiss frontier to the west of Berchtesgaden. For whatever reason, he carried the pistol with him instead of ditching what could be incriminating evidence.

Bavaud continued to ride the train past his ticket destination. Soon the conductor caught him without an authorized ticket and with no money to pay for his passage onward. Police took him off the train at Augsburg, and he was routinely turned over to the Gestapo because he was a foreigner.

The Gestapo seemed to swallow his story that he usually carried a pistol with him because target shooting was his favorite recreation. He was given back to the civilian police to face charges of trying to ride the German railways without paying. A week later, the Swiss was sentenced to sixty days in the Augsburg jail for fraud.

Bavaud no doubt felt enormous relief. He had been caught almost red-handed with a weapon but had gotten away with a short term of confinement. His good luck was soon shattered. In January 1939, only days before Bavaud would be released, two Gestapo agents called on him in his cell. They had not been taken in by his target-shooting story, it became known, and instead had gone about tracking down the would-be assassin's movements from one town to another. Finally, they located the place and date of his purchase of the pistol.

After a lengthy and brutal grilling of the suspect, the Gestapo agents wrung a confession from Bavaud that he had come to Germany to kill Adolf

Hitler, the antichrist. Tried before a so-called People's Court, the defendant was quickly found guilty and sentenced to death.

Meanwhile, at his home town of Neuchâtel, Maurice's mother and father received a letter from their son. He concluded the missive by stating: "Ah, if only I had remained at the seminary in God's service, if I had not forsaken the light for the darkness, I would not be here now."

The next day, Maurice Bavaud was taken from his prison cell by the Gestapo and beheaded.[6]

Standard Oil's Nazi Connection

ALTHOUGH NAZI GERMANY was furiously preparing for war in the late 1930s, numerous U.S. corporations continued to do business with Adolf Hitler. One of those maintaining close ties with I.G. Farben, a huge chemical conglomerate, was Standard Oil Company. Standard and Farben had what they called a "full marriage": Standard had a free hand in oil anywhere in the world in exchange for giving the German firm no global competition in the chemical field.

Farben, whose directors had unanimously endorsed the Nazi Party because it opposed free enterprise, was among the biggest of the fifteen large German corporations that provided a base for Adolf Hitler's "revitalization" of the Third Reich. Many of these firms operated companies in the United States, masquerading under Swiss ownership.

After war in Europe broke out in September 1939, Standard Oil negotiated a scheme of operation with Farben that would allow a continuing partnership whether or not the United States would or would not get involved in the conflict.

Curiously, the leading figure to generate action against the Standard Oil–I.G. Farben "marriage" was young Nelson A. Rockefeller, who had offices in Rockefeller Center in New York. In 1863, while the Civil War was raging in the United States, Nelson's once-penniless grandfather, John D. Rockefeller, and partners organized the firm of Andrews, Clark and Company, and began to develop a global industry that became the Standard Oil Company.

Nelson Rockefeller was aghast to learn that the company his grandfather had founded nearly eighty years earlier was now dealing with a German firm fueling Hitler's military juggernaut. Although the Dartmouth graduate lacked the clout to directly influence the corporation's policies, he decided to unlimber a potent weapon to corrode Standard Oil's "business as usual" mentality. That weapon was the white glare of publicity, which would have to be generated undercover for maximum efficiency.

Not long after President Franklin D. Roosevelt appointed the thirty-two-year-old Rockefeller to a new post, Coordinator of Inter-American Affairs, in mid-1940, Standard Oil's top executives offered a huge cash award—no questions asked—to anyone who would identify the source of a book titled *Sequel to the Apocalypse: How Your Dimes Pay for Hitler's War.* The volume detailed the cozy relationship between Standard Oil and I.G. Farben.

There were no takers, for good reason. Nelson Rockefeller had arranged for the book to be written and published secretly. It charted the links from Nazi Germany to Standard Oil, Ford Motor Company, and dozens of dummy corporations in the United States.

Rockefeller arranged to have thousands of copies shipped covertly to American embassies throughout South America, from where copies were distributed among government and military leaders and opinion makers in the media. Many in those categories learned that Standard Oil tankers were operating under the Panamanian flag from ports in Mexico and in other South American countries, ostensibly bound for neutral Spain. Actually, this precious cargo was refueling German U-boats and other Nazi ships operating in the Western Hemisphere.

Meanwhile, in the United States, large numbers of the "mystery book" found their way into media newsrooms, resulting in blaring headlines and articles castigating Standard Oil. Consequently, early in 1941, a Senate investigative committee, headed by a peppery legislator from Missouri, Harry S Truman, probed into the activities of Standard Oil.

Truman's investigation disclosed that Standard Oil was continuing to sell fuel to German "airlines" in the face of ongoing protests by the State Department. In Venezuela, Standard Oil was giving Germans preferential treatment in the development of oil fields.

Although Nelson Rockfeller's "publicity campaign" had caused Standard Oil to pull back from its association with I.G. Farben and other Nazi corporations, it was not until Germany went to war against the United States in early December 1941 that federal agencies, acting on wartime powers, decreed that Standard Oil's "marriage" to I.G. Farben would be granted an immediate "divorce."[7]

Theft of Maginot Line Secrets

THICK, BLACK WAR CLOUDS had been spreading over Europe in early 1939 when Winston S. Churchill, a political figure of long standing, was speaking out forcefully in Parliament about the need for Great Britain to rearm in the face of the ongoing saber-rattling by German dictator Adolf Hitler. During his anti-Nazi crusade, Churchill accepted an invitation by French general Alphonse Georges to inspect France's Maginot Line.

Named after André Maginot, a former French minister of defense, the two-hundred-mile-long series of fortifications extended northward from Switzerland along the border with Germany to the Belgian border. Thick concrete

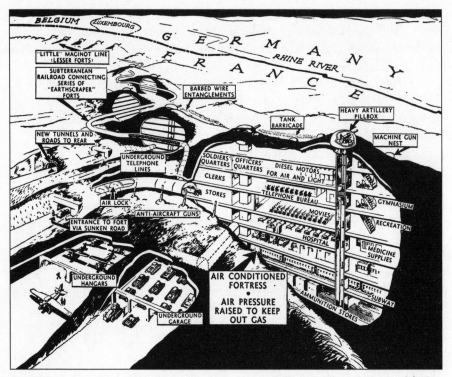

German agents stole blueprints of France's "impregnable" Maginot Line. (Author's collection)

forts stood aboveground, flanked by pillboxes and barbed-wire entanglements. Underground chambers provided space for communications systems, hospitals, storage rooms, garages, and living quarters for tens of thousands of officers and men.

Puffing on one of his seemingly ever-present cigars, Winston Churchill, who had extensive military experience in World War I, traipsed for hours through, in, and around the vaunted Maginot Line. He was deeply impressed. On his return to London, he presented a highly upbeat and secret report to the War Office.

"The French Front cannot be surprised," the future British prime minister wrote. "It cannot be broken at any point except by an effort that would be enormously costly in lives."

Churchill failed to realize that the "unbreakable" Maginot Line had already been broken—not by frontal attacks by infantry and panzers, but by agents of Admiral Wilhelm Canaris, the diminutive, wily chief of the German Abwehr. A special branch of the Berlin-based intelligence organization, Section I, had been created for the specific purpose of cracking the secrets of the Maginot Line.

For two years, beginning in 1937, countless clandestine approaches had failed. Finally, persistence paid off, mainly through the perfidy of a French captain, Georges Froge, who was in charge of distributing provisions to troops on the Line.

Froge, German agents had learned, was critical of the French government and seemed to admire the dictatorship of Adolf Hitler. Once Froge had been fingered as a potential spy with a wealth of crucial and secret information, Section I set up Operation Z, a special program to ensnare Froge.

Soon the Z agents learned that Froge was heavily in debt and being hounded by his creditors. He was desperate for money. After that, it didn't take long for Admiral Canaris's net to haul in the French captain, the bait being heavy bundles of cash.

Froge proved to be an intelligence bonanza. During his frequent tours up and down the Maginot Line, he gained access to maps, papers, and other documents relating to the fortifications and army units manning them.

As valuable as was Froge's information, it paled by comparison to the jackpot the Abwehr hit the day after Adolf Hitler sent his booted legions into Czechoslovakia on March 15, 1939. Charging into Prague with the panzer spearheads was a contingent of Abwehr agents with orders to seize intact the files of the Czech general staff and especially its intelligence branch, the Second Section.

What the Abwehr men did not know was that the Czechs had decided to build their own fortifications as a bulwark against German invasion and to pattern them after the Maginot Line. A panel of Czech officers had been allowed by the French to inspect the Maginot Line and make drawings and notes of anything that appealed to them.

Now, after the Abwehr agents arrived at the headquarters of the Czech general staff in Prague, they immediately made contact with a traitor, a Czech colonel at the headquarters, and he took his new "friends" to a hidden safe. When the safe was opened, the Germans could not believe their luck. The container held France's greatest secret—a detailed blueprint of the entire Maginot Line.[8]

The Pope's Clandestine Peace Plan

AT SIX O'CLOCK IN THE EVENING of March 2, 1939, the elevation of Cardinal Eugenio Pacelli to pope by a conclave of cardinals in Rome was announced by the traditional puffs of smoke from the Vatican. The Italian became Pope Pius XII.

The new leader of the world's Catholics' first public message, read to the princes of the Church in the Sistine Chapel, was one of peace. It had been the

Holy Office's historical role to remain neutral in political conflicts and to strive to keep mankind free from war.

Only a month after Pope Pius XII had been elected, however, he was being bombarded by ordinary Catholics around the world, especially those in English-speaking nations, asking him to intervene in the quarrels in Europe to prevent a major conflict. The *Catholic Herald*, published in London, demanded that the pontiff call a peace conference to settle the angry differences.

Perhaps spurred on by these demands and suggestions, the pope set into motion secret behind-the-scenes machinations to test European leaders' views toward a five-power peace conference. Instructions were sent from the Vatican to the papal nuncios in Warsaw, Paris, Rome, and Berlin, and to the apostolic delegate in London to sound out political bigwigs on the prospects of a successful outcome of a papal call for a parley of peace.

Reactions were diverse. British Foreign Secretary Edward Halifax was typically noncommittal. "Halifax has a unique gift," an acquaintance once wrote. "He is always at the center of [failed] events, yet manages somehow to leave the impression that he is not connected with them."

Father Tacchi Venturi, the papal delegate to the Italian government, talked on two occasions with Benito Mussolini, the bombastic dictator, who conveyed mild enthusiasm for a conference of Italy, Poland, Great Britain, France, and Germany to discuss major problems that could lead to war.

Jozef Beck, the Polish foreign minister, who was given to intrigue, had been military attaché in Paris after World War I when he was caught red-handed selling French army secrets to the Czechs and was expelled. Now Beck was bitter against Benito Mussolini, telling Monsignor Filippo Cortesi, nuncio in Poland, that the Italian leader was too cowardly to stand up to Adolf Hitler, thereby failing to take a lead in maintaining peace in Europe.

In Paris, Alexis Saint-Léger Léger, secretary general in the French government, was violently outspoken, claiming that the call for a peace conference was a Mussolini plot. Il Duce (leader), as the Italian strongman liked to call himself, had been scheming for a long time to coerce the major powers into a peace meeting so he could take credit for favorable results, if any.

At his Bavarian retreat on a mountain high above the village of Berchtesgaden, Adolf Hitler rolled out the figurative red carpet for Monsignor Cesare Orsenigo, the papal nuncio, who had flown to Germany in a special airplane provided by the führer. The monsignor was served tea during a long conversation in the Berghof, Hitler's ornate mansion.

Had Hitler not seized control of Germany, he could have enjoyed a fabulous living as a con man. As Monsignor Orsenigo listened, presumably in delight, the German leader with the brush mustache emphasized that there was no danger of war in Europe. Sure, Italy and France had major differences, but these could easily be ironed out. There was no chance of Poland getting involved in a conflict with Germany, even though the führer had been making what he called "minor territorial demands" from the neighboring nation.

Speaking without apparent rancor, Hitler singled out the culprit that could possibly endanger peace—Great Britain. The leaders of that country were scheming to incite Poland against Germany, just as they had incited Chinese leader Chiang Kai-shek against peaceful Japan and the Communists against Spanish dictator Francisco Franco, the führer declared.

Monsignor Orsenigo chose to remain silent to this strange revision of history. Hitler had been far more conciliatory toward peace than he had anticipated, even though the führer made no definite commitment to a five-power European conference.

While the papal nuncio was sipping tea and providing an influential forum for the führer, four hundred miles away in Berlin, the Oberkommando der Wehrmacht (German High Command) was putting the final touches to Case White, code name for the invasion of Poland.[9]

An American Forum to Promote Germany

ON MARCH 16, 1939, a group of mostly well-to-do New York business executives and professional men held a dinner meeting at the Lexington Hotel in Manhattan and founded the American Fellowship Forum. The name was misleading. Most members indeed were American, but their goal was to promote the interests of Nazi Germany.

The group masqueraded behind a stated purpose of focusing public attention on solutions to American social and economic problems. However, appointed national director of the forum was a tall, stylishly garbed former professor of German literature at prestigious Columbia University, Dr. Friedrich Ernest Auhagen, who was a paid Nazi agent.

A lieutenant in the German army during World War I, he had emigrated to the United States in 1923. After Adolf Hitler seized power in early 1933 and set his sights on rearming the Third Reich, Auhagen became an agent of the German secret service. His advanced degrees in economics and engineering allowed him to secure a teaching job at Columbia, an ideal cover for his covert activities.

Auhagen was able to live and dress in a style far higher than could be expected solely on a professor's salary. He raked in regular sums of money from Dr. G. Kurt Johannsen, a Nazi paymaster at the Hamburg, Germany, branch of the Abwehr.

The professor may have loved the Fatherland, but he was infatuated with Uncle Sam's greenbacks as well. On a regular basis, he received hefty cash sums from a wealthy American industrialist, Dr. Ferdinand A. Kertess, president of the Chemical Marketing Company of New York City.

Kertess did far more than merely stuff greenbacks into Auhagen's grasping hands. He himself was deeply involved in espionage work for the Third Reich. Drawing on his extensive business connections, Kertess shuttled information on ship movements in New York harbor to the German consulate in Manhattan, from where it was relayed to the Nazi naval attaché at the German Embassy in Washington, D.C.

The headquarters of the American Fellowship Forum was set up in a high-rise on Fifth Avenue in Manhattan. In June, the group produced the first issue of *Today's Challenge*, a slickly done magazine that was sent by the hundreds to American press and radio outlets.

Auhagen was listed as the editor, and the first issue featured an article by him titled "The New Europe." It was profuse in praise for the "visionary leader of Germany," Adolf Hitler, and his recent actions in seizing by armed might the tiny countries of Austria and Czechoslovakia.

Those actions by the German führer, Auhagen wrote, were "a most hopeful beginning of the New Europe." Contributing articles to the first issue of *Today's Challenge* were two prominent members of the U.S. Congress, Representative Hamilton Fish of New York and Senator Ernest Lundeen of Minnesota.

The American Fellowship Forum lasted for three years. Then its existence came to a screeching halt. In mid-1942, after the United States had been at war for six months, the Chemical Marketing Company went out of business, seized by the U.S. Treasury Department's Foreign Property Control Division. At about the same time, Dr. Friedrich Auhagen was sentenced to two and a half years in a prison for failure to register with the government as an agent of a foreign power.[10]

Roosevelt's Secret Scheme
to Aid the British

WAR THUNDERHEADS WERE HOVERING over a fearful Europe and blowing inexorably toward the United States when President Franklin D. Roosevelt delivered one of his trademark fireside chats over the radio to the American people.

"This nation will remain a neutral nation, but I cannot ask that every American remain neutral in thought as well," he told a confused and divided country. It was early June 1939.

The fireside chats were Roosevelt's favorite way of skirting hostile media and political attacks and going straight to the people. Critics labeled it "show biz"—but it was highly effective.

In his resonant voice he would intone, "My friends," and most Americans felt they were. "Uncle Franklin," many fireside-chat listeners called him. His millions of fans never knew that behind the scenes in Washington, Roosevelt was exercising heavy clout in clandestine ways to aid Great Britain and France if and when war broke out with Nazi Germany. His actions were stealthy and could have violated neutrality legislation that Congress had enacted earlier. But desperate times called for desperate decisions.

On June 30, three weeks after Roosevelt had assured Americans that the United States would remain neutral in any European conflict, he summoned British Ambassador Ronald Lindsay to the White House. Lindsay sneaked in a side door to avoid being detected by inquisitive journalists.

Lindsay was greeted by the customary Roosevelt lopsided smile and friendly words. Then the president launched into the matter at hand. In the event Adolf Hitler triggered a conflict in Europe, the president said, he planned to create a U.S. Navy patrol over the entire western Atlantic as far away as five hundred miles from the eastern coasts of the Americas.

Lindsay, a veteran diplomat who had seldom been surprised by anything, was surprised. The American president was preparing to defy Congress's stance on neutrality. What Roosevelt would be doing, on his own initiative, was to declare the entire western Atlantic a neutral zone, theoretically, at least, denying that vast region to German warships and U-boats (submarines).

An ocean lifeline between the United States and Great Britain would be crucial in the event of war. So, Roosevelt explained, all cargo ships with goods from the Americas could rendezvous unchallenged at Halifax, a major port in Nova Scotia, a southeastern province of Canada. Great Britain then would have to provide armed escorts only after convoys had left the "neutral zone."

Then Roosevelt made another demand that again astonished Ambassador Lindsay. Without authorization from Congress, the president wanted the British to lease to the United States sites for sea and naval bases in the Caribbean, on Tobago and Trinidad, St. Lucia, and Bermuda.

After departing from the White House, Lindsay promptly contacted the Foreign Office in London and strongly recommended Roosevelt's entire clandestine scheme. Despite Great Britain's woefully weak military posture, legal advisors in the Foreign Office raised objections. It just didn't seem cricket for a neutral United States to use the ports of a belligerent to deny certain waters to the opposing adversary (Nazi Germany).

Ambassador Lindsay returned to the White House on July 8 to discuss with Roosevelt some of the criticisms raised by the Foreign Office attorneys in London. The president was stunned and angry, especially when he concluded that the British had become skeptical of his true intentions.

The strong-willed president, who subscribed to the famous saying of his cousin, Theodore Roosevelt, "speak softly but carry a big stick," refused to take what he considered to be a rebuff from a traditionally friendly nation he was trying to help. Without advising Lindsay, the president decided to covertly pursue his scheme.

In mid-August, five weeks after Lindsay's second visit to the White House, teams of two or three men in civilian clothes fanned out in the Caribbean to inspect possible sea and air sites. Actually, they were American military officers in disguise. Secretly, the outsiders began to lease land in Bermuda, Trinidad, and St. Lucia. It would be three years, and the United States would itself be plunged into global war, before the Americans had the military manpower, ships, and airplanes to make full use of these outposts.[11]

"Our Enemies Are Little Worms"

A CURIOUS EVENT WAS UNFOLDING in Munich early on the sun-drenched morning of August 22, 1939. Some forty-five to fifty German men, most of them middle-aged in civilian clothes, were milling around in front of the Nazi Brown House on the K"niglishesplatz.

The locale had nostalgic memories for Adolf Hitler. In the early 1920s, he had selected the house as the first headquarters of the National Socialist German Workers' Party (later the Nazi Party for short), a ragtag group that the former German army corporal had founded. The structure had received its name because it was painted brown, the color worn by his early storm troopers, the Sturmabteilung (SA).

Now the mystery in front of the Brown House deepened. A convoy of automobiles picked up the group of civilians and drove southward for some forty miles to the picturesque sixteenth-century Bavarian village of Berchtesgaden. The procession rolled along the cobblestone streets and onto a road climbing sharply up towering Kehlstein Mountain. Halfway up the steep incline, the convoy was halted at two massive metal doors guarded by black-uniformed, heavily armed men of the elite Schutzstaffel (SS).

The doors swung open and the cars drove through a tunnel to an underground garage where the passengers alighted and strolled a short distance to an elevator whose shaft had been blasted out of solid rock. Spacious, with plush red carpeting, the elevator whisked the newcomers upward, and when the doors opened, they were in the Berghof, Adolf Hitler's rustic retreat on the Obersalzberg, 6,208 feet above Berchtesgaden.

By midday, the men were seated in wooden chairs in the fifty-by-sixty-foot parlor, replete with large oil paintings, ornate tapestries, and classic statuary. When the führer entered the room, the audience collectively leaped to its feet. These were not civilians, but the flower of German military aristocracy—commanders of armies, Luftwaffe fleets, Kriegsmarine (navy) flotillas, and their chiefs of staff. The civilian-clothing machination had been conceived to thwart any lurking British or French spies.

*A spellbinding orator,
Adolf Hitler whipped
audiences into frenzies.
(National Archives)*

Hitler, a dynamic speaker, declared, "There will probably never again in the future be a man with more authority than I have. My existence is therefore a factor of great value. But I can be eliminated at any time by a criminal or a lunatic. There is no time to lose. War must come in my lifetime."

Hitler paused briefly. The room was hushed. Then he continued, "I have made a momentous decision. I will invade Poland on August twenty-sixth!"

The führer shocked the admirals and generals: He had signed a Treaty of Friendship with the Soviet Union, a communist nation, and as such a sworn archenemy of Hitler. It would be but a brief marriage of convenience, he pointed out. "Great Britain and France will not dare to come to Poland's rescue without the aid of Russia."

Now Hitler's face flushed crimson with anger as he lashed out at the leaders of Great Britain, France, and Poland. "Our enemies are little worms," he bellowed. "I saw them at Munich. I am only afraid that at the last minute some Schweinhund [hound dog] will produce a plan of mediation."

After several seconds of silence, Hitler asked: "Why must there be war? We have nothing to lose; we can only gain!"

The führer concluded his six-hour presentation with a ringing admonition: "Have no pity. Have a brutal attitude! Ninety million [German] people must get what is their right!" He added, "I have ordered to the East my [SS] units to kill without mercy the clergy, the intellectuals, the leaders, the Jews!"

Poland would be invaded by 1.5 million troops and hundreds of panzers that had already been secretly deployed along the frontier. Zero hour: 4:45 A.M.

After Hitler dismissed his commanders, they departed with set and seemingly anxious faces. None had asked a single question or spoken a single word that might be construed as questioning the führer's judgment. Still in civilian suits, they returned to their unit posts throughout the Third Reich and prepared for war.

Unbeknownst to Hitler, in his audience had been five generals and an admiral who were active in the Schwarze Kapelle, a small, tightly knit group of prominent military officers, civic leaders, and government officials who had been plotting for months to seize the führer, have him declared insane, and lock him in an asylum while a new, democratic regime was formed.

No doubt these conspirators left the Berghof with heavy hearts. Adolf Hitler was riding the crest of enormous popularity in the Third Reich, so there was no way they could carry out their goal before war rocked Europe. They would have to bide their time.[12]

Lulling Europe's Leaders to Sleep

DURING THE LATTER PART of August 1939, the Germans, spearheaded by the clever minister of propaganda, Josef Goebbels, intensified a deception campaign to lull European leaders to sleep while the Wehrmacht got ready for the invasion of Poland. Originally set for August 25, X-Day had been moved ahead to September 1 to provide time for all the intricate pieces of the deception puzzle to be put into place.

Hermann Göring, an Adolf Hitler crony since the early days of the Nazi movement in Munich, played a key role in the intrigue and trickery. The rotund Luftwaffe chief and number two in the Nazi pecking order behind the führer was the ideal figure for this ruse. Most European leaders regarded him as a voice of reason, a relative term, in Hitler's entourage.

Göring sent an invitation to Josef Lipski, the Polish ambassador in Berlin, to go on a shooting outing in the German state forests in October (at which time Hitler planned for his army to be firmly entrenched in Warsaw). Nevile Henderson, the British ambassador, received a similar invitation.

Scores of other invitations also were sent from the German chancellery to all members of the diplomatic corps in Berlin to join with German leaders in celebrating the twenty-fifth anniversary of Field Marshal Paul von Hindenburg's monumental victory over Russian armies at Tannenberg, after which he became a national hero.

Hitler himself played a key role in the deception. He was dinner host to Carl Burckhardt, the League of Nations commissioner for Danzig, a so-called free city four miles inland from the Baltic Sea. The bustling port had been in

Reichsmarschall Hermann Göring was the most pompous of the leaders around Hitler. (National Archives)

German hands for about one hundred and fifty years until the peace settle-. ment in World War I established its independent status in 1919.

Danzig then became a hybrid. Poland controlled the railroads and the collection of taxes, but the city had its own assembly and was supervised by a commission representing the League of Nations. For many months, Hitler had been demanding that Danzig be returned to Germany. Now, after seemingly endless verbal barrages fired against Carl Burckhardt, the führer was his genial host. Hitler knew that within two weeks, his armed forces would attack and seize the vital port at the same hour that the Wehrmacht would plunge into Poland.

X-Day for Hitler's launching of Case White, the invasion of Poland and the seizure of Danzig, was edging closer. On the night of August 31—six hours before the Wehrmacht would strike—Gestapo thugs under the direction of Albert Forster, Gauleiter (Nazi leader) of Danzig, burst into the home of Carl Burckhardt while he was asleep.

Burckhardt was told he was under arrest, and his telephone was cut off. Minutes later, Forster arrived with a large entourage in tow. Only the night before, Forster had been in Berlin and received his instructions directly from Adolf Hitler.

Forster was nasty. Burckhardt, he bellowed, represented the Treaty of Versailles (the harsh document the victorious Allies had forced a defeated Germany to sign at the close of World War I twenty-one years earlier).

"You are lucky, Herr Burckhardt," the Nazi leader exclaimed. "You have two hours in which to leave Danzig."

Burckhardt was helpless after being told that the Nazi swastika would be raised over the Danzig high commissioner's office in thirty minutes—meaning armed Nazis were seizing control of the city. The League of Nations official rapidly packed a few belongings, climbed into his automobile, and drove off into the night toward Lithuania.

Still following the precise instructions received from the führer, Forster, after daylight, announced over the public radio that he was now in charge of Danzig. He abolished the Danzig constitution that had guaranteed the citizens their freedoms, and he declared the city a part of the Third Reich. Forster's new exalted title, given him by Hitler, was Chief of the Civil Administration of Danzig.

Before dawn on September 1, at precisely 4:45 A.M., Danzig was awakened by the first bombardment of what would be known as World War II. The German warship *Schleswig-Holstein*, which had already been in Danzig harbor on a pretext, began blasting away at predesignated targets with eleven-inch guns. At daylight, Stuka dive bombers pounded the city.

Polish forces—military and civilian—in Danzig were assaulted by the Nazi Landespolizei. Workers at the main post office, with its thick walls, held out the longest. The result was inevitable: fifty-one post office employees had to surrender. All of the captives were shot to death on the pretext that they had not been wearing military uniforms, even though no war had been declared.

Part Two

A World Rocked by War

A German Spymaster
Plots against Hitler

AT DAWN ON SEPTEMBER 1, 1939, thousands of German artillery pieces launched a thunderous bombardment of neighboring Poland. Some 1,600 warplanes of the Luftwaffe joined in the unprovoked assault. It was Adolf Hitler's X-Day for Case White, the mammoth invasion of nearly defenseless Poland by five German armies that surged over the frontier at 4:45 A.M.

The führer's blitzkrieg was a spectacular success. In only twenty-seven days, the Wehrmacht (armed forces) had crushed an ill-equipped and partially trained army of 800,000 men and conquered a nation of 33 million people. Hitler was raised to an even higher pinnacle of popular admiration in the Fatherland.

Within days of the invasion, the SS began murdering targeted Poles— political leaders, intellectuals, Catholic priests, and Jews of all classes and ages. On September 14, detailed reports of the atrocities reached the desk of Admiral Wilhelm Canaris, the Abwehr chief in Berlin. Canaris was aghast. He covertly created a task force of Abwehr officers to conduct an investigation.

The five-foot-five Canaris had been appointed to his command by Hitler and formally took office in 1935. A secretive man, nervous and intense in disposition, he had a slight lisp and walked with a stoop. Highly educated and widely traveled, he could speak the languages of Germany's most powerful enemies—England, France, and Russia—almost as well as those of her friends Italy and Spain.

Canaris's hair was white even as he had taken office in the Abwehr headquarters at 76/78 Tirpitzufer, overlooking the chestnuts and limes of Berlin's magnificent Tiergarten. Only two years after becoming head of the Abwehr, Canaris had began an odyssey of intrigue that has seldom been matched in history. At the same time he was providing the Teutonic warlord, Adolf Hitler, with intelligence for widespread conquests in Europe, he was also plotting with other conspirators the downfall of the führer.

Even while the invading Wehrmacht was wiping out the few remaining pockets of resistance in Poland in late September 1939, Canaris made a monumental decision that might cost him his life—he could be hanged for treason. He covertly sent the detailed information about SS atrocities in Poland to all of

*German master spy Admiral
Wilhelm Canaris. (Author's
collection)*

Hitler's commanding generals. These documents were also smuggled to Pope
Pius XII in the Vatican in Rome; the leader of MI-6, the British secret service
responsible for overseas operations in London; and the Deuxième Bureau, the
French intelligence agency in Paris.

Only one army general mildly protested the SS atrocities in Poland—and
he was immediately sacked by Hitler. That example was not lost on the other
German generals: if they cherished their careers—and most of them did—they
would carry out the führer's orders, however brutal those orders might be.

Admiral Canaris would not survive to learn how his secret action would
eventually convict many of those involved in atrocious conduct in Poland.
Hitler had the deposed Abwehr chief hanged on April 9, 1945, a month before
the war ended. At war crimes trials in Nuremberg after the German surrender,
the six-year-old reports by the Abwehr chief would be instrumental in death
sentences being meted out to many SS officers.[1]

The Polish Assassin Wore Pigtails

OBERGRUPPENFÜHRER REINHARD HEYDRICH viewed Adolf Hitler's campaign
to destroy Poland as a nation as a golden opportunity to grasp even more power
than the heavy clout he already possessed as head of the all-powerful RSHA
(Reich Security Main Office), which included the Gestapo and Kripo (Krimi-
nalpolizei). Cunning, ruthless, and opportunistic, the thirty-five-year-old SS
general set his sights on sending Einsatzgruppen (special extermination squads)
charging into Poland on the heels of the German panzers.

Jews of all classes were dragged from their homes and herded together like cattle for eventual extermination. Other Jews were flogged out of synagogues with whips. Jews and Gentiles alike were torn to shreds by savage dogs, and they kneeled before open pits and were shot down in droves.

By October 1, 1939, when the Wehrmacht campaign to crush Poland had concluded, Obergruppenführer Heydrich proudly reported to Adolf Hitler: "Of the Polish upper classes, only a maximum of three percent is still present."

Typically, to feather his own nest, Heydrich had vastly exaggerated the percentage of political leaders, Catholic priests, and intellectuals that had been murdered. But the number had been enormous, one of history's great blood-baths.

Consequently, out of desperation, a Polish underground slowly emerged. Most of its activities were centered in Warsaw, a city of some 1.3 million people that had been left largely a pile of rubble from German bombardments.

One of the early Polish resistants was twenty-two-year-old Niuta Teitel-baum, who had been born into a family of Hassidim, a sect of especially devout Jews. She had beauty and charm, and her blond pigtails made her look like a child. On volunteering for the underground, she made it known that she expected to fight.

"I am a Jew," she declared. "My place is in the struggle against the Nazis for the honor of my people and for a free Poland!"

Niuta's clever mind, personality, and her pigtails, which seemed to make her a sixteen-year-old girl, allowed her to get into closely guarded German facilities. One day she strolled up to the guards in front of Gestapo headquarters in Warsaw. Bowing her head as if embarrassed over the revelation, she asked if she could see a certain officer (whose name she had earlier obtained) about "a very personal matter."

The guards smiled. Clearly this youngster was in a "family way" and she wanted to see what the "father" was going to do about it. The guards gave her a pass to roam about the headquarters and told Niuta her "boyfriend's" room number.

Nonchalantly moving about the building until she found the designated room, Niuta entered and saw a tall officer dressed in the black uniform of the SS seated behind a desk. Without a word, the woman whipped out a concealed pistol with a silencer and shot him through the head. He fell forward onto the desk—quite dead.

Niuta then walked along a corridor and down the stairs. She smiled coyly at the guards at the front door. They grinned back. Clearly, this "pregnant" girl had received a warm reception from the SS officer she had come to see. Moments later, she was swallowed by the crowds of pedestrians.

A short time later, Niuta learned where another SS officer lived, having singled him out almost at random. She silently broke into his dark house in the middle of the night and began stealthily peeking into bedrooms until she spotted the target deep in slumber. She could have shot him as he slept, but she wanted this Gestapo officer to know that the last thing on earth he would see was a Jewish woman bent on revenge.

She gently tugged him awake, and he raised onto his elbows and rubbed his eyes in disbelief. Standing only a few feet in front of him was a girl with pigtails aiming a pistol with a silencer in his direction. Moments later, the German was dead.

Niuta continued raising havoc with the Germans in her role as an assassin. Then the Gestapo began hunting for the unknown resistant, and they called her *"kleine Wanda mit die Toepfen"* — Little Wanda with the Braids. A heavy price was put on her head. Yet she continued her activities, including joining with male resistants in pitching grenades into a posh Warsaw nightclub reserved for Gestapo and SS officers.

Miraculously, perhaps, Niuta escaped capture for nearly three years. Then her luck vanished. In July 1943, Gestapo agents, no doubt tipped off to her hideout, burst into her room and seized her before she could swallow a poison pill. After weeks of brutal torture, the Heroine of Warsaw, as she became known to the Polish underground, was executed.

Niuta's activities had a curious twist. On occasion, female resistants across Europe had used various schemes to get out of buildings in which they were being held by the Gestapo. But Niuta may well have been the only resistant who tricked her way *into* German-occupied buildings.[2]

An American Celebrity Aids the Führer

IN NOVEMBER 1939, two months after Adolf Hitler ignited war in Europe by invading neighboring Poland, a German aristocrat, Baron Ulrich von Gienanth, arrived in Washington to take up duties as Second Secretary at the German Embassy. Although it was a modest post, Gienanth, scion of an old and wealthy Prussian family, was soon in demand by the society lionesses in Washington.

A jovial, outgoing man with a keen sense of humor, the German mingled easily with the great and near-great at these lively parties. The social graces and elegance acquired from his affluent upbringing served as an ideal cover for his true function: Gestapo chief in the United States.

Known in Gestapo circles as "The Baron," Gienanth had been ordered to concentrate on subverting prominent Americans whose backgrounds or actions reflected sympathies to Adolf Hitler and the Nazi cause. So he promptly focused on thirty-eight-year-old Laura Ingalls, a renowned aviatrix, socialite, dancer, and actress.

Many who knew Ingalls regarded her as an eccentric. She had first come to the attention of the Nazi bigwigs in Germany when on September 26, 1939, she made global headlines by piloting her airplane above and "bombing" the White House with thousands of keep-out-of-the-war leaflets.

Soon after his arrival in Washington, Gienanth recruited Ingalls as a paid agent in the secret employ of the Third Reich. Considering her renown and established contacts with the elite in the United States, she worked cheaply—$300 per month.

"The Baron" was delighted with Ingalls's work. She became a tireless speaker, traveling throughout the United States to exhort large and boisterous rallies to fight President Roosevelt's plan to "drag the United States into the war in Europe."

Gienanth wrote his superiors in Berlin about the fiery, rabble-rousing speeches the aviatrix was giving to wildly cheering crowds. "It's just what the King and Mama did in the early days," the master spy stated. In the code used in the letter, "King" meant Adolf Hitler, "Mama" was Gienanth, and the "early days" referred to the Nazis' bitter and often bloody struggle to seize power in the 1920s and early 1930s.

Ingalls had long been in the sights of J. Edgar Hoover, the scrappy, astute director of the Federal Bureau of Investigation, but he could not arrest her for merely making rabble-rousing speeches damning the United States. But in early 1942, about a month after the United States had been bombed into war at Pearl Harbor, Hoover sprung his trap.

On February 24, Ingalls was tried in court and sentenced to a prison term of from eight months to two years for failure to register as a German agent.

It was brought out during the trial that the aviatrix had written a letter to the president of a "peace group" in the United States in which she said, "I want to invite you to visit me in my chalet in Berchtesgaden after the war." Berchtesgaden was the site of Adolf Hitler's retreat atop a towering mountain in southern Germany.

Baron von Gienanth, meanwhile, was back in the Third Reich, having been expelled from Washington when the führer declared war on the United States four days after Japan bombed Pearl Harbor.[3]

A Civic-Minded Spy in Miami

CARL HERMAN SCHROETTER was the amiable skipper of a charter boat, *Echo of the Past*, based in Miami, Florida. He had come to the United States in 1939 and soon was a naturalized citizen.

Schroetter promptly joined in Miami's community life and was an exemplary American. He displayed his civic-mindedness by volunteering for election duty as a registration clerk in Dade County's Precinct 34. He was also a spy for the German Abwehr, and his main assignment was to report on the naval facilities and other military installations in the Miami region.

Swiss-born Schroetter had been traveling in Germany when war broke out with England and France in September 1939. Unbeknownst to him, the Abwehr had been tailing him. He had two sisters living in the Third Reich, and by threatening his siblings, the Abwehr coerced the bewildered Schroetter to return to Miami and become a "sleeper" agent. He was to lead a normal life, but would be available for a mission when called upon by Berlin.

In 1940, Schroetter was activated and ordered to report on ship movements along the Florida coast, a task he could perform without attracting undue attention while piloting *Echo of the Past* on legitimate excursions.

Perhaps out of concern for his sisters in Germany, Schroetter became an eager spy. Throughout 1940 and into the spring of 1941, while Adolf Hitler was conducting widespread conquests in Europe, the Miami resident mailed to his Abwehr controller in New York City a heavy stream of coded messages, some of them written in invisible ink.

In the meantime, the Abwehr was demanding information on the growing naval air station outside Miami, but Schroetter was unable to get inside the facility. Security was tight.

So Schroetter got a job as night chef at the Greyhound Club, a popular bar and grill near the air station that was a haunt for navy officers and men. The spy had deliberately applied for a night job. At that stage, many of the servicemen would be well intoxicated after a few hours of drinking, and their tongues would be loosened.

Unaware of any spy menace in Miami, the navy officers and sailors talked freely to the affable chef, who carefully plied them with questions that the Abwehr in Berlin wanted answered. After his shift at the nightclub was over each night, Schroetter returned to his modest lodging and fired off to his New York contact all the detailed information he had gleaned at the club.

After the United States was bombed into global war at Pearl Harbor, Admiral Karl Dönitz, commander of German submarines, had sent his ace U-boat skippers to the East Coast of the United States to pounce on Allied cargo ships bound for England and North Africa. No doubt the high-grade intelligence provided by Carl Schroetter had contributed greatly to the loss of hundreds of lives and scores of Allied vessels during the first half of the year.

The carnage was a national disaster for the United States, comparable to saboteurs blowing up ten of the country's largest warplants. In mid-1942, the U-boat wolf packs became even bolder. Instead of attacking only at night, they now sank Allied merchantmen in broad daylight.

The highly motivated U-boat skippers and their crews appeared to be enjoying their field day off America's coastline. Often they gave water, cigarettes, and food to survivors of sunken ships in lifeboats before sending them on their way with a standard joke: "Don't forget to send the bill for that ship to Roosevelt or Churchill."

At his headquarters in a thick bunker at the French port of Lorient, Admiral Dönitz could not resist boasting. As German and neutral-nation newsreel cameras turned and photographers' flashbulbs popped, the admiral declared: "Our U-boats are operating close inshore along the coast of the United States so that bathers and sometimes entire coastal cities are witnesses to that drama of war, whose visual climaxes are often constituted by the red glorioles of blazing tankers."

In the meantime, Carl Schroetter had gone undercover, telling his Abwehr controller in New York City that he was being tailed by agents of the Federal Bureau of Investigation. However, he had not holed up in time. A week later, the G-men, as they were known, arrested the spy.

Although Schroetter pleaded guilty to espionage, he refused to identify other Abwehr agents with whom he was connected in the United States. Consequently, he received a term of ten years in prison.

A few days after Schroetter entered the federal prison in Atlanta, he committed suicide in his cell by hanging himself with a sheet.[4]

A Swedish Professor's Intelligence Coup

FINLAND IS A COUNTRY of lakes, swamps, and forests, covering an area a little smaller than the combined areas of Minnesota and Mississippi in the United States. Finland's neighbor along its eastern border was the Soviet Union, about a hundred times larger than Finland and with some eighty times more population. Yet Soviet dictator Josef Stalin coveted the tiny nation, and in the bitter cold of the last day of November 1939, he sent the Red Army plunging into Finland.

Stalin had told his generals that Finland would surrender before the first of the year. It was a David and Goliath confrontation. No doubt Stalin was astonished to find that Goliath was outwitted and outmaneuvered by tiny David.

As the free world looked on in admiration, the 175,000-man Finish army under seventy-two-year-old Field Marshal Carl Gustaf von Mannerheim harassed and delayed Stalin's one million Red Army soldiers. By the first week of 1940, instead of surrendering, Mannerheim's "Skiing Ghosts," as his white-clad soldiers were dubbed by the world's press, were inflicting heavy casualties. They seemed to be at the right place at the right time to surprise Soviet units.

There was good reason for Baron von Mannerheim's apparent strategic omniscience. A hulking, easygoing professor of mathematics, Dr. Arne Beurling, in neutral Sweden, had intercepted and decoded Stalin's plans to invade

Finland. Beurling had warned Mannerheim, who had his troops in defensive positions when the Red Army struck. In the weeks ahead, the professor continued to slip word to the Finns about Red Army intentions after decoding messages between the Russian fighting formations and their headquarters.

Dr. Beurling's incredible intelligence coup resulted in the Soviet army paying a horrible price in blood. But the outcome was inevitable. Goliath vanquished David. The Finns were forced to surrender on March 10, 1940.[5]

Greta Garbo: A Secret Agent

NEUTRAL SWEDEN WAS BLANKETED by deep snow in January 1940 when William S. Stephenson, a forty-three-year-old self-made Canadian millionaire, arrived in Stockholm, a hotbed of intrigue. He owned a factory that built airplanes and controlled the largest movie studio outside of Hollywood, among other holdings. But he was in Stockholm as a secret agent to orchestrate a major sabotage operation against the Third Reich.

Earlier, Winston Churchill, the First Lord of the Admiralty, decided that vital materials in Sweden bound for Nazi Germany "must be prevented from leaving by methods which will be neither diplomatic nor military." Therefore, he had his Naval Intelligence create Strike Ox, named for Oxelosund, an ice-free port some sixty miles southwest of Stockholm.

Targets of the covert operation were tons of Swedish iron ore which, if destroyed or sidetracked, would leave Adolf Hitler with only enough stockpiled to keep his steel industry going for another nine months. Churchill chose Bill Stephenson, who had extensive commercial interests in England and combined business with freelance intelligence missions, to spearhead Strike Ox.

When Churchill spoke of halting certain vital supplies from reaching Germany, he, Stephenson, and a small group of British scientists knew that heavy water also traveled this route from Norway to the Third Reich. And heavy water, Churchill had been informed, was a key ingredient to creating the ultimate weapon, a revolutionary atomic bomb.

Stephenson's cover story was that he had to go to Sweden to look after his commercial interests there. The secondary cover for the benefit of German intelligence was that he had come to sabotage Oxelosund's loading ramps and cranes to keep the iron ore from being shipped. Actually, the Canadian would be on the trail of heavy water, and try to learn what progress the Germans had made toward building an atomic bomb.

As expected, German agents soon learned of Stephenson's arrival in Stockholm. It seemed logical to the Nazis that the destruction of Oxelosund's facilities would badly cripple the German arms industry.

Strike Ox, as hoped, became an open secret in Sweden. King Gustav V was both furious and frightened. He urged King George VI in London to call off the sabotage operation. So Strike Ox was cancelled, and Bill Stephenson launched his true function of learning German atomic secrets and reinforcing a network of friendly Swedes to help achieve his goal.

Because of his movie studio, Stephenson had many contacts in the entertainment community, and one of these he sought out was Greta Garbo, the world-famous Swedish actress who had worked in his studio and was a close friend. Described by some in the industry as "the most celebrated actress the screen has ever seen," she was widely known for her secretive lifestyle. In a profession where a performer would do almost anything to get her photo taken, Garbo shied away from press cameras.

Born in Stockholm, she had appeared in several Swedish movies; then, at age nineteen, she went to Hollywood, where she starred in such acclaimed films as *Camille*, *Anna Christie*, and *Ninotchka*.

Now back in her native country at age thirty-four, Garbo had been working undercover for the British, reporting on Nazi sympathizers. When Bill Stephenson showed up in Stockholm to expand his information network, Garbo carried messages for him and introduced him to her high-level friends. What Garbo could not be told was that the Canadian also was quietly arranging an escape route for Neils Bohr, a Dane, one of the world's foremost physicists.

Bohr, British intelligence knew, was experimenting at the Institute for Theoretical Physics in Copenhagen on projects thought to be related to atomic energy. In early 1940, friends had been urging Bohr to flee to England in anticipation of a German invasion of Denmark. But the nuclear physicist had always refused.

Apparently Bill Stephenson planned to launch an operation to "escort" Bohr to Great Britain, whether the Dane liked it or not.

In the meantime, Adolf Hitler in Berlin had ordered his generals to launch Operation Weseruebung (Weser Exercise). It kicked off at 5:15 A.M. on April 9, 1940, and German troops charged into Norway and Denmark.

*Movie superstar
Greta Garbo. (MGM)*

The Danes were in a hopeless position. Their flat little country was incapable of defense against German panzers. The Danish army fought a few skirmishes, but by the time the citizens had finished their breakfasts, it was all over. King Christian X was forced to capitulate.

That unexpected German invasion effectively concluded Bill Stephenson's plan to "escort" Neils Bohr to England. However, after he had left the country, Greta Garbo continued to keep him informed about Nazi machinations in Sweden.[6]

"You Will Spy for the Fatherland!"

NEW YORK CITY WAS BLANKETED with snow on the morning of February 7, 1940, when the SS *Washington* arrived from Europe and tied up at a wharf. Three grim-faced men scrambled up the gangway and walked rapidly to a cabin. They knocked on the door and a passenger, identified on the ship's roster as William G. Sawyer, answered the summons.

The strangers slipped into the cabin, and for long seconds, Sawyer and the others stared at one another. Then one of the newcomers flashed a badge and said "FBI!" The passenger was visibly relieved. Only a few weeks earlier in Germany, he had agreed to become a spy in the United States, and he had been fearful that the visitors were Gestapo agents.

Sawyer was an alias. The man's real name was William G. Sebold, and his nightmarish adventure had its roots several months earlier in San Diego, California, when he had grown nostalgic to see his native Germany again. During World War I, he had fought in the Kaiser's army as a corporal on the Western Front and had been seriously wounded.

About two years after the conflict had ceased, he came to the United States under his real name (Wilhelm Georg Debowski), changed his name to William G. Sebold, and obtained a job as a machinist, a trade at which he was skilled. He married a young American woman, loved the United States, decided to become a citizen, and was determined to be loyal to his adopted land.

In June 1939, Sebold took a leave of absence from his well-paying job as a draftsman at the Consolidated Aircraft Company, bid his wife goodbye, and crossed the Atlantic on the SS *Deutschland*, docking at Hamburg.

While waiting to clear customs, Sebold was approached by two agents of the Geheime Staatzpolizei (Gestapo). They told Sebold to come with them, and the three men climbed into an automobile and rode to a large brownstone building.

The naturalized American was ushered into a cavernous office to be greeted by a smiling SS officer. "Welcome to the new Germany!" the black-uniformed official said graciously. "My name is Colonel Paul Kraus, chief of the Hamburg Gestapo."

As Sebold took a seat and puffed nervously on a cigarette, Kraus pulled a file folder from his desk and reeled off a lengthy recital of Sebold's past, going back to his boyhood days in his birthplace of Mülheim-on-Ruhr. The Gestapo chief also gave details about Sebold's aging mother, two brothers, and a sister, all of whom still lived in Mülheim.

Colonel Kraus took out another folder and began ticking off production figures at the Consolidated Aircraft Company. Sebold was stunned. Those figures were precisely accurate. Seeing Sebold's astonished look, the German explained, "We have a Gestapo agent in the Consolidated Aircraft plant, near where you work."

When Sebold refused to confirm the aircraft plant figures, Kraus took off the kid gloves. He snapped, "I would remind you, Herr Debowski, once a German, always a German!" Pausing briefly, the Gestapo man said, "Your relatives live in Mülheim. If you refuse to cooperate, we cannot guarantee their safety . . ."

Kraus's voice trailed away, casting an even more sinister connotation to the threat: "You will spy in the United States for the Fatherland!"

Bill Sebold, American as apple pie, baseball, and the hot dog, felt trapped. Loyalty to his adopted land or to his mother, brothers, and sister — which would it be? Before he could reply, Colonel Kraus, pleasant once again and blowing cigarette smoke rings, told Sebold to think over his proposal for a few days.

Sebold promptly caught a train for Mülheim, and since the family home was crowded, he checked in at the Hotel Handelshof. Hardly had he finished unpacking than he set off by foot for his mother's home. A Gestapo agent tailed him, and another went into the Handelshof and confiscated a letter and a postcard that Sebold had mailed to his wife in San Diego.

After a joyous reunion between the former Wilhelm Debowski and his family, the bewildered American wandered around the ancient city of his birth, mulling over the situation in which he had been trapped. He had no choice: either he spied for the Nazis in the United States or his mother, brothers, and sister were doomed, and it would be unlikely that he himself would get out of the Third Reich alive. Colonel Kraus was delighted to hear Sebold's decision and told the spy recruit that he would live in Hamburg for three months while taking espionage training at the Abwehr Academy.

Early in September, Sebold enrolled at the Academy. Emphasis was given to radio operations. The American was told that he would be provided with a thousand genuine U.S. dollars, and when he reached New York, he was to buy radio parts and establish his own clandestine station for communicating directly with the Abwehrstellen (branch), also known as Ast X, at Hamburg. In late

December, he "graduated" from the Academy and was given the alias William G. Sawyer.

After paying a final visit to his family in Mülheim, Sebold, at the risk of his life, managed to give the Gestapo tails the slip and crossed the Rhine River to Cologne. There he informed officials in the U.S. Consulate that he had agreed to spy for Germany in the United States but that he would cooperate with the Federal Bureau of Investigation when he reached New York.

During the Atlantic crossing, Sebold was haunted by the specter that the Consulate in Cologne might have failed to notify the FBI about his coming. So when there had been the knocking at his cabin door on the *Washington*, he had not known if it would be G-men, as the American sleuths were popularly called, or a Gestapo hit squad.

Now, in the small cabin of the ship, Sebold handed the FBI agents the $1,000 (a sizeable sum at the time) that the Hamburg controllers had given him to buy radio parts. Sebold also handed over the names and addresses of four persons listed by the Abwehr on a slip of paper. It was rightly decided by the G-men that these four people were key agents in a New York–based Nazi spy ring.

The G-men felt that the Gestapo may have sent spies to the *Washington* to see who got off the ship with Sebold and where the party went. So they told Sebold to go to a certain hotel in Yorkville, the German-American community on the Upper East Side of Manhattan, and the sleuths would contact him that night.

While Sebold holed up in the hotel, FBI technicians enlarged the four microfilms that the Abwehr in Hamburg had concealed in the back of their recruit's watch. All of the messages were the same, written in German and containing the same "shopping list" of fourteen weapons and equipment used by the U.S. armed forces—secrets that the spies were to steal.

Sebold had been told in Hamburg to give one microfilm to each of the four persons whose addresses he had been given. His first call was on sixty-two-year-old Frederick Duquesne at his office, Air Terminal Associates, in a Wall Street building. The title was meaningless; it served as a front for his role as head of the Nazi spy network in greater New York.

On Sebold's arrival, Duquesne eyed the visitor suspiciously. "I am William Sawyer," the newcomer said, adding the passwords that had been given him in Germany: "I bring you greetings from Rantzau, Berlin, and Hamburg."

Duquesne, who told Sawyer that he had spied for Germany since the Boer War forty years earlier, confessed that he had a major problem. So much intelligence was being brought to his office on Wall Street by his spies that he was having a hard time getting the data to Hamburg.

No problem, Sebold assured him. Hamburg had instructed him to set up a shortwave radio station in the New York City area.

FBI agents took photos through dummy mirrors of German spies calling on double-agent William Sebold (back to camera) in his "office" in New York City's Knickerbocker Building. (FBI)

Before Sebold had left Hamburg, Colonel Kraus told him the secret radio station might be unmasked if a parade of Nazi spies traipsed in and out of the facility. So five thousand dollars had been deposited in a New York bank for Sebold to open an office in midtown Manhattan where he could talk with the German agents and collect their information. Sebold took space in the Knickerbocker Building on 42nd Street and gave his dummy firm the name Diesel Research Company.

Sebold had several silent partners in his company—FBI agents who created elaborate props to allow the firm to operate more efficiently. A mirror on the wall of Sebold's office reflected the image of anyone looking into the glass—but in the adjoining room this mirror became a window through which G-men could take movies of everything that transpired in the research firm's office. The walls were painted white in order to produce clearer pictures.

Hidden microphones would carry each word spoken to a recording device. There were other deft touches. On Sebold's desk was a clock and behind it a flip-over day-by-day wall calendar, which would reveal on film the precise time and date when Sebold had a visitor. There was only one extra chair in the room, and it was placed near Sebold's desk so that the visiting spy would always have to sit facing the mirror—and the movie camera. Now all was in readiness for the cat-and-mouse game between the Federal Bureau of Investigation and the espionage masterminds in the Third Reich.[7]

Hitler Finances an FBI Coup

SOON AFTER THE GERMAN WAR MACHINE had plunged into Poland on September 1, 1939, J. Edgar Hoover, the robust supersleuth who headed the Federal Bureau of Investigation, rose to speak at a convention of police chiefs in San Francisco. Hardly had the applause receded than he rocked the audience by declaring, "We have a distinct spy menace in the United States!"

It was a gross understatement. For much of the decade, German spies had penetrated nearly every major U.S. military, government, and industrial entity. Hundreds of supposed secrets had poured across the Atlantic to the Abwehr branch in Hamburg.

Hoover told his mesmerized law enforcement listeners at San Francisco, "President Roosevelt has instructed the FBI to take charge of all investigative work in matters involving espionage, sabotage, and subversive activities."

For the first time in its one-hundred-and-sixty-three-year history, the United States would have a single federal agency designated to fight insidious forces seeking to subvert the nation from within.

Now, six months after the FBI had taken on its massive new assignment, Hoover's agents in New York advised him that they were working with William G. Sebold, who had volunteered to be a double agent. Realizing that Sebold's situation had great potential for both unmasking Nazi agents in the United States and tricking the Abwehr leaders in Europe by plying them with false information, Hoover took a direct interest in the project. He ordered his G-men to acquire a house off the beaten path in the New York suburbs and build the radio station over which Sebold was to keep in contact with Hamburg.

Masquerading as a New York City businessman seeking a house in a quiet suburb as a hideaway to escape from daily business pressures, Hoover's man picked out and purchased, with the American money that the Abwehr had provided Sebold, a small frame house in a sparsely populated area in Centerport, Long Island, a short drive from Manhattan, as the location of the station. It would be operated by FBI agents M. H. Price and J. C. Ellsworth. One of them had been a "ham" (licensed amateur radio operator) for several years and could send thirty words per minute in code, while the other had once lived in Germany and spoke the language like a native Berliner.

The final step was to register the Centerport operation as an approved amateur station, just in case any radio hams around the United States happened to become suspicious.

*The small house in suburban New York City from which FBI agents radioed doctored
intelligence to the Abwehr in Hamburg, Germany. (FBI)*

Now the FBI would have a direct pipeline into the Abwehr hierarchy in
the Third Reich—if all went well.

Toward the end of April 1940, Wilhelm Siegler, the head butcher on the
SS *Amerika* and a veteran Abwehr courier, brought news for Sebold from
Hamburg: He was to open radio communication at precisely 7:00 P.M., Eastern
Standard Time, on May 15. He was to use the call sign CQDXVW-2 and con-
tact Station AOR, a radio transmitter in Hamburg.

Sebold's (that is, FBI Agents Price and Ellsworth's) transmission would be
encoded in a key picked from a current bestseller by Rachel Field, *All This and
Heaven, Too.* (Which triggered an FBI quip: "All This Is Heavenly.") The key
to the code was in the date a radio message would be sent. The day and month
were totaled up and twenty was added to the sum, indicating the page of
Field's book on which the message would be contained. Starting with the first
line on that page, the agents manning the Centerport transmitter would work
up and down in a complicated series of squares.

At the appointed time, the two G-men in the Centerport cottage tapped
out the call sign CQDXVW-2. Anxiously they awaited a response. There was
none. For two more nights, they tried to get through to Hamburg, but met with
only silence.

Had the Gestapo and Abwehr been tipped off about "William Sawyer's" double-dealing? If so, his mother, two brothers, and a sister in Mülheim would suffer hideous deaths in Gestapo torture chambers.

On the night of May 18, the G-men at Centerport continued to tap out signals in what appeared to be a blown machination. Suddenly, at midnight, they were electrified: Their receiver began to crackle. A message was coming through from Station AOR in Hamburg. Decoded by the FBI agents, it read:

Send only two times per week. We are prepared to send and receive daily. We are prepared 7:00 A.M., 1:00 P.M., and 5:00 P.M.—AOR

The two Feds let out whoops of joy, then dispatched a coded reply:

Your signal weak. Can you improve it? I will send Tuesdays and Thursdays 1:00 and 5:00 P.M. Will listen daily except Saturday night and Sunday.—CQDXVW-2

J. Edgar Hoover formed a "little brain trust" of his most devious-minded men to create an ongoing script for Sebold's shortwave transmissions. These early days would be crucial, for the Abwehr would instruct agents in the United States to check on the validity of the information Sebold was sending to Hamburg. So the scriptwriters had to include true facts and data along with a mass of twisted or bogus military secrets. Magnified to enhance their significance, the phony secrets were largely outdated information or that deemed relatively harmless. Aircraft that had been declared obsolete by the army could be described in great—and accurate—detail.[8]

Japanese Fishermen in the Caribbean

WHILE ADOLF HITLER was engaged in his widespread campaigns of conquest in Europe, the Japanese fishing industry was displaying keen interest in the waters of the Caribbean, nearly 10,000 miles from Tokyo. The warm, gentle waters not far from Florida in the United States were swarming with fishing craft. Mainly they were angling for information that would be valuable to the Imperial High Command back home. It was the early 1940s.

Unseen by the casual outside eye, the entire "fishing" operation in the Caribbean was closely supervised by a soft-spoken, middle-aged businessman whose base jumped about from island to island. Actually, he was Captain Ketarino Kabayama of the Japanese navy. To keep up appearances, fish were caught and the harvest from the fleet of small boats was taken to Japan by

Shoicki Yokoi, who moved about the Caribbean masquerading as an exporter. He was a commander in the Japanese navy.

There were more than hauls of fish on board the boats. Most had two-way radios and an officer in disguise from the Department of Naval Intelligence in Tokyo.

On occasion, one of the fishing fleet would dock in the harbor at Colón, Panama, where the U.S.–controlled canal was crucial to the security of America itself. One or two of the Japanese secret agents would pay a visit to a small haberdashery shop at Calle 10a. The firm was owned by an attractive, elegantly garbed woman in her early thirties, Lola Osawa.

That name was an alias and the shop was a blind. She was in reality Chiyo Morasawa, wife of a Japanese naval officer. The couple formed a husband-and-wife espionage team, specializing in stealing secrets of the vital Panama Canal. The wife's popular business firm was actually the unlikely headquarters for several Japanese spy rings scattered about the region.[9]

Confiscating Nazis' Stolen Art Treasures

DURING THE 1930S, the United States had been invaded by the most massive espionage penetration of a major power that history had known. Admiral Wilhelm Canaris, Nazi Germany's chief spymaster, employed ingenious ruses and sinister schemes to extract intelligence from American industry, government, and armed forces.

German diplomats, whose main function was espionage in the United States, had no problem with sending stolen or acquired secrets to the Fatherland—they were carried by couriers in bulging diplomatic pouches that were free from inspection by American customs officers. But the swarm of ordinary Nazi agents operating in the United States had to send reports and documents to Germany through the regular mails.

The United States was officially neutral, so it could take no direct action to put a crimp in this flow of intelligence to Germany. However, the British secret service established the Imperial Censorship Station in Hamilton, Bermuda, a British crown colony about 670 miles east of New York City.

The nerve center for the operation was in the Princess Hotel, a pink colonial structure. It was staffed by hundreds of handwriting experts, chemists (to detect invisible inks), cryptanalysts (to solve complicated codes), and assorted sleuths.

All Pan American Clippers, huge flying boats that traveled mostly between Port Washington, outside of New York City, and the neutral European nations of Spain and Portugal, were required to halt at Bermuda. So were

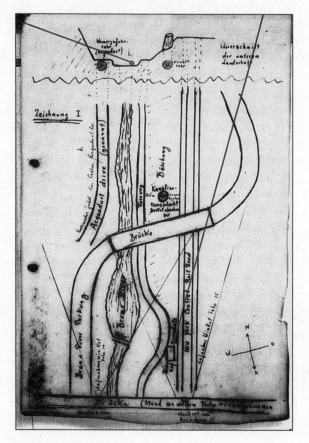

German spies sketched scores of strategic sites in the United States, including the waterworks in Westchester County, New York, to guide saboteurs. (FBI)

ocean liners. The planes and ships had to deliver their bags of mail to the censorship stations.

On an average stopover by an oceangoing ship loaded with passengers, the experts at the Princess Hotel would inspect as many as 200,000 pieces of mail, looking for espionage clues. The tedious and difficult process uncovered information that pinpointed large numbers of spies that the German Abwehr chief Canaris had planted or recruited in the United States.

The British sleuths at Bermuda also learned that the Germans were raising money for Adolf Hitler's war juggernaut by shipping through neutral ports art treasures stolen by the Nazis in conquered nations and sold for millions of dollars in New York City. Wealthy American buyers of the purloined masterpieces were not too picky about their sources.

These stolen art treasures also passed through the Bermuda censorship station on the way to New York City. In one instance, the American Export Lines' ship *Excalibur* carried valuable paintings in a sealed strongroom. British authorities asked the captain to open the compartment, but he refused.

Like skilled safecrackers, the British burned the sealed room open with blowtorches and discovered a large cache of rare and valuable paintings. These works of art were confiscated and stored in the vaults of the Bank of Bermuda. It would be nearly four years, after the Wehrmacht was driven out of France in late 1944, before the 270 Impressionist works were returned to their astonished owners.[10]

A Propaganda Blitz against the United States

WHILE A BRUTAL WAR WAS RAGING in Europe, and Japan was inflicting one of history's bloodiest onslaughts against China, in the early 1940s, most Americans were peacefully preoccupied with their own homegrown affairs.

Americans felt that they were safe from the "trouble" taking place overseas. They assured themselves that there were two broad oceans to protect them, and the national slogan seemed to be "keep out of other nations' quarrels." A poll taken by Elmo Roper in December 1939 disclosed that 67.4 percent of Americans were opposed to taking sides.

Franklin D. Roosevelt, who would soon be running for an unprecedented third term as president, typically sensed the mood of the American people. In one of the radio broadcasts he called fireside chats, he declared: "I have said this before, but I shall say it again and again. Your boys are not going to be sent into any foreign wars."

During the preceding two decades, the United States had allowed her armed forces to disintegrate to those of a fourth-rate country. But, as Adolf Hitler told confidants, America was a sleeping giant—and the führer intended to lull her into even deeper slumber while his plans for widespread conquest unfolded.

Consequently, Hitler called in two of his top officials, Propaganda Minister Josef Goebbels and Foreign Minister Joachim von Ribbentrop, and told them to launch an all-out propaganda blitz against the United States to keep that potentially powerful adversary neutral. He had picked the right men: both Goebbels and Ribbentrop were proven masters of deceit and fraud.

Barely five feet tall and walking with a bad limp, the forty-two-year-old Goebbels was a Hitler favorite because of his aptitude for demagogic broadcasts and print stories while spreading the Nazi message. By 1940, he had become one of the five most powerful men in the Third Reich, having total control over all communications media.

Ulrich Friedrich Willy Joachim von Ribbentrop was handsome, arrogant, charming, and said by critics to be empty-headed. He had gained entrée into high society by marrying the daughter of a wealthy wine merchant. A year later, he added "von" to his name.

Josef Goebbels, the Nazi propaganda genius, controlled all of the German media and often spoke over the radio. (National Archives)

Ribbentrop, whose enemies in the Nazi hierarchy abounded, was nevertheless a good salesman for the Third Reich. Hitler held him in high esteem.

In Berlin, Goebbels and Ribbentrop concocted a broad outline for the propaganda blitz against the United States. Hans Thomsen, a slick operative who masqueraded as the chargé d'affaires in the German Embassy in Washington, would orchestrate the offensive.

Thomsen, an ambitious and energetic type, was elated over being designated to play such an important role for the führer. Early on, he excitedly dispatched a coded message to Berlin: "A prominent Republican Congressman who is working closely with the [German] Embassy has offered, for three thousand dollars, to invite fifty isolationist members of Congress to the [forthcoming] Republican convention so they can influence delegates to adopt a stay-out-of-the-war foreign policy platform."

Moreover, Thomsen added, this congressman had asked for $30,000 (equivalent to some $350,000 in 2001) to help defray the cost of full-page newspaper ads to be headlined: "KEEP AMERICA OUT OF WAR." The German official did not estimate how much of that hefty sum would find its way into the congressman's pocket.

The Nazi campaign to keep America dozing had no shortage of domestic allies. New York City's *Daily Worker*, parroting the Communist party line from Josef Stalin (with whom Hitler had recently signed a "friendship pact") in

Moscow, screeched constantly: Don't send American boys to die for the war-monger Churchill and the ill-gotten British Empire. The *Daily Worker* rantings made an impact on thousands of dispirited, jobless Americans caught in the center of the Great Depression.

Hans Thomsen, the German Embassy official, energetically sought out American reporters and authors to enlist them in the Nazi campaign. On June 13, Thomsen again wired Berlin: He was negotiating a deal through a New York City literary agent in which five "well-known American authors" had agreed to write "keep out of the war" books. This propaganda bonanza, Thomsen added, would cost only $20,000. Ribbentrop promptly approved the expenditure.

Many American newspapers, patriotic but isolationist in viewpoint, were perhaps duped by Goebbel's media machinations. When the führer gave a speech in Berlin in mid-June, Hans Thomsen arranged to have advance copies of a news release distributed widely to American newspapers and radio stations. He wired Berlin that he had personally slipped an advance (translated) text of the führer's address to a New York City reporter for a chain of large American newspapers.

Only a few hours after the final echo from Hitler's Berlin speech had died down, millions of Americans were greeted by blaring newspaper headlines that declared: "HITLER WANTS PEACE." Few editors bothered to probe into the Nazi warlord's price for "peace": the capitulation of Great Britain and the permanent merging of the conquered nations into Hitler's Greater Reich.

Thomsen was ecstatic over the German propaganda bonanza's impact. He wired Berlin that he had arranged for "an isolationist Congressman" to enter the führer's "peace speech" in the Congressional Record on June 22. The German Embassy official was especially elated over the dramatic play given the Nazi dictator's views in Hearst's *New York Journal-American*. He had one hundred thousand reprints made and distributed to opinion leaders throughout the States, Thomsen informed his boss, Ribbentrop.[11]

The Secret Looting
of Conquered Europe

ARTUR RÜMANN, a wealthy Bavarian art dealer, was playing host at a luncheon with eight or ten prominent German industrialists in a plush dining club in Dusseldorf, the business center of the coal-and-steel-producing Ruhr Valley. When Adolf Hitler came into power in early 1933, he had promptly set about harnessing the vast power of the Ruhr to arm and equip the huge armed forces he began to create. It was Saturday, May 18, 1940.

At 2:00 P.M., Rümann and the other movers and shakers interrupted their meal when they heard a radio announcer state he had important news from the Western Front. Hitler had launched Case Yellow, a massive offensive against the British and French armies in France, Belgium, and the Netherlands, eight days earlier. Now, the radio broadcast said, General Gerd von Rundstedt's Army Group A panzers had broken through French lines and had raced two-thirds of the way across northern France. General Fedor von Bock's Army Group B had charged halfway across Belgium.

Cheers erupted from the industrialists and business executives glued to the radio in the dining establishment. One of the men pulled out a map of the Netherlands, which had already surrendered, and as the radio announcer called out the place names, eyes darted back and forth to pinpoint the Dutch business firms and manufacturing plants now in German hands.

These German entrepreneurs had long known the Dutch industrialists and the plants they had operated. "There is Müller," called out one German, pointing to a spot on the map the Dutchman owned. "He is yours," he added, nodding toward a dining companion. Chimed in another: "There is Schmidt. He has two plants; we will have him arrested."

One of the diners, thirty-two-year-old Alfred Krupp von Bohlen und Halbach, scion of the Krupp family that had virtual control of the German arms and munitions industry, had been a heavy financial backer of Adolf Hitler when he had been rising in power. Krupp's family had become fabulously wealthy and influential after the führer began rearming the Third Reich in 1935. Now, clustered with the others around the radio, young Krupp said to one man, "You can have those two [Dutch manufacturing plants]."

These German industrialists were busily dividing up the spoils that they felt were rightfully theirs because of their staunch support of Hitler. They were not alone. Throughout the Reich, a legion of expectant Germans—public officials and private entrepreneurs—were poised to pounce on the riches of the newly occupied nations.

These wealthy scroungers would be sort of freelance thieves. On the other hand, Field Marshal Hermann Göring, known behind his back as *Der Dicke* (Fatty), was an official looter. He had been appointed by Hitler as head of the führer's Four-Year Plan for economic expansion. Göring had organized a systematic mass looting of conquered nations.

"We will exploit everything to the utmost," Göring told General Georg Thomas, who was named to head the day-to-day operation of the pilfering of other countries' resources. Thomas created economic staffs and field units (called Wirtschaftstruppen) that went with the invading German forces to locate, catalog, and seize essential goods. They had been ordered to ship "trainload after trainload" back to German factories or to confiscate operating plants within the occupied regions.

Throughout the German occupation of much of western Europe, with a total population of some seventy million, long trains and convoys of trucks, loaded with stolen booty, converged on the Third Reich. "The real profiteers of this war are ourselves," Hitler boasted to confidants. "We will give nothing and take everything we can make use of!"

Göring joined in making his views known. "I intend to plunder," he told his subordinates, "and plunder copiously!" The field marshal, whom Hitler had designated as his heir in September 1939, found himself refereeing bitter disputes among various government agencies and private enterprises, such as the Krupps, who were competing ferociously for the spoils.

Göring, in his own right, had become something of an expert on pillaging. He had his agents scour the galleries of Paris, Amsterdam, and Brussels and "acquire" valuable original paintings by Rembrandt, Rubens, and other masters. He had no intention of sharing this art collection, which enriched him by hundreds of millions of dollars.[12]

A Hollywood "Warrior" Is Knighted

ENGLAND WAS AN ISLAND under siege. She stood alone against the threat of Adolf Hitler's awesome Wehrmacht, which was poised across the English Channel to invade the British Isles. Contingency plans had been drawn up to evacuate the royal family to Canada. Unprepared for total war, Britain reeled in tumult and confusion. It was June 1940.

Winston S. Churchill had been appointed prime minister by King George VI on May 10, just in time to preside over the destruction of the Dutch, Belgian, French, and British armies by the German offensive code-named Case Yellow. The rotund, keen-witted Churchill and other British leaders knew that if their country were to survive, the sleeping giant United States, with its largely untapped industrial potential and huge manpower, would have to be drawn into the European conflict—covertly or otherwise. But first, the American isolationist mindset of "keeping out of other nations' quarrels" would have to be reversed.

Secret service leaders in Britain began focusing on Hollywood, which had the impact to chip away at the American people's reluctance to get involved in a major war. In the celluloid paradise created by Hollywood during the Great Depression era of the 1930s, Tinseltown moguls like Louis B. Mayer and Samuel Goldwyn produced movies that provided escape for the masses. Some eighty-five million Americans each week scraped up the dimes or quarters needed to enter through the magic portals of movie theaters.

While Hollywood produced such escapist fare as child star Shirley Temple in *Rebecca of Sunnybrook Farm* and teenage superstars Mickey Rooney and

Hollywood's pro-British blockbuster movies featured superstars Tyrone Power and Betty Grable (left) in A Yank in the RAF *and Greer Garson with Helmut Dantine (right) in* Mrs. Miniver. *(MGM Studios)*

Judy Garland in *Love Finds Andy Hardy*, the British sought to exploit the propaganda potential of the movie capital of the world.

Movies, the British knew, had a mesmerizing impact on viewers, who subconsciously accepted as their own opinions those emphasized in films. In one box-office hit, Clark Gable, the romantic hero of the time, was shown in a scene removing his shirt, thereby revealing that he was wearing no undershirt. Nearly all men and boys wore undershirts. But after that scene, undershirt sales in the United States plummeted nearly 70 percent.

Ronald Colman, a Briton and a suave lover in many Hollywood movies, had been asked by the British to make certain that England would look good on the silver screen. Leslie Howard, another Briton who had gained fame in the United States for his role in the blockbuster movie *Gone With the Wind*, also was encouraged to do what he could to put a favorable face on England before millions of avid moviegoers.

One of Hollywood's best-known and most successful producers, British-Hungarian Alexander Korda, had been recruited to help bend America's isolationist viewpoint toward aiding embattled Great Britain by a crusty old pro in the British Secret Service, Colonel Claude Dansey.

Dansey, who had organized a widespread espionage network in Europe during the 1930s, was assistant chief of MI-6, Great Britain's secret service responsible for overseas operations. Described by friends as "crusty" and by his British enemies as "that cantankerous old son of a bitch," he must have felt out of place in his campaign to sway public opinion toward helping England. He was known to have been critical of anything American. But Great Britain was fighting desperately to survive, so Dansey focused his acknowledged slight-of-hand skills on Hollywood through Alexander Korda, Ronald Colman, Leslie Howard, and others.

One of Korda's first movies was *That Hamilton Woman* (*Lady Hamilton* when shown in Britain), a tearjerker that, it was alleged, Winston Churchill had seen five times—and wept after each showing.

Korda, the husband of the alluring Hollywood actress Merle Oberon, had finished *That Hamilton Woman* in an incredible six weeks. Its propaganda value was high. Most of the millions who saw it on the screen came away with the desired sympathetic view toward England.

The British offensive against Hollywood was conducted almost like secret missions launched against Nazi-occupied areas—without the physical mayhem. H. Montgomery Hyde, an MI-6 officer, was sent to Hollywood to "assist" Alexander Korda. Years later, Hyde would state that Korda was, in essence, "a clearing house for British intelligence."

Isolationists in the United States took notice of the British filmmakers in Hollywood. At a huge rally in St. Louis on August 1, 1941, U.S. Senator Gerald Nye, a staunch advocate of isolationism, bellowed that "Hollywood is a raging inferno of war fever." Demanding that America "be freed of foreign propaganda," Nye later declared that Hollywood's "interventionist propaganda films have served to change, if not warp, a lot of clear thinking in American minds."

Across the Atlantic, British Prime Minister Winston Churchill, clearly agreed with Senator Nye. On Churchill's staunch recommendation, Alexander Korda was awarded a knighthood in 1941, only weeks before the United States totally shed its isolationist tag after the sneak Japanese attack on Pearl Harbor.[13]

Roosevelt: Conniver or Country Bumpkin?

DRAWING ON A LONG BLACK CIGAR and peering through eyeglasses resting near the tip of his nose, the pudgy, not very large but somehow indomitable man was seated at his desk in his bombproof command post deep beneath the pavement in London. His habits were somewhat owlish, and he often worked throughout the night. Winston Spencer Churchill was in a grim mood as he pored over reports of Operation Dynamo. It was June 6, 1940, and he had been prime minister for only four weeks.

Dynamo had been an incredible rescue mission by some eight hundred and fifty mainly civilian vessels that had evacuated from France to England 337,131 British and French troops that Adolf Hitler's triumphant Wehrmacht had trapped at the English Channel port of Dunkirk.

Great Britain had suffered one of the worst military disasters in her long history. Left behind in France were 120,000 vehicles, 2,300 artillery pieces and mortars, 8,000 Bren guns, 90,000 rifles, and 7,000 tons of ammunition and shells.

Churchill was stunned. Now Great Britain stood alone against the powerful German army arrayed across the English Channel. "If they come, we'll have to hit them over the head with bottles!" Churchill confided to an aide. "That's all we've got to fight with!"

In this hour of mortal danger for Great Britain, the new prime minister, a veteran of forty years of political service in war and in peace, had been handed an awesome challenge when he had been appointed by King George VI: Save the British Empire.

Now sixty-six years of age, Churchill, to those who knew him, seemed to have spent his entire life training for this hour of destiny. Surrounding himself with a youthful, blue-blooded staff, he swiftly established procedures and methodologies to fight a total war. Although there would be no written directives, Churchill gave the highest priority to a subtle campaign of machinations to drastically influence American public opinion and nudge the sleeping giant into the war.

Seducing the people of America into the crusade against Adolf Hitler would seem to be a towering mountain to climb. "Keep out of other nations' quarrels!" was the slogan among most Americans. One isolationist group, based in Chicago and led by a wealthy businessman, Avery Brundage, was the Citizens Keep America Out of the War Committee. Lanky, boyish-looking Charles A. Lindbergh, who had gained enduring fame in 1927 when he became the first person to fly the Atlantic alone, was the keynote speaker at a massive rally produced in the spring of 1940 by Brundage's group at the 100,000-seat Soldier Field in Chicago.

President Franklin D. Roosevelt was among American leaders who tried to guide the nation toward at least helping beleaguered Great Britain with supplies and shipments of military equipment. But each time he spoke out, he was loudly branded a warmonger.

No doubt Roosevelt's view that Hitler needed to be stopped was paramount in his thoughts when he approved a unique situation for the United States: permitting a foreign power (Great Britain) to establish in the United States a counterintelligence service ostensibly designed to help catch Nazi spies throughout the Western Hemisphere. Actually, the primary secret function of the agency's head, William Stephenson, was to be Winston Churchill's "chief nudger" to draw the United States into the war in Europe.

Stephenson, a wealthy Canadian industrialist who had been a fighter pilot in World War I and was later an amateur boxer, set up his command post in a most unlikely place: the thirty-fifth and thirty-sixth floors of the International Building in Rockefeller Center in New York City.

The whole affair was so hush-hush that Roosevelt had not even informed Secretary of State Cordell Hull about it. An innocuous title, British Security

Coordination (BSC), was adopted by Stephenson, a man of stout heart, enormous drive, and a keen and devious mind.

Almost at once, the man designated to coerce American public opinion toward war launched his shadow campaign of plots and intrigue. He learned that Major Elias Belmonte, the Bolivian military attaché in Berlin, was scheming with German intelligence against Bolivia's pro-American president, Enrique Penaranda. Britain, and indeed the United States, had vested interests in continuing to trade with Bolivia, the fifth-largest South American country. A pro-Nazi takeover of the government could threaten American and British access to wolfram, a mineral essential to aircraft manufacturing.

Stephenson sent one of his top men, H. Montgomery Hyde, to investigate the threat to a strategic material in Boliva. On his return to New York, Hyde began implementing a disinformation scheme designed to get a reluctant Uncle Sam to pick up his rifle and go to war. It was a devious stratagem—but these were desperate times in Great Britain, and neither Hyde nor Stephenson could afford to be picky.

Hyde put a group of researchers to work and called on gifted forgers in the British Security Coordination office to craft a letter by Major Belmonte, describing his conspiracy with the Nazis to overthrow the Bolivian president.

Then Hyde hatched a phony but convincing scenario in which a German courier based in La Paz, the capital of Bolivia, flew to Buenos Aires, Argentina, where he was robbed at gunpoint by a British spy. The briefcase snatched from the Nazi purportedly contained the letter that Hyde had fabricated.

Hyde's counterfeit letter from Major Belmonte to the German minister in Bolivia, Ernst Wendler, said that the "coup will take place in the middle of July" and stressed that "we must rescind the wolfram contract with the United States."

William Stephenson passed the bogus letter along to Secretary of State Cordell Hull, who rushed it to President Roosevelt. Both men presumably never questioned the validity of the letter, a testament to its graphic and literary excellence.

Roosevelt clearly was angry. Hull promptly notified Bolivian President Penaranda about the blockbuster information. A state of siege was immediately proclaimed in Bolivia, and there were mass arrests of suspected Nazi agitators. Meanwhile, Roosevelt took to the radio to tell Americans about the despicable plot described in the phony Belmonte letter.

Montgomery Hyde's disinformation masterpiece had scored heavily, far more than even he had anticipated. Not only was U.S. public opinion nudged a little more toward involvement in the war, but the German legation in La Paz was forced to close, denying the Nazis a valuable espionage base in South America, and the Third Reich would no longer be permitted to buy wolfram.

Moreover, the bogus Belmonte letter established a climate favorable for the Pan-American Conference a few months later when Bolivia and eighteen other Latin American nations broke with Adolf Hitler and established a unified system of hemisphere defense.

Stephenson next produced a "secret" German map of Nazi designs on the Western Hemisphere in September 1941. The map went up the customary channels: Secretary of State Hull to Roosevelt. Again the president apparently took the forged map at face value, and he referred to it in one of his famous fireside chats as proof of a "Nazi design, not only against South America, but the United States as well."

Roosevelt told American radio listeners—millions of them—that the map proved that Adolf Hitler and his Nazi cohorts planned to "seize the vital Panama Canal and then to take over Latin America, joining its fourteen republics into five vassal states."

Americans were outraged.

Stephenson had scored yet another psychological triumph. But had President Roosevelt, an astute politician, really been taken in as though he were some country bumpkin? Or had he suspected the map and Belmonte letter were forgeries and chosen to use them to promote his own objectives? The answer will probably never be known.[14]

"Smuggling" Five Ships to England

FORTY-NINE-YEAR-OLD GEORGE BINNEY, the British Iron and Steel Control representative in Scandinavia, opened the top-secret document that had just arrived at his office in Gothenburg, a major port in southwestern Sweden. The message was from the chairman of the civilian organization for whom he worked:

> It is of paramount importance that we receive all the war stores on order in Sweden (ball bearings, machine tools, special steels, Swedish iron, etc.). You must, repeat must, at all costs get them to England.

Two months earlier, on April 9, 1940, Binney had been in Norway when Adolf Hitler had sent his powerful armed forces plunging into that peaceful nation. The British official had escaped to nearby neutral Sweden to continue the economic war against Nazi Germany. The British Ministry of Economic Warfare's task was to slow the flow of essential matériel into the Third Reich and to mount clandestine operations to acquire these vital goods for Britain.

As soon as he had arrived in Gothenburg, Binney warned London that if the British government did not promptly pay for the matériel ordered from Sweden at the start of the conflict in September 1939, these goods would fall

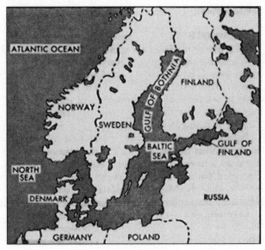

Locations of
Scandinavian
countries.

into German hands. London paid up at once, and now Binney's boss in England was directing him to get this precious cargo to Britain as soon as possible.

Binney had been handed a tall order, a seemingly impossible task. He would have to round up the purchased matériel, find ships to haul them westward through a German naval blockade, then recruit large numbers of civilian seamen who would be willing to risk their lives to do the job. All of this enormous effort would have to be achieved in secrecy.

If this feat were to be accomplished, Binney would seem to be the type of man to pull it off. Energetic and clever, he had what colleagues called a "pugnacious and piratical spirit." Moreover, he had developed a wide circle of influential contacts in Scandinavia.

The fact that the clandestine operation would be a gross violation of Sweden's neutrality and could draw that small nation into war with Germany bothered Binney not at all. Nor did the British government reflect any concern about the possible consequences for Sweden. These were desperate times, and no one in the British camp could be too squeamish about "technicalities."

Through his covert contacts, Binney learned that the Swedes would be happy to continue undercover trading with the British. But high-level officials in Stockholm were worried about German reaction if purchased materials were kept in storage in Sweden for a long period of time.

Now Binney focused on a means to smuggle the huge amount of war stores from Gothenburg along a five-hundred-mile sea passage to the Orkney Islands, the location of the British Royal Naval base at Scapa Flow. His eye fell on the twenty-six Norwegian merchant ships stranded at Swedish ports when Norway had been invaded. The Swedish government had resisted Berlin's efforts to seize these Norwegian ships.

The ticklish and complex procedure dragged on into August before London, in clandestine negotiations, presumably with the Norwegian government-in-exile in England, secured the charter of five merchant ships at Gothenburg. To keep the suspicious Germans confused, British undercover agents in Sweden put out word that the vessels were to be used to store nonessential goods bought from Swedish manufacturers.

Meanwhile, Binney had run into major problems when he began rounding up crew members for the five blockade-running ships. Their Norwegian captains refused to get involved. Covertly contacting seamen was time-consuming and hazardous. Any one of those approached might tip off the Gestapo, of which there was no shortage in Sweden.

Finally, the Briton recruited enough volunteers from the original Norwegian crews, from the crews of two British destroyers sunk during the German invasion of Norway who had escaped to Sweden, and Swedes themselves. Altogether there were 147 crewmen, each of whom had been promised a bonus of fifteen hundred pounds sterling on the arrival of their ships in the Orkney Islands. Three of the captains were British; two were Norwegian.

A pragmatic man, Binney confided to an associate that he estimated that the project to smuggle five large merchant ships out of Sweden under the noses of the Germans had only a fifty-fifty chance of success. If the tons of precious war matériel failed to reach the British Isles, he wanted to make certain that the Kriegsmarine (German navy) did not seize the booty at sea.

Binney called on a Gothenburg representative of Lloyd's of London, a large insurance firm whose underwriters will issue a policy on almost anything. Two large losses by Lloyd's included the ocean liner *Titanic,* which sank in 1912, and the German dirigible *Hindenburg,* which crashed and burned in 1937. How, Binney wanted to know, can a ship be scuttled rapidly at sea?

The insurance executive reflected puzzlement. "This must be the first time Lloyd's has been consulted on how to sink a ship!" he exclaimed. Explosives could not be used: Sweden had strict laws about allowing such matériel in the country. So the Lloyd's agent came up with an ingenious scheme.

Four holes were cut into each side of each hull before the cargo was taken aboard, and remote-control valves were fitted. Once the ship was loaded, the holes would be below the waterline. In a crisis, the remote-control levers for opening the valves would be pitched overboard, the holes would be opened, and the sea would rush in. The ship would sink in less than an hour.

With the approach of December 1940, Operation Rubble, as the project was now code-named, had been in existence for five months. Now, with as much secrecy as possible, the crews began loading the five ships at Gothenburg. This was one of the project's most crucial time frames. Had it not been for a dedicated Swedish ally, Captain Ivar Blucker, chief of the harbor police, Binney might not have been able to get the cargo out of the port before it was sabotaged by the Germans.

Blucker knew many of the hundreds of seamen based at Gothenburg, and he made certain that Nazi sympathizers had not been planted in the crews that Binney had recruited. When the ship loading began, Blucker arranged to have his men "detain" other known German sympathizers among the seagoing community in Gothenburg.

By January 1, 1941, the five cargo ships had been painted battleship gray to help hide them from Luftwaffe scout planes and German warships. They were ready to sail, but the weather failed to cooperate: It remained clear and sunny. Finally, on January 23, with a heavy snow providing natural camouflage, the ships headed out to sea.

Now Ivar Blucker, at great personal risk, arranged for the disruption of all telephone communications in the area. Even if German spies spotted the vessels leaving port, the ships would have several hours' head start before word of their departure reached German air and naval bases in nearby Norway.

About halfway to its destination, the tiny armada of blockade-busters was joined by an escort of British warships and circling Royal Air Force planes. At dawn the next morning, the "smuggled" vessels reached the Orkney Islands.

Operation Rubble had been an astonishing accomplishment. It brought to hard-pressed England 25,000 tons of crucial war matériel and five badly needed merchant ships. For his orchestration of the daunting feat, George Binney was knighted by King George VI. The five ship captains were awarded high British decorations, and several members of the crews received civil medals.

The British officials now pondered how Captain Ivar Blucker, the Gothenburg harbor police chief, could be suitably recognized. Without his efforts, Operation Rubble could never have been pulled off. Clearly, he could hardly be given a British award. As a show of gratitude, a pair of gold cuff links with a British royal crest on them were sneaked to him from King George's private secretary by way of undercover agents in Sweden.[15]

Plastic Surgery for a British Spy

LIKE A CONQUERING ROMAN CAESAR of old, Adolf Hitler entered Paris in triumph. His Wehrmacht had defeated the once vaunted French army—it had been stronger than Germany's both in men and matériel, but not in spirit, nor in boldness and skill—in a shocking forty-two days. That day the crestfallen French generals received their armistice terms from the führer in the railway carriage of Marshal Ferdinand Foch at the Compiégne Forest—the same carriage in which Germany had surrendered at the end of World War I. It was June 21, 1940.

Now England was a lion at bay. She was confronted across the English Channel by the most powerful military force that history had known and a new front that stretched from the Arctic Circle for three thousand miles to the Pyrenees Mountains of Spain.

Hitler issued his first orders for the invasion of England ten days after his humbling of the French generals in Paris. Directive No. 16-40 was cloaked in the utmost secrecy: Only seven copies were prepared, one each for the top Wehrmacht commanders. The invasion would be code-named Operation Sea Lion.

Britain was in dire peril. Her military was woefully weak. If the nation were to survive the looming cross-Channel assault by the Germans, it was crucial to infiltrate spies along the French coast to discover at close quarters what the Germans were doing.

Agents for the critical espionage mission had to be found in England. French informants were not yet available. Among the Britons who seemed to qualify was prominent and wealthy R. E. Hutchinson, who had vacationed for many summers along the French coast. Moreover, he had background knowledge of artillery, tanks, and other accoutrements of war.

Hutchinson was willing to take on the perilous mission. But he was well known along the Channel coast in France, so he might be betrayed by someone who recognized him.

British intelligence officers presented a unique approach to the candidate, who promptly agreed. Hutchinson's bushy mustache was shaved off and he underwent plastic surgery to alter his features. Four weeks later, the restructured agent sneaked ashore at night in France at an area known as the Pas de Calais.

Dressed in genuine French clothes that had been borrowed from a recent refugee in England, Hutchinson traveled up and down the coast, making mental notes of troop formations, tanks, and presumed German army command posts. Two weeks later, the agent—who had said that even his own mother wouldn't recognize him—returned to Britain with a wealth of detailed intelligence.[16]

Part Three

Nazi Germany on the March

Nazi Diplomat Spies in
the United States

CAPTAIN ELLIS M. ZACHARIAS, who had been in U.S. Naval Intelligence since his graduation from Annapolis in 1920, was suffering pangs of frustration in his new post of Naval Intelligence chief for the West Coast of the United States. It was the same malady that gripped many American military officers in mid-1940.

Recognized as one of the genuine authorities on intelligence matters in the United States, Zacharias's frustration was fostered not only by the nation's almost total apathy toward her peril from two powerful countries, Germany and Japan, but because he knew that the Nazis had clandestinely invaded the United States with the most massive espionage penetration of a foreign power that history had known.

Zacharias's domain was staggering in scope, extending along the Pacific Coast states from the Canadian border to the Mexican border. However, from his post in San Diego, he launched a gargantuan campaign to locate and record the addresses of five thousand persons in his district who were on the Naval Intelligence loyalty-suspect list. There had never been a security program of this magnitude conducted in the United States.

Despite the enormous obstacles, the immense cataloging project was completed, and Zacharias sent the list by courier to the Office of Naval Intelligence (ONI) headquarters in Washington, D.C. He urgently recommended that each of the several naval districts compile similar lists. The recommendation was approved, and if the United States went to war, enemy agents and sympathizers could rapidly be picked up.

Zacharias discovered, but was not surprised, to learn that the German consulate in San Francisco and its leader, Fritz Wiedemann, were engaged in widespread espionage activities. Because the United States and Germany were officially "friendly," no direct action could be taken against Wiedemann, the espionage chief on the West Coast.

Zacharias was well versed on Wiedemann's background. Debonair and articulate, the husky, handsome "diplomat" was a widely known figure in the Third Reich and in embassies around the world. He had been the infantry company commander of a corporal named Adolf Hitler during World War I.

Fritz Weidemann, Hitler's spy chief on the U.S. West Coast, was a "victim" of a trick played by an American Navy officer. (Author's collection)

Since the führer came to power in the early 1930s, Wiedemann had been a confidant of and troubleshooter for the leader of Nazi Germany.

Knowing that he could take no legal action, Zacharias hatched a devious scheme to harass Wiedemann, to keep him off-balance, and to focus his attention away from spying and onto his personal status. Zacharias's weapon would be trickery.

Zacharias called in one of his double agents, a German who had important contacts in Berlin and was supposed to be spying for Wiedemann. No doubt with impish delight, the navy officer outlined his scenario, in which the double agent was to play the star's role.

Then the man was dispatched to San Francisco to put on the show. He would perform with Barrymore-like stage skill.

The double agent sought out Fritz Wiedemann and, in a conspiratorial tone, disclosed alarming (and phony) news. The man said that he had learned from his contacts in the Third Reich that Wiedemann had fallen into disfavor with the führer and would soon be relieved of his post and brought back to Germany in disgrace.

Customarily unflappable, the spymaster was visibly upset over the news, so disturbed that he reacted in a manner that exceeded Zacharias's fondest hopes. Wiedemann promptly sent a member of his staff to Berlin, seven thousand miles away, on a wild-goose chase to find out from Hitler himself how he had failed. In the meantime, the San Francisco consul general put espionage activities on the back burner.

In the months ahead, as war clouds continued to drift toward the militarily ill-prepared United States, it became clear to Washington leaders that

Fritz Wiedemann's San Francisco outpost was not the only one masquerading as a German consulate while being operated, in essence, as a branch of Nazi intelligence.

In Los Angeles, it was an open secret that Consul General George Gyssling was the Kreisleiter (Nazi Party district leader) for California. He had a string of spy posts stretching along hundreds of miles of coastline, and much of the information he collected from these agents was of particular interest to the Japanese, who soon received the data.

Consul General Karl Kapp in Cleveland was an especially industrious diplomat/spy who penetrated the Cleveland civil defense system, procured voluminous information on plants that were converting to war production, and even sent an experimental U.S. army gas mask that had been stolen by one of his American agents. With the active connivance of a sixty-year-old Akron, Ohio, attorney who compiled mailing lists, Kapp sent out tens of thousands of pamphlets whose theme was that President Roosevelt was "a captive of international Jewry."

Then there was Baron Edgar von Spiegel, New Orleans consul general, a former U-boat skipper and a crude but often effective operative. Spiegel's clumsy effort to blackmail an American newspaper publisher in his region brought about a noisy State Department investigation—but no other official action.

In Chicago, Consul General Hans Krause-Wichmann's domain was the Midwest, and about ten Abwehr and SD agents took orders from him. Krause-Wichmann wrote Berlin that for a few dollars per month, an American was supplying him with the takeoff airfields and dates of departure of warplanes being flown to England.

In Boston, the debonair diplomat Dr. Herbert Scholz, who had been the toast of Washington society until being transferred to New England in late 1939, had rapidly recruited a staff of agents. One of them was a reserve captain attached to U.S. Army Intelligence who kept Scholz informed on steps being taken to counteract German espionage activities in New England. Scholz also made contact with a group of hoodlums who claimed to be members of the Irish Republican Army and who hated the British. Their professed goal was to blow up British shipping in Boston harbor, and one freighter was sunk in the Charles River under mysterious circumstances.

German spies masquerading as consular officials had no problem in sending stolen or acquired intelligence to the Fatherland—couriers carried the information in bulging diplomatic pouches that were immune to inspection by any outside authority.[1]

Secret Trysts in Berlin Theaters

FORTY-EIGHT-YEAR-OLD Sam E. Woods was going through his morning mail at his desk in the U.S. Embassy in Berlin. For the past six years, the unassuming

Texan with a passion for anonymity had been commercial attaché-at-large, and in that humdrum post, he had made many friends among the Germans. It was early August 1940.

Because of his low key personality and seeming total disinterest in political matters, the Gestapo had paid no attention to him, although the sleuths had been tailing several members of the embassy staff thought to be collecting Nazi military and diplomatic intelligence. Actually, it was the nondescript Woods who had been highly effective in eliciting secrets from usually unsuspecting Nazi officials.

Now, with Adolf Hitler preparing to launch his powerful Luftwaffe against England as a prelude to invasion of the islands, Woods slit open an envelope and saw that it contained only a single ticket for a reserved seat in a large Berlin movie theater, although he had ordered none. Wise to the machinations of clandestine activities, the American decided to go to the theater on the specified night and see what developed.

In the dim light, Woods recognized the man in the adjoining seat, a German acquaintance of several years whom he knew had high-level contacts with the Reichsbank, Germany's top financial institution. The American also knew that the man was a staunch anti-Nazi and that he was astute enough to conceal those sentiments.

Seated side by side, the two men seemed to be deeply engrossed in the film, and they gave no sign of recognizing one another. However, Woods became aware that his acquaintance had gingerly slipped an envelope into the American's side coat pocket.

When the movie concluded, each man went his own way. On arriving home, Woods took out the envelope and removed a piece of paper. It stated that Adolf Hitler and his high-ranking generals were holding exhaustive discussions in the Reichskanzlei (German chancellery) to plan an invasion of the Soviet Union.

Woods knew that his informant had solid credentials and access to state secrets. So he forwarded the blockbuster information to Washington, where Secretary of State Cordell Hull and his advisors put minimal credence to the report. After all, as the entire world knew, Hitler was massing his mighty Wehrmacht for an invasion of militarily weak England.

Seventy-year-old, white-haired Cordell Hull, the last great American to be born in a log cabin (in Tennessee), like other leaders in Washington, was living in an Alice in Wonderland world. The United States was the only major nation that had no global intelligence agency, so Hull and other top officials customarily had to reach crucial decisions based on "gut reaction."

As with all astute politicians, Hull had one inflexible rule: always remain flexible. So he had word sent to Sam Woods to keep in touch with his undercover German contact, whom he had not identified.

In the weeks ahead, several more covert meetings were held in various Berlin movie houses. The German kept the attaché informed of the latest developments in Hitler's plans for the Soviet invasion. The informant disclosed that the Nazis had appointed military and economic groups for each of the twenty-one government districts in the Soviet Union. Later he advised that the Germans were secretly printing huge bales of forged Soviet banknotes.

On December 18, 1940, Hitler issued Directive No. 21 for Barbarossa, the code name for the invasion of Russia. It contained details for elaborate camouflage and deception programs. Although the Barbarossa directive had been distributed to only a limited number of high-ranking military officers and government officials, Woods's contact managed to obtain a copy and slip it to the American attaché.

By early February 1941, even Secretary Hull had been convinced that the Germans were indeed preparing to attack the Soviet Union, even though Hitler and Josef Stalin had signed a "friendship pact" in late 1939. So Hull finally got around to taking the astonishing intelligence to President Franklin D. Roosevelt.

At the time, top officials in the U.S. State Department and Soviet diplomats were holding a series of secret conferences in which Roosevelt was seeking to loosen the ties between Stalin and Hitler. Presumably with Roosevelt's approval, or even suggestion, Undersecretary of State Sumner Welles, at the conclusion of one of these covert sessions, disclosed to Soviet Ambassador Konstantin Oumansky the information about Hitler's invasion plans.

Apparently, this had been the first warning Stalin had received. The Soviet dictator brushed it off as a clumsy plant by British intelligence, using naive Americans as go-betweens to drive a wedge between Stalin and Hitler. Stalin harshly criticized Ambassador Oumansky's decision to even forward the nonsensical report to the Kremlin.

On June 22, 1941, the greatest ground campaign of the war was kicked off by some three million German soldiers. Just as the Barbarossa strategic plan Secretary Hull had received from Sam Woods detailed, the Wehrmacht struck simultaneously with three wedges into Russia, the main one being in the center and aiming at Moscow.

In the Kremlin, there was massive disbelief. None was more shocked than Josef Stalin.[2]

J. Edgar Hoover: Rumormonger

J. EDGAR HOOVER, a robust, iron-jawed supersleuth, fought crime with a vitality that bordered on passion. When the Federal Bureau of Investigation chief spoke, his words emerged in crisp, staccato bursts. Since September 1939, he

*Federal Bureau of
Investigation Director
J. Edgar Hoover. (FBI)*

had been in charge of all investigative work in matters of espionage, sabotage, and subversive activities.

Like other leaders in Washington, the FBI boss was fully aware that the White House was secretly behind Great Britain and bitterly opposed to Adolf Hitler and his Nazi regime. So while his G-men steadily rooted out German spies in the United States, Hoover gladly served as a conduit for rumors that British cloak-and-dagger agencies wanted planted on Berlin.

Washington was a hotbed for never-ending rumors, most of which would collapse under their own weight—or lack of it. But when a figure of Hoover's towering stature instigated the rumors, Nazi agents working out of the German Embassy on Massachusetts Avenue accepted the rumors as gospel and shuttled them along to the Abwehr in Germany.

Hoover had to be careful about sowing the disinformation so as not to give away the fact that it was only rumor. Moreover, he had to disseminate the phony reports to officials in Washington who, more than likely, would pass along the rumors.

In late 1940, London got word to Hoover that it would like him to palm off a rumor that British scientists had developed a startling new weapon—glass balls that would be dropped from bombers. The balls supposedly contained a new explosive that gave off tremendous heat that could not be extinguished, thereby causing buildings and houses to be destroyed by fire.

There was, of course, no such thing as these glass balls. But Hoover dutifully planted the rumor among Washington officials who talked too much, knowing that they could not resist displaying their inside information at cocktail parties attended by neutral-nation diplomats, some of whom were secretly in league with the Germans and could be counted on to pass along the glass balls rumor.

Several weeks after Hoover had launched the glass balls canard, he got word back, through British intelligence circles, that scientists in Berlin were desperately trying to solve the glass balls riddle with a view toward devising a means for counteracting the devious new British weapon. This time-consuming effort had perhaps kept the scientists away from developing new weapons of war to be used against the British.[3]

An Unlikely Counterfeit Traitor

WHEN ADOLF HITLER began rearming Germany in the mid-1930s, he often told aides that the United States, a sleeping giant with gargantuan industrial potential, would be the "decisive factor" in any future world war. So he ordered his master spy, cagey Admiral Wilhelm Canaris, his chief of secret intelligence to flood the United States with spies.

Canaris employed all the ruses and sinister schemes he knew to penetrate the United States with a highly formidable array of subversives. Because no single federal agency was charged with fighting espionage in the United States, Canaris's spies, by mid-1939 when Hitler had been planning to invade Poland, had stolen nearly every American defense secret.

Many of the Nazi spies infiltrated the United States under various disguises, but hundreds of American citizens joined in the undercover espionage operation, which stretched from coast to coast, but was mainly centered in the New York City area.

One of the most productive of the Nazi spies was Carl Alfred Reuper, a German-born American citizen who had returned to the United States in December 1939 after taking an espionage course at the Abwehr Academy in Hamburg, Germany.

The thirty-seven-year-old Reuper was a skilled mechanic, and he found the ideal job for a German agent: working for Air Associates in New Jersey on secret U.S. government contracts.

Reuper was a gung-ho spy. He organized his own network, mainly men who worked in several vital defense plants in New Jersey and eastern Pennsylvania. Each agent received from him a precisely worded directive: collect code books, documents, specification, blueprints, and photographs "relative to the national defense of the United States."

Each evening after work, Reuper returned to his home on Palisade Avenue in Hudson Heights, New Jersey, after an eight-hour workday at Air Associates. He changed clothes and took a bus across the George Washington Bridge to Manhattan, where he held secret meetings with his operatives amid the hustle and bustle of Pennsylvania Station.

On January 4, 1941, Reuper approached a fellow employee at Bendix, Walter Nipkin, a German-born American citizen who was a lathe operator.

*A German spy built this powerful radio transmitter in his New York City
apartment to send intelligence messages to Hamburg. (FBI)*

After a lengthy recital of the glories of the new Germany, Reuper disclosed that
he worked for the Abwehr. Sensing from Nipkin's silence that the potential
recruit was eager to help the cause of Nazism, Reuper glanced around to make
certain that no one was watching, then pulled from his pocket several sketches
and blueprints. These were the kinds of materials needed by the Fatherland.
Would Nipkin show his loyalty by pilfering similar ones?

For the first time, Nipkin seemed hesitant. How could he get away with
stealing secret blueprints? Easy, Reuper replied. Nipkin would simply slip the
documents to him. He would photograph them and have the originals back to
Nipkin within an hour.

Nipkin was not sold. How much money would he get for that? Reuper
flushed in anger. How could Nipkin think of money when the Fatherland was
fighting for its life? When the spy prospect insisted that he should receive
something for his efforts, Reuper brightened and told him that indeed he
would be rewarded—with an autographed picture of Der Führer.

Reluctantly, Walter Nipkin agreed to cooperate—for Der Führer.

A week later, the two men huddled in a secluded nook of Air Associates,
and Nipkin, nervous and perspiring, deftly slipped secret drawings to the spymaster. Reuper was delighted. Within ten days, copies of the blueprints were
on the way to Germany.

However, the blueprints would only mislead German aviation engineers, for the drawings bore about as much resemblance to Air Associates secrets as J. Edgar Hoover did to Adolf Hitler. After Reuper had first identified himself as an Abwehr agent, Nipkin had gone to the FBI office in Newark and told his story. The G-men had advised Nipkin to play along with the spymaster, so when Reuper demanded secret blueprints, the FBI accommodated him—with phony drawings.

For five months, the mild-mannered Nipkin would continue in his masquerade as a Nazi agent and periodically slip Reuper authentic-looking but worthless blueprints and specifications, mainly those of obsolete military aircraft. At no time would Reuper gain an inkling that Nipkin, who loved the old Germany but cherished his adopted land, was putting the finger on nearly every member of the Nazi's gang.

On the morning of June 29, 1941, scores of FBI agents fanned out in greater New York City. Before dusk, their dragnet had hauled in thirty-three spies of "a foreign power." Even the most naive Americans knew the identity of that "foreign power"—Nazi Germany. Among those in jail was Carl Reuper and most of his ring. All thirty-three suspects were charged with conspiracy to violate American espionage laws.

On September 3, the trials began for the accused in the high-ceilinged room in the Federal Courthouse in Brooklyn. Hoping to save their skins, many of the Nazi spies "sang like canaries." Consequently, the FBI's case had been watertight, the evidence devastating. All of the defendants were convicted on assorted counts.

Walter Nipkin, the counterfeit traitor, was hard at work at his lathe at Air Associates when Carl Reuper was sentenced by Judge Mortimer W. Byers to sixteen years in prison.[4]

The Spy Who Fooled Both Sides

JUAN PUJOL, a soft-spoken young Spaniard, had been leading a quiet life in Madrid as manager of a small hotel before war broke out in Europe in September 1939. While the bloodletting continued and Adolf Hitler conquered vast expanses of territory, Pujol became steadily more outraged.

In January 1941, Pujol went to the British Embassy in Madrid, spoke to the military attaché, and offered his services as a spy. Convinced that the caller was a German plant, the Briton rejected Pujol.

Disheartened, but refusing to be thwarted, Pujol hatched a scheme to strike at the hated Nazi regime from within. He called on Gustav Lenz (real name Gustav Leisner), a former German navy officer, who was Abwehr chief in the Iberian Peninsula (Spain and Portugal), and offered to spy for Germany.

Lenz had been recruited into the Abwehr in 1937, and after a short training course, he was sent to Madrid. Posing as a respectable businessman, he conducted his activities from the offices of the Excelsior Import and Export Company, a commodity brokerage firm.

When the Wehrmacht invaded Poland, and England and France declared war against the Third Reich, Lenz shifted his base to the German Embassy at 4 Castellana and rapidly built an espionage network that British electronic snoopers estimated had fifteen hundred agents in Spain and a thousand in Portugal.

Madrid was a beehive of cloak-and-dagger machinations. An enormous volume of secret information was passing from Lenz's operation in the embassy to an Abwehr relay station near Wiesbaden, Germany. Almost every word being radioed to Madrid or from the Third Reich was being intercepted by the Radio Security Service (RSS) at Hanslope Park in Great Britain.

Typical of those in his profession, spymaster Gustav Lenz was suspicious of Pujol's motives. Why would this young Spaniard suddenly decide that he wanted to spy for Germany against England? Because he hated the British, Pujol explained.

Lenz had his agents conduct an investigation of the spy candidate's background, and nothing unusual was discovered. So Lenz decided to send Pujol to England in June 1941. He provided his new agent with a questionnaire concerning military secrets to be ferreted out, secret ink, the British equivalent of three thousand U.S. dollars (a hefty sum at the time), and the code name Arabel.

The new spy had no intention of going to England. When he reached Lisbon, Portugal, on the first leg of his trip, he remained there. A week later, he radioed to Lenz that he had arrived in England and would start sending intelligence reports soon.

Using tourist guides and reference books found in Lisbon libraries, and scanning British newspapers, which were in abundance in Portugal, Arabel began fabricating clever intelligence reports (purported to come from England) that had an authentic ring. From time to time, the Spaniard shuffled fictitious and real military units around Great Britain. On occasion, he happened to send accurate reports.

So detailed were Arabel's intelligence nuggets that Lenz radioed that he thought the spy should be more careful while hopping around England. Because the British secret service had collared nearly all of the Nazi agents in England at the beginning of the war (many became double agents), Arabel soon became a hero at Abwehr headquarters in Berlin.

Arabel's stature with the German spymasters soared even higher when he radioed Madrid from his tiny Lisbon apartment that he had "recruited" three subagents (all fictitious)—one in Liverpool, one in Glasgow, Scotland, and one in western England. This ploy cemented the Abwehr's view that their ace agent was really roaming the British Isles.

For months, the British, through the customarily highly efficient Radio Security Service, knew about Arabel being in Great Britain (which he was not). How had he slipped past the tightly knit British security? MI-5 (which handled counterintelligence matters) was "going crazy" (in one official's words) trying to locate the Abwehr's ace spy in England.

By now, Arabel decided that his hoax was on the verge of collapsing. He could understand only minimal English, knew nothing about the composition of the British armed forces, and was finding it increasingly difficult to provide the Abwehr with the specific intelligence matters it was demanding. So he concluded that he could best advance his private war against Nazi Germany by contacting British officials in Lisbon and telling his entire story.

Pujol (Arabel) arranged a meeting with Gene Risso-Gill, a British intelligence officer in Lisbon. They met at a secluded old inn overlooking the Atlantic Ocean. The Spaniard, for the second time in a year, offered his espionage services to Britain.

Three days later, Risso-Gill contacted Pujol and said that he had received orders from London to sneak him into England. The new agent, with the new code name Garbo, arrived in Britain on April 25, 1942. He was provided with documents identifying him as Juan Garcia, a translator for the British Broadcasting Corporation (BBC).

Within only a few months, Pujol, under the direction of his British controllers, had fabricated an even larger phony network—fourteen agents and eleven well-placed contacts, including a key one in the Ministry of Information, where Allied secret matters were regularly handled.

Garbo (formerly Arabel) was tireless. His morale and enthusiasm soared even higher when British secret agents managed to slip his wife and young child out of Spain under the noses of Nazi informers, and bring them to England. During the next two years, Garbo sent some two thousand messages—all of them phony or half-truthful about the military and government situation in Great Britain.

Admiral Wilhelm Canaris, the astute chief of the Abwehr in Berlin, was delighted with the work of his ace spy in England. So Garbo was financed by the Germans to the tune of 20,000 pounds sterling ($96,000), a whopping sum at that time, and more than Prime Minister Winston Churchill's annual salary.[5]

Nine Germans Capture Belgrade

EARLY IN 1941, the mighty German Wehrmacht was stalled in the west at the English Channel, but Adolf Hitler and his generals were already putting the final touches on Operation Barbarossa, the invasion of the Soviet Union. At the same time, the führer was planning on conquering North Africa to reach his dream of a Teutonic empire in the Middle East.

Success in these two huge endeavors hinged on the nations of the Balkans, and Hitler wooed Bulgaria, Rumania, and Hungary into his fold. Then, through only slightly veiled threats, Prince Peter of Yugoslavia agreed to become Hitler's ally, signing a pact with the Third Reich on March 24, 1941.

In London, Prime Minister Winston Churchill was both furious and worried. Prince Peter had assured the British leader that Yugoslavia would remain neutral. So British agents in the capital of Belgrade coerced anti-Nazi Yugoslavian army and air force officers into launching an armed rebellion. Key points were seized in Belgrade, including the palace, where King Peter II was arrested and hustled off to exile in Greece.

General Dusan Simović, whose office in the Air Ministry had been the core of opposition to German penetration of Yugoslavia, took over the reins of government. When the sun set that day, the coup had been accomplished without bloodshed.

In Berlin, Hitler was fuming. He ordered his generals to "destroy Yugoslavia militarily and as a national unit." He directed that the Luftwaffe bomb Belgrade with "unmerciful harshness."

Admiral Wilhelm Canaris, the diminutive, white-haired chief of the Abwehr who was in league with the British, learned of the forthcoming bombardment, code-named Operation Punishment, and secretly warned Yugoslav leaders. Consequently, Belgrade was declared an open city, for centuries a term meaning a place that was not going to be defended; therefore, it should be spared destruction.

On the morning of April 6, 1941, the Luftwaffe struck. In an action that lasted for three days and nights, Belgrade was devastated. Some 17,000 civilians were dead in the rubble. A sickening stench of death hovered over the once beautiful city of about a half-million population.

Hard on the heels of the massive Luftwaffe assault, German panzer and infantry divisions surged into Yugoslavia from three sides and raced toward Belgrade.

On the morning of April 12, a motorcycle assault company of the SS Das Reich Panzer Division approached the city along the northern bank of the Danube River at the eastern outskirts. The flood-swollen river seemed a barrier to the ravaged capital because the bridge over which the motorcycle vanguard had hoped to move had been blown up by the Yugoslavs.

Despite the seemingly insurmountable obstacles, Hauptsturmführer (SS Captain) Fritz Klingenberg could see the prize off in the distance, and he was determined to try to reach it even though he was far out in front with only a relative handful of men.

A diligent search turned up one motorboat, and in midafternoon, Klingenberg, along with a platoon leader, two sergeants, and five privates, scrambled into the small boat and headed for the far bank. Although nearly swamped by the raging river several times, the craft made the crossing. The SS men jumped onto the sandy shore, and Klingenberg waved his men onward, bound on a seemingly impossible task—capturing the sprawling capital with only himself and eight men.

Klingenberg banked on two factors—stealth and surprise. The Yugoslavs were still bogged down in confusion from the Luftwaffe bombing, and they wouldn't be expecting to encounter a tiny band of German soldiers in the center of the city. The scenario unfolded almost precisely as the SS captain had envisioned.

Soon after leaving their motorboat, the SS group ran onto a contingent of twenty Yugoslavian soldiers. Shocked to encounter an enemy force in Belgrade, they surrendered without firing a shot. Minutes later, several military trucks loaded with soldiers approached the Germans, who fired a few rounds, and the mesmerized Yugoslavians capitulated.

The gods of war were still smiling on Klingenberg. One of the prisoners was an ethnic German who volunteered to be a guide and interpreter.

Taking over the captured trucks, Klingenberg and his eight soldiers headed for the Yugoslavian war ministry, but they found it an empty shell: the high command apparently had fled. So the SS men drove to the German legation, where the military attaché, who had remained during the Luftwaffe bombardment, greeted the newcomers enthusiastically. He was astonished, however, to learn that Klingenberg and only a few men had been masquerading as the entire potent Das Reich Panzer Division.

If the military attaché was stunned, no doubt Yugoslavian civilian authorities would also believe that an entire German division had penetrated the city. So Klingenberg launched a bold bluff. A Nazi swastika flag was run up the legation's flagpole, and Klingenberg sent a Yugoslavian civilian to contact the mayor and tell him that Belgrade was in control of the Das Reich Division.

Two hours later, the mayor and several of his top officials arrived at the German legation to formally surrender. The trick had worked magnificently. It was not until the next day that panzers roared into Belgrade to back up Klingenberg and his eight men.[6]

The "Directress of Masquerades"

COLONEL MAURICE BUCKMASTER, a former manager of the Ford Motor Company in Paris, was in charge of the French Section, a branch of the Special Operations Executive (SOE). F Section, as it was known, was concerned with cloak-and-dagger missions against the Germans in France and French territories. Each nation in which the London-based SOE functioned was represented by a section—Belgian, Dutch, Danish, Polish, Norwegian, French.

These various sections relied almost exclusively on nationals of their own countries—except for the F Section. Because the London-based Bureau Centrale de Renseignements et d'Action (BCRA), the intelligence and operations service of General Charles de Gaulle's French government-in-exile, insisted on securing the services of its compatriots, SOE created "honorary Frenchmen" for F Section.

Buckmaster had to recruit anyone prepared to spy on or kill Germans, resulting in a ragtag collection of would-be agents. In the main, they were ordinary people who knew nothing about cloak-and-dagger operations.

Although Buckmaster was a man of great administrative ability and energy, he was immersed in forming in France what he called "an army of the shadows," which one day would help pave the way for the return to the Continent by powerful Allied forces. Therefore, much of the day-to-day direction of F Section was left to his aides.

Foremost among his top lieutenants was Vera Atkins, a young, energetic, and highly intelligent Englishwoman. An officer in the paramilitary organization FANY, a woman's auxiliary service in Great Britain, she was regarded by many as the real brains that made the F Section function.

Atkins was designated as the intelligence officer of F Section, but this role rapidly expanded to cover a multitude of duties. Cool, extremely competent, and analytical, she became known in F Section as the "Directress of Masquerades." In her capable hands rested the lives of countless spies, radio operators, and couriers parachuted into Nazi-occupied France.

Through a myriad of sources, Vera collected hundreds of scraps of information about life in France under the German occupation. In her orderly and encyclopedic mind, she stored a large volume of regulations that could daily confront spies in France, such as working conditions, police registrations, travel, documents, curfew, and food rationing.

This tedious process was unending. In an effort to trick Allied agents, regulations and rules were changed or added almost weekly. The Gestapo in France was vigilant, so the F Section operatives had to be doubly so—their lives depended on it. On entering a bistro, Atkins told her recruits at the Special Training School, they should loiter inconspicuously until they learned if local residents were ordering alcoholic beverages that day. On arbitrary occasions, the Gestapo, seeking to identify outsiders, would suddenly forbid cafes and bistros to serve alcoholic drinks, a fact known to the locals but not to outsiders. Bartenders, under threat of arrest, were forced to report anyone who ordered wine or beer.

While prowling around France, Vera emphasized to her "pupils," they should enter cities walking beside their bicycles, because on irregular days, the German authorities would suddenly prohibit riding two-wheeled vehicles (pushing a bicycle was acceptable, indicating that the pushee was a local).

After entering a cafe to eat, the spy should spend at least ten minutes seeming to inspect the menu. During that time, he or she could cast furtive glances to see if locals were ordering meat. On some days, the Gestapo ordered meat to be withheld, again a fact known to the natives in the community, but not to the spy.

Despite her heavy workload, the Englishwoman found time to teach the British agents French manners. As a French native, he or she would wipe the gravy with a piece of bread and eat it with gusto. On the other hand, a Briton, in a proper manner, might leave a few chips or petits pois on his plate, then carefully align his knife and fork alongside when finished. If a Gestapo agent were watching, the latter technique could result in the spy's capture and execution. Such tiny details about up-to-date conditions in occupied France could determine if the F Section agent lived to carry out his or her mission or met a brutal death at the hands of the Gestapo.

There were secret laboratories scattered about London that provided forged documents for the spies, but Vera always enhanced the agents' authenticity by adding a few items such as "family" photos (of strangers), a letter from an imaginary girlfriend, or a fake clipping from a Paris newspaper.

After an espionage recruit or two had "graduated" from the Special Training School, Vera took part in the final briefing sessions, which were held in a small but comfortably furnished apartment retained by F Section at Orchard Park in London. It was always a relaxed atmosphere. Atkins and the other officers chatted with the nervous would-be agents, not as their superior officers, but as friends offering helpful advice tips.

Forty-eight hours after their arrival at the briefing hideout, the recruits were driven to F Section's secret airbase at Gibraltar Farm, near Tempsford, about forty miles north of London. In a small shack, a final check was made of the spies' pockets, often turning up British cigarettes and British money, a forgotten London bus ticket, or similar small but telltale items.

When Vera and other officers were finished with their tedious inspections, nothing remained to show that the agents had ever been in England. Their clothes, shoes, hats, haircuts—all bespoke lifelong Frenchmen and women.

Before boarding a waiting airplane from which he or she would parachute into the ominous darkness over France, the agents were handed a tiny poison pill. A not too believable remark from Atkins or other officers was: "I'm sure you won't have to use it."

Atkins always remained at the dimly lighted airfield until the plane had lifted off and was consumed by the night. She knew in her heart that many of her "pupils" would never survive to see eventual Allied victory.

Back at SOE headquarters, Vera waited anxiously for hours—sometimes days—for receipt of the coded wireless message that indicated an F Section agent had landed safely and was proceeding to his or her predesignated base of operations. But that act did not divorce her from future contact with her flock in France. She concocted a scheme to utilize the BBC (British Broadcasting Corporation) to pass along messages from her.

Listeners to the French programs broadcast by BBC were puzzled by the series of seeming nonsensical phrases, many of which were repeated numerous times in a day. Most theorized, however, that these terse blurbs had something to do with Allied cloak-and-dagger operations in France.

"Johnny has a new Sunday suit," "the crow flew out of the tree," or "the cow jumped over the moon" often had life-and-death meanings to a lonely and frightened F Section agent holed up in a French barn with the Gestapo on his or her trail.

Vera arranged to inject a special sideline into the "official" system of personal messages. She used this means to inform an agent about his or her home life and family. Such messages had to be prearranged either before the spy left or by earlier Morse signals.

Some of the agents' wives were expecting a birth when their husbands had to leave. As soon as possible, Vera informed the spy over BBC that he had become a father and that mother and child were doing well. When she received news from an agent's family (they were never told of his or her whereabouts), she flashed it to the agent by means of a personal message.

Much later, many F Section spies would say that the Englishwoman had preserved their sanity. Often cut off from homes and families for a year or more, hounded by the Gestapo, ill or injured but not daring to go to a hospital, these men and women in the field called Vera Atkins their "guardian angel."[7]

Ruses to Aid Trapped British Force

ONLY THREE MONTHS after a relatively unknown German general named Erwin Rommel had arrived in Tripoli, North Africa, to take charge of the crack Afrika Korps and Italian formations, 36,000 Australians and other British Commonwealth troops were trapped in the unpretentious Libyan port of Tobruk. With their backs to the Mediterranean Sea and hemmed in on three sides by Rommel's panzers and infantry, the defenders had taken up positions behind strong concrete defenses that Italian engineers had built in earlier years. It was April 1941.

Hard-bitten Major General Leslie J. Morshead, a one-time Australian schoolmaster who was in charge of the Tobruk garrison, warned his beleaguered men: "There is to be no surrender!"

Rommel, on the other hand, was directing his iron will and skills to capturing the town, which had a population of only four thousand people living in a few hundred houses among a handful of palm trees.

Both Rommel and British leaders were acutely aware of the great military importance of this tiny village. Tobruk was the best port for hundreds of miles in North Africa, far superior to Rommel's main port at Tripoli. Without Tobruk,

British deceptionists in besieged Tobruk burn old rubber tires to give the Luftwaffe the illusion that bombs had hit a vital target. (National Archives)

Rommel had to haul supplies and reinforcements overland from Tripoli, a few hundred miles to his rear. With Tobruk in his hands, Rommel would have an excellent forward base for an all-out offensive eastward into Egypt and then on to the rich oil fields of the Middle East.

At his underground command bunker in London, Prime Minister Winston S. Churchill had quickly grasped the enormous significance of Tobruk. On April 7, he informed General Archibald Wavell, his commander in the Middle East: "Tobruk is to be defended to the death without thought of retirement!"

Four major assaults were launched by Rommel, and all of them were beaten back. Rommel was furious, obsessed with siezing the port. He set about cleaning house with a vengeance, sacking several of the higher German commanders he had inherited on arrival in North Africa.

Rommel was deeply frustrated by the stubborn holdout of the "doomed" garrison in Tobruk. In one of his frequent letters to his wife Lucie back in southern Germany, he acknowledged: "The Australian troops are fighting magnificently. Tobruk can't be taken by force, considering our present [strength]."

Rommel had to settle for a long, exhausting siege of Tobruk. He ringed the port with strong forces, but his main bodies of German and Italian troops swept on eastward almost to within sight of Cairo, Egypt, headquarters of the British Middle East Command.

For months, the siege of Tobruk continued. The trapped garrison could be supplied only by sea, and to keep this crucial lifeline open, the British utilized a variety of ruses and tricks.

Supply ships with their precious cargoes sneaked into the harbor at night. But with dawn, they were sitting ducks for German fighter-bombers as they waited to be unloaded. So British camoufleurs were called in to "hide" these vulnerable vessels.

From earlier German air attacks, there were many wrecked and half-sunken ships in the harbor. So the camouflage teams painted wreckage scenes on large pieces of canvas and connected them. Then the canvas was attached to the side of a truly damaged ship and held up by poles. From high in the air, it appeared to German pilots that the resulting canopy was part of the genuine wrecked ship.

At night, small vessels entered Tobruk harbor and moored under the canopies next to the wrecked ships. In the days ahead, the Luftwaffe continued to attack unconcealed ships, while ignoring the ones that were huddled next to the damaged craft.

Throughout the seige, the "Tobruk Air Force" consisted of three Hurricane fighter planes that used a small strip of ground. Two of the planes were hidden in caves dug into a nearby wadi, the bed of a stream that was usually dry. The entrances were concealed by nets and painted canvas, which blended into the immediate surroundings.

The third plane was hidden in a large excavation scooped out at night. A giant wooden lid on which sand was spread during the day covered the huge hole. When ready for a mission, this Hurricane was hoisted out of the excavation with a winch and cable; then the lid was replaced.

Reinforcing the masquerade, a decoy airstrip was scratched out of the packed sand a considerable distance from the real landing site. A few dummy planes, made of wood and canvas, were placed about the phony strip and moved about periodically as real aircraft would be. Throughout the four-month siege, the pilots flew many missions without once being impeded by the Luftwaffe.

From the beginning of the seige, General Morshead knew that it was only a matter of time until German planes attacked the Tobruk plant that was capable of distilling the salt out of 40,000 gallons of sea water daily. It supplied nearly all of the garrison's drinking water. Trying to hide the plant or to create a decoy would be useless, the British camoufleurs knew, because it had been built by the Italians, who knew its precise location.

Army Captain Peter Proud, a prewar art director of British movies, was in charge of keeping the distillery from being destroyed. He trained a special squad of "wreckers" who were hidden near the inviting target to await the arrival of the Luftwaffe.

On a clear night, a flight of Junkers bombers zoomed in and dropped explosives. Their aim was faulty, and the bombs landed close to the distillery but did no real damage. That was precisely the scenario for which Captain Proud had been hoping.

A few minutes after the final bomber headed for its base, the "wreckers" plunged into their task, digging many shell craters among the buildings of the distillery. These excavations were accented with shadows made of oil and coal dust. Rubble and debris, which had earlier been stacked into nearby piles and covered with camouflaged canvases, were scattered about the facility.

On the roof of the main building, other damage was simulated with canvas and paint. Finally, unused structures were blown up to reinforce the ruse. At dawn, piles of worn-out rubber tires were set afire to give the impression that the distillery was still smoking from the accuracy of the Luftwaffe raid.

As anticipated, German photo-reconnaissance planes flew over at high altitudes that morning. A few hours later, a broadcast over Radio Rome declared that a distillery vital to the trapped garrison on Tobruk had been blown to smithereens.

Throughout the seige, the distillery continued to produce fresh water without interference from the Germans.[8]

"We Stand behind Every Camel!"

EARLY IN MAY 1941, a British convoy steamed through the entrance to the Mediterrean Sea at Gibraltar, continued for more than two thousand miles eastward while dodging lurking German U-boats and warding off German bomber attacks, and churned into the huge British naval base at Alexandria, Egypt. Rapidly offloaded were 238 new tanks to reinforce General Archibald Percival Wavell's Middle East Command.

These tanks had arrived with a terse message from Prime Minister Winston Churchill, who exclaimed in biblical terms:

"Behold, now is the day of salvation." Translation: launch a massive attack westward against the vaunted Afrika Korps of General Erwin Rommel, whose force was fifty miles inside Egypt preparing an offensive to capture Cairo, the location of Wavell's headquarters.

Now Wavell rushed to inspect the new shipment of tanks. He was shocked to see that they were painted with forest-green camouflage, because they had originally been assigned to Greece. In the North African desert, these green tanks would stick out like the proverbial sore thumb, providing ideal targets for German gunners.

Wavell was a burly, one-eyed man who, during the early months of the war when Great Britain was a lion at bay, virtually ruled a vast empire in Arabia with an agile brain and a few battalions of infantry. All of his adult life, he had been a student of the art of modern war, particularly as it related to deception.

In a memorandum to the British chiefs of staff in the dark days of late 1940 during which the mighty German Luftwaffe was pounding Great Britain in an effort to destroy the Royal Air Force as a prelude to invasion, Wavell had written: "Practically all the ruses and stratagems of war are variations or developments of a few simple tricks that have been practiced by man on man since man was hunted by man.

"The elementary principle of all deception," he continued, "is to attract the enemy's attention to what you wish him to see and to distract his attention from what you do not wish him to see. It is by these methods that the skillful conjuror obtains his results."

Now, after inspecting the green-colored—and, therefore, useless—tanks, General Wavell hurried back to Cairo, bent on putting his deception and camouflage principles to work. He had an officer immediately contact a small group of prewar magicians, artists, professors, and craftsmen who had only recently arrived in the Middle East. Not knowing where to assign the Britons, Wavell made them an independent unit and gave it the official designation Camouflage Experimental Section.

Now Wavell's emissary told the men of the Camouflage Experimental Section about a crucial and urgent mission that was being assigned to it. With the greatest of speed, the green tanks were to be repainted with a substance that would blend with the desert.

"General Wavell wants you to whip up a batch of suitable paint," the officer told Lieutenant Frank Knox, in peacetime a don (professor) at England's prestigious Oxford University.

"How much of a batch?" Knox asked.

"Ten thousand gallons," was the reply.

Knox winced. There wasn't a pint of desert camouflage paint in North Africa—except for that held by the Germans.

A mini-crisis was at hand. The crucially needed new tanks could not be used on the desert without the camouflage paint, and it would take weeks before an emergency paint request from London could arrive.

Creating ten thousand gallons of sand-colored coating, one tough enough to withstand the blast-furnace heat of the desert, would be a daunting task. Solving the riddle was largely put in the hands of Lance Corporal Philip Townsend, a skilled painter who had worked mainly in oils in civilian life.

When the brooding Townsend had been interviewed to join the group of British conjurers, he said, "I know all there is to know about paint. I know pigment, I know mixing." He added: "I know hard work. I'm not here to make new pals. I just want to be left alone to do my job."

Now the artist was indeed being "left alone" to solve the seemingly unsolvable problem: miraculously causing a huge amount of desert-colored paint to suddenly appear. What was needed, he explained to the other six members of the Camouflage Experimental Section, was a substrate (or base) to hold fast the color, and a pigment to provide it.

"Almost anything that hardens can be used as a base," he added. "All we really need is to find a liquid or powder that is soluble to whatever pigment we use. Then we'll need some coloring substance."

All seven Britons scoured Cairo and its environs for a suitable substrate. Finally their efforts were rewarded when they discovered a huge dump just north of Cairo. An old-timer among British officers in the Middle East called it "the largest military junk pile in the world."

While rooting through the cargo raised from a torpedoed freighter, the scroungers came upon scores of sealed tin drums that contained a thick brown substance. A tiny taste solved the riddle: Worcestershire sauce. Hundreds of gallons of it. Townsend knew he had the paint base.

More scrounging at the dump turned up tons of spoiled flour and an equal amount of cement. All these materials were loaded into trucks and taken back to the group's tent camp, where paintmaster Townsend could experiment until he had developed the proper mix of Worcestershire sauce, cement, and flour. He developed the mix, but it was bright red, making it useless in the desert. Now they needed a pigment to turn the paste a sand color.

Townsend tried every coloring substance he could find to put in the mix, including assorted inks, powders, and melted crayons. Nothing worked. He was about ready to concede defeat. Then one day he was strolling down a dirt path and accidentally stepped into a pile of camel droppings.

The paintmaster felt a surge of elation. He reached down and picked up one of the dried, hard, sandy brown chips. "This is it!" he exulted. It was the perfect color, and the supply was unlimited. After several tests, he hit on the proper mix. Camel dung made a perfect, although malodorous, desert-brown paint pigment.

Now the "Dung Patrol" was born. One of the magicians or an Egyptian worker hired for the job trailed every camel caravan leaving Cairo. Oases in the surrounding desert were inspected daily. Each dawn, the streets of Cairo were swept for night leftovers.

The Dung Patrol operated with military precision. A small metal scoop was designed and assigned to each man. A tongue-in-cheek slogan was conceived: "We stand behind every camel!"

Watching the Dung Patrol in action, large numbers of Arabs were angry. For hundreds of years, camel droppings had fueled the local bread ovens, so the Britons had to hustle to beat angry Arab men and women to the suddenly prized camel pats.

In the tiny tent encampment, the ingredients for the paint were mixed by Townsend and his Egyptian helpers in huge washing tubs that had been "borrowed" late one night from an army field laundry unit. Soon some two thousand gallons per week were being produced. The finished product was turned over to a British engineer company, which did the actual tank painting.

Now General Wavell was ready to launch Operation Battleaxe, an offensive to inflict a crushing blow on General Rommel's force, which was arrayed near the western border of Egypt.[9]

An Enemy Agent in the Spymaster's Family

ITALIAN NAVY COMMANDER MAX PONZO was dark-complexioned, and his darting eyes gave him a shifty, sinister expression. He was brilliant and resourceful, and in the late 1930s, he built SIM, the naval intelligence agency, into a highly effective network such as Italy had never known.

Ponzo established several small but tight espionage rings in customarily neutral countries such as Portugal, Spain, Turkey, and Switzerland. A minor network was created in Washington, D.C., headed by a room service waiter at the posh Wardman-Park Hotel, where Secretary of State Cordull Hull lived.

Although information poured in from his spies abroad, Ponzo concentrated on the office of the U.S. naval attaché in Rome, Captain Thomas C. Kinkaid. His office was badly understaffed, and Washington refused to send him personnel. So he was compelled to hire a few Italians.

One of these natives, a high-placed clerk, worked for Ponzo. The agent had occasional access to the office safe and managed to make a duplicate key. Thereafter, Ponzo knew of every American plan or move from the contents of the safe.

In mid-1941, Captain Kinkaid, who would later distinguish himself as commander of the U.S. Seventh Fleet in the Pacific war against Japan, was recalled. His replacement, Captain Lester N. McNair, recruited a few local spies, presumably on orders from Washington. Freelance espionage had become something of a fad in Rome. It was a fascinating experience, earned money for the agent, and if he or she were unmasked, the worst penalty was to be exposed to Benito Mussolini's government.

One of Captain McNair's prize recruits was a charming and attractive young woman who went by the name of Signorina Elena. She was well situated in Roman society to collect useful pieces of information.

After a few weeks, Elena, at the instigation of McNair, called on Commander Ponzo, disclosed that she was an American spy, and offered to become a double agent, working for Ponzo.

The Italian spymaster was delighted to have a pipeline right into the Rome branch of the U.S. Naval Intelligence Service, so he made arrangements for Elena to pass on to him whatever information Captain McNair sought. McNair, in turn, provided her with phony information for Ponzo.

When Benito Mussolini declared war on the United States on December 11, 1941, Elena became even more valuable to McNair, because she was the only spy the U.S. Navy had in Rome. Arrangements were made for Elena to send her information to Colonel Barwell R. Legge, the U.S. military attaché in Bern, Switzerland, after the American Embassy in Rome closed and its personnel left for home.

A courier from Legge would call at Elena's apartment in Rome to pick up her information and take it to Bern. Ponzo posted agents around Elena's building. When the courier left with a briefcase of papers, the Italian sleuth's men tailed him in an effort to identify other American agents in Rome.

In the meantime, Ponzo was feeding the Italian navy headquarters a steady flow of intelligence on British ships in the Mediterranean. As soon as a British vessel passed through the narrow Straits of Gibraltar, either entering or leaving the Mediterranean, a signal was flashed to the Italian navy leaders.

The Italian consul in Algeciras, a Spanish city bordering the Rock of Gibraltar, was a key member of Ponzo's espionage apparatus. He lived at the Hotel Reina Crisina, whose Spanish owner was sympathetic to Italy and Nazi Germany. So the landlord looked the other way while the consul built an observatory on the roof.

The observatory had powerful telescopes, long-range binoculars, and cameras with telescopic lens. In a room in the hotel, the Italian had installed a clandestine transmitter. Within minutes after a British ship passed into or left the Mediterranean, Ponzo knew about it in Rome.

On occasion, when his pressing work permitted, Ponzo paid a call to an old but ornate house on the via delle Botteghe Oscure to visit one of Italy's best-known and most distinguished lawyers, Giovanni Serao. His clients included some of Italy's greatest corporations and a string of big foreign firms. For many years prior to the outbreak of war in Europe, he had been the legal advisor of the British Embassy in Rome. He had performed so well that he was knighted for his services to the British Crown.

Giovanni Serao was Max Ponzo's father-in-law and the idol of the younger man. Perhaps Ponzo never knew that his idol detested the Fascist government of Benito Mussolini and disapproved of Italy fighting against Great Britain.

Serao sneaked to British agents in Rome a wealth of high-grade information, which he had obtained in the course of his legal practice that brought him close to many of Italy's leading lights.

In essence, the father-in-law of Italy's leading spymaster was the clandestine chief of the British secret service in Rome.[10]

Mission: Hide Alexandria Harbor

FORTY-NINE-YEAR-OLD General Erwin Rommel was elated. At his command caravan in the scorching desert of Libya in North Africa, he had just read a decoded message sent by the U.S. military attaché in Cairo, Colonel Bonner Fellers, to Washington, D.C. Unbeknownst to General Archibald Wavell, British commander in the Middle East, the Germans had cracked the Black Code used by the Americans in various embassies around the world. It was June 15, 1941.

Three days earlier, Wavell, with high hopes for a smashing victory, had sent his Western Desert Force in an all-out assault, code-named Operation Battleaxe, against Rommel's vaunted Afrika Korps. The Desert Fox, as the wily German general had become known, had been forewarned of the British attack through wireless intercepts of the Black Code. He set an ambush of powerful 88-millimeter guns.

Battleaxe, Rommel gleefully learned from the intercept, had been a disaster for the British. The Western Desert Force had lost ninety-nine tanks out of the two hundred and twenty-five in the assault, and numerous others had broken down. More than a thousand Tommies (as British foot soldiers were called) had been casualties.

Rommel, who had become a legend on the homefront, stood at the Egyptian border with Libya, waiting for a green light from Adolf Hitler to plunge forward, seize Alexandria, then capture Cairo and the nearby north-south Suez Canal, Great Britain's lifeline to the Middle East.

Now the bloody conflict in North Africa had become a race for supplies. Rommel also had suffered sizeable losses in crushing Battleaxe, so before he could strike, he would have to receive large amounts of weapons, ammunition, food, clothing, and other war gear. His supply line stretched from Europe southward across the Mediterranean Sea to Tripoli, Libya, then hundreds of miles eastward by truck to the front lines.

Wavell was resupplied almost entirely by convoys dodging German U-boats and bombers on the Mediterranean to Alexandria, a city of one million Egyptians.

If Wavell could replenish his force by sea before Rommel could get his needed supplies across the vast distances of barren desert, the British might be able to hold Alexandria, Cairo, and the nearby Suez Canal.

Both Wavell and Rommel were acutely aware that the harbor at Alexandria was the key to the looming showdown. So the British rushed in all the antiaircraft guns that could be spared from other locales in the Middle East and ringed the Alexandria harbor with them. The Royal Air Force, also hard-pressed, brought in more fighter planes.

Rommel, meanwhile, stepped up Luftwaffe bombing assaults against Alexandria, especially its waterfront and the shipping there. Almost every other night, the air raid sirens wailed over the large city, searchlights criss-crossed the dark sky, and bomb explosions rocked the region.

In the wake of the Battleaxe disaster, one of General Wavell's staff officers called on Major Geoffrey Barkas, head of Middle Eastern camouflage, and gave him a seemingly impossible task: conceal Alexandria harbor to protect it against German bombing attacks.

Barkas was a prewar film producer who had volunteered for the army within days of the outbreak of war in September 1939. At the time, he told senior officers that he would serve in any worthwhile job, never dreaming that his eventual mission would be to try to outsmart the craftiest of German generals, Erwin Rommel.

Now Barkas promptly called on an old friend from the peacetime entertainment world, Lieutenant Jasper Maskelyne, who had been born into the world of magic thirty-eight years earlier. For sixty-six years, he, his grandfather, and his father had been Europe's first family of conjuring. Jasper had been only nine years old when he made his debut on the stage—and mystified the audiences.

On May 10, 1940, Jasper had been on a London stage drinking a glass of razor blades. When he began withdrawing from his mouth the six sharp blades, knotted to a cotton string that kept him from swallowing them, a British army officer burst into the crowded theater. "Hitler's just invaded France, Belgium, and the Netherlands!" he shouted excitedly.

Patriotic fervor swept the British Isles, just as it had when Great Britain declared war on Nazi Germany on September 3, 1939, two days after Adolf Hitler had sent his potent war juggernaut charging into militarily weak Poland. Among those standing in long lines to enlist was Jasper Maskelyne. Other men were volunteering to take up arms against the Nazis, but Jasper stunned the recruiting officers by declaring that he planned to mobilize the domain of magic against the führer.

High-ranking British army officers were reluctant to grant a commission to a man, albeit a famous one, who apparently wanted to help win the war by waving magic wands or casting spells over German leaders. However, with the surrender of France on June 22, 1940, England was in dire danger of invasion. In this desperate situation, even a magician might be useful, so Maskelyne was awarded a lieutenant's commission.

Now, at the encampment of the Camouflage Experimental Section in the desert outside Cairo, Major Barkas told Maskelyne that "hiding" Alexandria harbor was in his hands. Jasper seemed to be elated by the herculean task. Alexandria harbor would be by far the largest stage on which he, or any

German aerial photo of Alexandria harbor. British magicians "moved" the entire port to a new location to hoodwink the Luftwaffe. (Author's collection)

magician, had ever performed. During his conjuring career, he had vanished people, motorcycles, and even an elephant. But an entire harbor!

Soon after dawn the next day, Maskelyne and his Magic Gang—six magicians, artists, movie set designers, and cartoonists—were standing on a bluff looking down on Alexandria harbor, which was crammed with vessels of all types and sizes. Guarding the entrance to the busy waterfront was the giant lighthouse on Pharos Island, one of the Seven Wonders of the Ancient World. The beacon had been built around 240 B.C. and was higher than a thirty-six-story skyscraper.

The Britons were sobered by the thought of concealing such a large and bustling area. Alexandria harbor was an easily located target for German bombardiers. They would home in on the Pharos lighthouse from a long distance in the desert. A pathfinder plane preceding the main flight would follow the familiar Egyptian coastline, then light Alexandria harbor with flares and incendiary bombs. Succeeding waves of bombers would unload their lethal cargoes into the brightly burning fires.

At the end of a day of inspection of the harbor, members of the Magic Gang set up their operation in a quonset hut and traded fanciful ideas on how to hide the vast target. Finally, Jasper Maskelyne declared: "There's only one solution. We've got to move it!"

As his associates watched eagerly, Maskelyne tapped his pipe on a large wall map of the Cairo–Alexandria region. "Here's Alexandria harbor," he stated. "And over here"—he moved his finger a few inches across the map—"is Maryut Bay, about a mile down the coast."

Now the others were getting the picture. "See how the Maryut shoreline curves? Almost like here in Alex!" Jasper pointed out.

"At eight thousand feet, a Jerry bombardier would have trouble telling one from the other," one man chimed in. Exclaimed another: "Particularly at night, and with ack-ack shells exploding around him!"

"Exactly!" Maskelyne declared. "The beauty of the idea is that we won't have to move or cover anything. All we've got to do is to lay down a network of ground lights and structures at Maryut resembling those in Alex. When we know Jerry planes are on the way, we just turn out the Alex harbor lights and switch them on at Maryut. Then we set off explosives we've planted at Maryut, and the fires will draw Jerry like bees to honey!"

"Well, what about the next morning when Jerry recon planes come over to take pictures of the damage at Alex harbor?" one man asked.

"As long as the Jerry recon boys see rubble around Alex harbor, they'll become convinced that their bombardiers had been right on target," Jasper said. "If Jerry wants rubble, we'll give him rubble—plenty of it!"

Maskelyne and his gang plunged into their daunting task. The area around Maryut was sealed off to keep out inquisitive natives—and German spies. Some two hundred army engineers and other craftsmen were assigned to the project.

Working with Royal Navy people, one member of the Magic Gang supervised the creation of canvas ship superstructures. Dim night lights were placed on these dummies. Tall wooden stakes with similar lights atop them were planted in Maryut Bay to give the impression from high above that scores of other ships were at anchor.

Night aerial photos of Alexandria harbor were used as a pattern for Maryut, where hundreds of electric lanterns were staked into the sand and mud.

Then they were wired together to be switched on when Luftwaffe bombers were approaching.

Scores of plywood sheds and small buildings were built. Many of them were packed with explosives that would give off flash and smoke identical to that of detonating bombs.

"Duplicating" the towering Pharos lighthouse was a major task in itself. The masquerade was built around the fact that German bombardiers, high in the sky in the blackness, would be unable to determine how high a structure was. A working "lighthouse" was created by mounting truck searchlights on a plywood slab held up by six stilt legs. These genuine lights were connected to a timer that would switch them on and off, giving the impression that the platform appeared to be rotating.

Making this ploy work would require delicate timing. Once German airmen had time to take a bearing on the phony lighthouse, it would be switched off, just as the Pharos lighthouse had been.

Jasper Maskelyne clearly was reveling in his role of master manipulator for the entire project. All of the lights and explosives detonators at Maryut Bay were connected to a console that Jasper would operate atop the genuine Pharos lighthouse.

In the meantime, feverish work was underway to "bomb" the real harbor at Alexandria when the time came. Thousands of tons of rubble were trucked in and distributed in numerous places, then covered with tarpaulins. After a Luftwaffe attack—hopefully on Maryut—the entire rubble would be uncovered for the benefit of German aerial photographs after daylight.

Bomb craters were painted on huge slabs of canvas, and these would be laid on the ground or hung from Alexandria buildings to simulate heavy damage. Scrap piles were raided throughout the region. Truck and vehicle hulks, already wrecked, were hauled in and would be put next to the phony craters.

Thousands of papier-mâché bricks were rapidly manufactured, and these would be strewn about the premises. As a mute testimony to the "accuracy" of German bombardiers, dummy masts would protrude from the water in the harbor, graphic testimony that ships had been sunk.

If the Maryut machination was to bamboozle the Germans, bombers would have to be met by a good-sized amount of antiaircraft fire. So Maskelyne coerced the Alexandria harbor defense commander to shift—reluctantly—many guns and crews to Maryut. At the same time, orders were given to the gunners remaining at Alexandria not to fire unless directly attacked.

Now everything was ready for the Great Performance. The show's schedule had been refined, the scenery and props were in place, and the performers had been rehearsed. Like actors in prewar music halls of Europe, all the thespians were nervous. "Opening night" was at hand. Only the "audience"—the German bomber force—would decide if the performance would be a hit or a miserable failure.

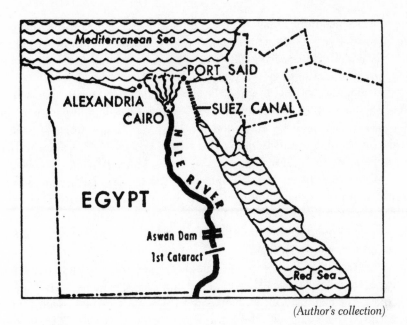

(Author's collection)

Two nights later, reports from the desert told Maskelyne and Frank Knox, an Oxford professor, that a German bomber force was winging toward Alexandria. The two men were both elated and anxious. Atop the Pharos lighthouse, they were prime targets to be killed.

"Don't worry about it," Maskelyne reassured the other. "If we get done in, we won't have to explain why our project had been a disaster!"

Minutes later, after it was estimated that the lead Luftwaffe bombardier had taken his bearings from the powerful illumination atop Pharos lighthouse, Maskelyne slammed down a switch—and Alexandria harbor was gripped by blackness. Another lever was activated, and the dummy lighthouse at Maryut was ablaze. Then the searchlights at Maryut began to crisscross the sky, and as the Luftwaffe flight neared, the antiaircraft guns at Maryut opened fire.

When the sky force came ever closer and the magicians in the Pharos lighthouse felt the bombardiers were close enough to spot the Maryut illumination, the dummy harbor was suddenly blacked out, just as had been the case for months when Alexandria had been attacked. Much to the delight of Maskelyne and his companion, the Luftwaffe bombers ignored Alexandria and began dropping bombs on the phony harbor at Maryut.

Now, as planned, a series of blasts were set off at Maryut by the two men in the Pharos lighthouse. Thick fingers of flame—all planted earlier by the Magic Gang—leaped into the black sky. Piles of dry timber, previously placed, were ignited. Succeeding flights dropped their explosives on the sandy desolate beaches. The dummy harbor had been virtually "destroyed."

In the meantime, Maskelyne's "rubble strewers" raced through the dark streets and alleys of Alexandria, removing the tarpaulins from the crushed masonry and bricks, spreading the canvases with painted bomb craters, and scattering thousands of papier-mâché bricks.

As soon as the final German bomber headed back to its base, scores of Royal Engineers went to work at Maryut. Fires were extinguished, the genuine wreckage was covered by sand, and the destroyed "stage props"—shrubbery, cardboard buildings, and harbor lights—were replaced. The dummy harbor had to be ready for a return engagement by the Luftwaffe.

All that day, the joy of the Magic Gang was tempered. After receiving aerial photos of the "damage" inflicted on Alexandria harbor, would the Germans realize that they had been duped? Only if another bomber force swallowed the bait and again pounded the dummy harbor at Maryut would it be known if the deception had been successful.

That night, the bombers roared in lower than usual, no doubt bent on inflicting even more damage. They pounced on Maryut, which soon was engulfed in flames. For eight successive nights, the Luftwaffe returned. Each morning, the Magic Gang, along with the Royal Engineers, replaced the "destruction" at Maryut and created "wreckage" at Alexandria.

Suddenly, the Germans lost interest in Alexandria. Ultra, the ingenious British interception and decoding machine at Bletchley Park, north of London, disclosed the reason. Adolf Hitler was about to launch Operation Barbarossa, a massive invasion of the Soviet Union, and large numbers of bomber units were transferred from North Africa to support Barbarossa.

In the next twenty months, millions of tons of the accoutrements of war would land safely at Alexandria harbor, supplies eventually used to help drive the Germans out of North Africa.[11]

Nazi Spies Visit the White House

THIRTY-FIVE-YEAR-OLD Karl Victor Mueller was born in a small Austrian village, but he emigrated to the United States in 1936, and became a naturalized citizen. However, in 1941, with Adolf Hitler's Wehrmacht fighting the Red Army inside the Soviet Union, Mueller yearned to return to Austria, which the führer had "annexed" a few years earlier.

In the meantime, Mueller was recruited as a German spy, and he did all he could in the United States for Nazi Germany. He teamed up with another crack Nazi agent, Kurt Frederick Ludwig, on visits to American defense plants.

Ludwig was born in Fremont, Ohio, but had been taken to Germany as a child. An insignificant-looking, diminutive man, he had been a successful businessman in Munich and knew several figures high on the Nazi totem pole, including Gestapo chief Heinrich Himmler. In 1939, shortly after German

*German master spy
Kurt Ludwig paid a
visit to the White
House. (Author's
collection)*

panzers swarmed into Poland, Ludwig told Himmler that even though he was still an American citizen, he was eager to contribute to Germany's war effort. Himmler, a one-time chicken farmer, sent Ludwig to the United States to spy out American military secrets.

Leaving his wife and children in Munich, Ludwig took a course in espionage techniques before sailing for New York City, where he arrived in March 1940. His orders were to organize his own spy network, and Karl Mueller became one of his ace recruits.

Ludwig purchased a powerful car—courtesy of Adolf Hitler's pocketbook—and he and Mueller would race along the highways at the then breathtaking speed of eighty miles per hour while heading for jaunts to defense plants. Hidden in the automobile was a portable shortwave radio set over which he could send coded messages to clandestine Nazi stations in Brazil or to U-boats off the eastern seaboard of the United States for relay to Germany.

Ludwig and Mueller functioned smoothly as a team. Each carried a camera on these spying jaunts, and even though both men had thick German accents, guards and attendants at war production plants and airfields often went out of their way to assist the two Nazi spies in getting the photographs they sought. Mueller and Ludwig took one trip to the U.S. Naval Academy at Annapolis, Maryland, where they got scores of excellent pictures of cadets drilling, training facilities, and buildings.

On a trip to Washington, the two men ventured into the White House on a regular guided tour, and Ludwig was delighted to report to Berlin a vivid personal description of what it was like for a Nazi spy to be sauntering around inside the house of the president of the United States.[12]

Escaping in Disguise from a Death Camp

CAPTAIN IAN GARROW, whose 51st "Highland" Division had been cut off when German armies trapped most of the British forces at the French port of Dunkirk in the spring of 1940, chose to remain in France and help other British soldiers escape to England. Despite enormous obstacles—other than the quite real threat of being arrested by the Gestapo and summarily shot—Garrow organized an escape line from Paris (where evaders from northern France were collected) westward to the Pyrenees, at the French-Spanish border.

Garrow's escape apparatus shuttled hundreds of British evaders to sanctuary in Spain, from where they were able to get to England by boat or airplane. Disguised in civilian clothes, they traveled by foot, bicycle, bus, car, train, and horse and cart.

Finally, after a year and a half of dodging the Gestapo, Captain Garrow's luck ran out and he was arrested by French police of the puppet Vichy government. He had been betrayed by a veteran escape worker, Harold Cole, who had told friends that he was a British army captain who had escaped from Dunkirk. In fact, he had been a sergeant who had deserted before Dunkirk, taking with him the funds of the company's mess. Only much later would it be learned that Cole had a long record of civilian convictions for burglary and fraud.

Through underground sources, Patrick Albert O'Leary (nom de guerre of Albert-Marie Guérisse), a former medical officer in the Belgian army, learned that Garrow had been arrested. He immediately began a search to locate where the captain was being held.

Back in 1940, when the German army had rapidly overrun Belgium, O'Leary escaped to England, where he volunteered to be sent back to France as a spy for the Special Operations Executive (SOE), the British cloak-and-dagger agency. While landing at night along the southern coast of France, O'Leary was detected and arrested. After spending several months in an internment camp, he escaped, made his way to Marseilles, and linked up with Captain Ian Garrow, who was in the city to forge links into his escape line to Spain.

After Garrow had been captured, O'Leary took charge of the escape line and steadily expanded it until it had more than 250 volunteers throughout France. They included the Misses Trenchard, two elderly Scottish ladies who operated a tea shop in Monte Carlo and provided meals for evaders hidden in a nearby villa; Paul Ulmann, a Jewish tailor from Toulouse who fashioned the clothing O'Leary's agents and clients needed for disguises; and Father Carpentier, a priest in Abbeville, who printed false identity papers on his own press.

Among other O'Leary escape-line workers were Louis Nouveau, a stock-broker in Marseilles, who contributed most of his considerable wealth to the evading operation; Georges Rafarrin, the rotund chef on the Paris-Marseilles express train, a favorite of German passengers because of his genial disposition, who also doubled as O'Leary's courier between those two cities; Mademoiselle Françoise Dissart, a white-haired woman in her middle sixties who was O'Leary's main organizer in Toulouse; and Madame Mongelard, owner of the Hôtel de Paris in Toulouse, where most of the rooms were occupied by fugitives from the Gestapo and Vichy police.

Toward the close of 1942, O'Leary learned through underground sources that Captain Ian Garrow was being held in Mauzac, a French internment camp, and was going to be sent to the German concentration camp at Dachau for execution. O'Leary, in the guise of a traveling salesman, reconnoitered Mauzac, and saw that it was heavily guarded and surrounded by three rings of barbed wire.

The nimble-witted Belgian quickly decided that the only hope of spring-ing Garrow was for the prisoner to dress in the uniform of the French soldiers guarding the camp and walk out with them when they went off duty. O'Leary cozied up to one of the guards and offered him 250,000 francs—about six years' salary—if he would smuggle a uniform into the camp. The man agreed to do the job, and O'Leary gave him half of the bribe, the funds provided by the British government.

O'Leary also learned from the same guard that time was running out for Captain Garrow. He would be shipped to the German death camp in a week. The Belgian traveled to Toulouse and had his escape line's Jewish tailor, Paul Ulmann, create a uniform that would fit Garrow.

Ulmann and his wife labored almost continuously for forty-eight hours to complete the job, and O'Leary rushed it back to Mauzac on November 30, 1942. On arrival, the Belgian was shocked: no longer were French soldiers guarding the camp. Now French gendarmes were in charge, so the uniform O'Leary had brought with him was useless.

O'Leary hastened back to Toulouse, and the Ulmann couple fashioned an authentic French gendarme's uniform, again in two days of frantic effort.

At 6:45 A.M. on December 6, 1942, a group of gendarmes walked through the Mauzac gate after finishing their guard shift. With them was a tall man who, unlike the others, did not engage in small talk. In his neatly fitting gen-darme's uniform was Ian Garrow, who was escorted to the Spanish border by Patrick O'Leary.

Three months later, O'Leary was meeting with his agents in a Paris cafe. Gestapo men burst in and arrested him. As with Garrow, he had been betrayed by a traitor, one of his volunteers. Soon the Belgian was sent to the death camp at Dachau, but he survived the war.[13]

The World's Strangest Business

WHEN WAR BROKE OUT in Europe in September 1939, thirty-eight-year-old Elder Wills had spent his adult life in the domain of disguise and make-believe. After studying architecture as a youth, he became a scenic artist at the Theatre Royal, Drury Lane, in London. Later, he turned to movies as art director, producer, and director, scoring several film successes.

After going to France with the ill-fated British Expeditionary Force, he was evacuated from Dunkirk to England with a leg injury. For a year, he was put to work camouflaging buildings and airfields, and designing cardboard tanks and planes, to help mystify the Luftwaffe and deter Adolf Hitler from launching Operation Sea Lion, the invasion of nearly defenseless England.

Early in November 1941, Captain (later Lieutenant Colonel) Wills was summoned by Professor Dudley M. Newitt, head of the Scientific Research Department of the Special Operations Executive (SOE), and given an incredible mission. Starting almost from scratch, Wills was to create a large collection of secret laboratories that would supply a fantastic variety of items needed by SOE spies and saboteurs to survive.

Wills tackled his task with typical enthusiasm and established several workshops in and near London. In this crucial endeavor—thousands of lives could be at stake—Wills was assisted by some of his former workers from Elstree movie studios: makeup artists, carpenters, wardrobe mistresses, plasterers—all skilled in the never-never land of make-believe. The largest "laboratory" was installed at the Thatched Barn, a highly popular nightclub in pre-war days.

Wills's first urgent job was to provide a satisfactory suitcase for the radio sets dropped with spies into Nazi-occupied Europe. Wills had been flabbergasted to learn that the suitcases in use had been bought in public stores and were of the same type. So if a Gestapo agent were to spot one of these containers, he knew he had an Allied spy trapped.

Wills and his helpers scoured junk shops to secure a wide array of Continental suitcases, the kinds that the average Frenchman, Belgian, or Dutchman would carry. Some of these containers were too new, so they had to be artificially battered to make them appear well worn. Into these suitcases were built double bottoms and secret compartments that might be overlooked in a hasty inspection by the Germans.

Initially, SOE agents were provided with codes written on ordinary paper. These scraps had proven to be a death warrant for some agents. Wills invented an invisible ink that could be seen only under infrared lighting. He also created small flashlights with concealed infrared discs to permit agents to read radio codes. The Gestapo would not be suspicious of flashlights; they were carried by millions in blacked-out Europe.

British agents showing forged identity cards at a German checkpoint in France. (National Archives)

Wills's secret laboratories produced microfilmed documents so tiny that they could be sealed in minute containers which, in turn, were hidden in various parts of the body, such as the rectum or navel.

Each agent would be provided with a box of ordinary matches, and only he knew that one match, identifiable only by a tiny nick, contained a microfilm with the equivalent of nine sheets of standard-size stationery.

A large number of other everyday items were altered: toothpaste tubes with special compartments; shoelaces with a soft tube inside; microdots, no larger than a speck of dust, that could be placed on the lens of eyeglasses, but when developed by a special photographic process would disclose messages up to five hundred words in length.

Operation Lavatory instructed agents where to hide their radios when they reached a safe house—in toilet cisterns. A specially designed pulling chain served as an aerial.

Telltale clothes could be a spy's death warrant. So Wills obtained the help of a Jewish refugee from Vienna, a master tailor, to be his chief adviser on "fashions." Clothes manufactured on the continent were quite different from those created in England, so details had to be correct down to socks, underwear, and brassieres.

Although the Jewish advisor spoke only fractured English, he set to work with enormous zeal and ingenuity. He recruited several Jewish tailors and seamstresses, established a small secret factory in the heart of London, and produced a wide range of men's and women's clothing to precise specifications.

Code-named Hans, the Austrian would visit synagogues around southern England and, without giving away his function, obtain labels that bore the name of a genuine Paris, Brussels, or Amsterdam store. Later, these labels were duplicated in Hans's secret factory, "aged," and sewn into the clothes, which were then properly tattered and frayed.

A British manufacturer, sworn to secrecy, made shoes and boots of types that were worn on the continent. The boots were provided with sliding heels to conceal a cavity for the storage of microfilms.

Wills and his men produced a wide variety of everyday articles, all of which were small and easy to carry or conceal on a person. The items were explosive devices. Milk bottles could be unobtrusively placed in a Gestapo or Abwehr office and would explode when the caps were removed. Fountain pens spewed out mayhem, and loaves of bread exploded when cut in half or broken by hands.

Wills enlisted the assistance of Professor Julian Huxley, secretary of the London Zoological Society, along with officials in the Natural History Museum, as advisors for the creations of ingenious booby traps. Horse, camel, elephant, and mule "droppings" were constructed of plastic and painted by hand. They were virtually indistinguishable from the real things.

Carefully packed into crates marked "shoes," "chairs," or other innocuous items, the booby traps were shipped to the appropriate locales: horse droppings to much of Europe, camel droppings to North Africa, elephant droppings to the Far East.

A lone underground warrior could sneak onto a road or trail being taken by enemy convoys or troops, and surreptitiously place a few of these lethal explosives in the midst of genuine droppings. On occasion, the resistance man would have the satisfaction of viewing from concealment a vehicle and its occupants blown up.

Tens of thousands of "cigarettes" filled with explosive and incendiary materials were sent to SOE agents in Nazi-occupied Europe. These innocent-looking items collectively caused much damage to German supply depots and other facilities.

French railwaymen were among the most eager and resourceful resistance members. They used nuts and bolts that were hollow and filled with explosives that could be attached to locomotives being used to haul troops, weapons, and supplies for the Wehrmacht. French factory workers also generated widespread damage by putting these nuts and bolts on vital machine tools turning out war matériel for the occupiers.

Wills and his imaginative helpers also created phony coal lumps and timber logs, items almost identical to those used in German headquarters, barracks, and other facilities. Filled with high explosives, the "coal" or "logs" were so realistic that resistance men could carry them openly on the roads and streets of Nazi-held Europe. By one ruse or another, these items found their way into Wehrmacht barracks or offices, with death and destruction to follow.

Colonel Wills and his highly imaginative helpers played a major but largely unsung role in preparing Europe for eventual invasion by Allied armies.[14]

French Gold Cache
Kept from Hitler

LATE IN 1940, the French cruiser *Emile Bertin* steamed into the harbor at Fort-de-France, the capital of Martinique, a French island about forty miles long and sixteen miles wide. Located about a thousand miles southeast of Cuba, Martinique had become a secret base for German U-boats. Within one thirty-day period, the underwater craft had sunk twenty British-controlled cargo ships in the region.

It was dark when the *Emile Bertin* tied up at the dock and crewmen began unloading some $3 billion (equivalent to $35 billion in the year 2001) in gold. The precious metal was put on the ammunition hoists of an old fort nearby and lowered into vaults designed for storing shells. This fortune in gold had been sent to Martinique for safekeeping by the puppet French government based in Vichy, France.

When Adolf Hitler's Wehrmacht shocked the free world by conquering the once vaunted French army in only six weeks in mid-1940, the armistice agreement specified that Germany would occupy roughly the northern half of France, while the French could establish their own government for the nation in the southern, or unoccupied, half of the country.

However, Adolf Hitler had no intention of allowing a potentially hostile, although defeated, France to govern itself. He installed a revered hero of World War I, eighty-four-year-old Marshal Henri Pétain, as the figurehead ruler of unoccupied France. The bewildered Pétain was never in control of the Vichy government and was helpless to halt the constant power struggles within his entourage.

Actually running the Vichy government was Pierre Laval, who had long been involved in French politics and was known as a master of duplicity and opportunism. So when Hitler, behind the scenes, arranged for Laval to "officially" be Pétain's successor, the ambitious Frenchman promptly announced that he intended to "collaborate in all domains" with the Germans.

Laval set about establishing Martinique as a Vichy French stronghold and dispatched Admiral Georges Robert to govern the island. In addition to being used by German submarines, the island was a relay station for German intelligence collected in the United States. Martinique also served as a base for secret agents of the Foreign Organization of the German National Socialist Party (Nazis) under Gauleiter (political leader) Ernst Wilhelm Bohle, whose task was to subvert Latin American countries thought to favor the Allies.

Through secret agents and intercepted radio messages, British intelligence learned of the gold shipment. The cache became a matter of deep concern. Although the riches rightfully belonged to the French people, it could be handed over to Bohle by Laval and used to promote pro-Nazi interests throughout the Americas. The gold could also be used by Bohle to purchase in South America the raw materials needed for the creation of weapons of war in Germany.

In early 1941, a Martiniquais, Jacques Vauzanges, called at the offices of the British Security Coordination (BSC), established a year earlier in a Rockefeller Center highrise in New York City. Its covert function was to identify and undermine Nazi clandestine activities in the Western Hemisphere. Vauzanges was an officer in the French Deuxiéme Bureau (military intelligence) who had become disenchanted with the Vichy government's collaboration with the Germans.

A swashbuckling, energetic type, the Frenchman told William Stephenson, a wealthy Canadian industrialist who headed the BSC operation, about the fortune in French gold on Martinique and how it might fall into the clutches of Adolf Hitler to help finance his campaigns of conquest. The visitor suggested that he return to Martinique, where he had many contacts with the French military on the island, to organize a rebellion against the Vichy government.

Vauzanges's scheme was to persuade French naval officers on the island to flee with several warships to the Canadian port of Halifax—after the gold cache had been put aboard one of the vessels.

Equipped with a two-way radio and secret codes, Vauzanges slipped back into his native Martinique in mid-1941. But the fortunes of war seemed to have turned against the British, so the French naval officers he contacted on the island were firmly committed to Marshal Pétain and the Vichy government. The proposed rebellion never got off the drawing board.

Despite this setback, British intelligence continued to focus on the gold cache. Prime Minister Winston S. Churchill asked the BSC if the riches were still in the old fort, or if they had been secretly removed and were floating around the open markets of South America.

To answer this riddle, Louis Franck, one of the world's leading specialists in bullion and arbitrage, was rushed to the BSC in New York City. He was descended from a long line of Belgian bankers. Franck painstakingly studied

Seer Sees Nazi Doom if U. S. Acts in 8 Months

The noted "Hungarian astrologist" was actually a captain in the British Army. (Cleveland News)

every financial transaction on the world market that might give clues that the gold was being infiltrated into South America. He could find no evidence that the treasure was anywhere except in the old fort on Martinique.

Franck asked Stephenson if there was any way of stealing the gold. The Canadian master spy shook his head: Great Britain was still hanging on by her fingernails against Nazi Germany, and there was no way a military expedition could be mounted to seize Martinique and its gold.

"Then neutralize the governor of Martinique [Admiral Georges Robert]," Franck suggested, "and prevent the gold from being taken from the island. In effect, that puts the gold under our control." He added reasonably, "You don't ask to see each bar of gold at Fort Knox [in the United States] each time you buy U.S. dollars."

"I think you've got something there," the wily Stephenson replied. "We make sure the gold stays in Martinique, but put over the fact that we've got the power to take it—even if we don't."

Acting with typical speed, Stephenson had a disinformation campaign launched on Martinique. The thrust was that the British navy was keeping a close eye on the island and might land a force at any time to seize the gold.

In the meantime, Stephenson sent for Louis de Wohl, who had been touring U.S. cities as "the famous Hungarian astrologer." An ever-growing audience had become convinced that he had supernatural powers. Wohl had been built up in the press about his amazingly accurate predictions on the course of the war in Europe. Actually, Wohl knew little about astrology.

A pudgy, middle-aged man, Wohl was a captain in the British army. He had been brought to the United States in mid-1941 as the centerpiece of an elaborate scheme by the BSC to help demolish the widespread point of view that Adolf Hitler's military juggernaut was invincible and he was bound to win the war in Europe.

There had been good reason for Wohl's "amazingly accurate predictions." British intelligence had been feeding him bits and pieces of information that he wove into astrology information he scrounged from textbooks.

Wohl was ensconced in a Manhattan hotel, and each night, a British agent would sneak up the fire escape and hand the "astrologer" the latest information about Martinique. Based on this data, Wohl wrote in his highly popular syndicated column, *Stars Foretell,* that a "prominent Nazi collaborator serving in some tropical island would shortly go *maboul* (crazy)."

Incredibly, a week later, Admiral Robert had indeed "gone mad," suffering from severe sunstroke that left him temporarily unable to speak with clarity. Wohl's credibility skyrocketed. Few knew that moles on the island had disclosed earlier that the admiral had been having dizzy spells from the heat.

As a component of the subtle campaign to convince Martinique officials that they were being closely watched, U.S. Admiral John W. Greenslade was dispatched by Washington to pay a courtesy call on the slowly recovering Admiral Robert. Although the United States was officially neutral, it was not lost on the Frenchman that Greenslade had been sent to convey the impression that Washington, along with London, the British navy—and even Louis de Wohl—were watching Martinique and searching for any sign that the gold was being moved.

The ongoing intrigue resulted in the French riches remaining in the fort's vaults for the duration of the war.[15]

The German "Butcher's" Gardener

BRITISH ARMY LIEUTENANT RICHARD PINDER was an expert in sabotage operations. After being parachuted into southern France in late 1942, he traveled between various *réseaux* (networks) to train the underground warriors in his specialty.

One day, Pinder and a few French resistants were seated in a cafe in the small town of Montauban when they were arrested by German police making a sweep to round up Frenchmen for forced labor. The Briton's identity card, forged in London, gave his occupation as *horticulteur,* although he hardly knew the difference between a rose and a tulip.

Because of his presumed skill, Pinder, who was not suspected of being an underground leader, was shipped to Prague, Czechoslovakia, where he was assigned as the gardener at the mansion of Karl Hermann Frank.

When the German armed forces had seized Prague in March 1939, five months after the outbreak of general war in Europe, Heinrich Himmler, chief of the Gestapo and the head of the Schutzstaffel (SS), named Frank as leader of the Gestapo in Czechoslovakia with the SS rank of Gruppenführer (lieutenant general).

On May 27, 1942, a few months before Lieutenant Pinder arrived in Prague, Karl Frank's immediate superior, thirty-eight-year-old Obergruppenführer (SS general) Rinehard Heydrich, was riding in his chauffeur-driven Mercedes from his ornate mansion in a Prague suburb to his headquarters in towering Hradcany Castle. A favorite of Adolf Hitler, the young general, whom the führer had appointed Reichsprotektor of Czechoslovakia, was so ruthless that his officers privately called him the Blond Beast.

At a hairpin turn in the road, the Mercedes slowed, and two Czechs, who had been parachuted near Prague to assassinate Heydrich, leaped from behind bushes and pumped bullets into him. A few days later, the man who had been "credited" with conceiving the Final Solution program for destroying the Jews in Europe died from his wounds.

Under the direction of Gestapo chief Karl Frank, the Germans reacted to the assassination with fury. In Prague, a *ratissage* (rat hunt, Gestapo vernacular for a manhunt), was unleashed upon the Czechs. Over ten thousand were arrested, and some 1,300 executed.

Frank saved the most horrific of his reprisals for the small mining village of Lidice, whose citizens, he believed wrongly, had harbored the resistants who had killed Heydrich. Several hundred SS and German army troops descended upon Lidice at night and assembled the entire population in the village square. All males between sixteen and seventy-five years of age were herded into a nearby field and riddled by SS machine guns. The women and children were carried away in trucks and, with a few exceptions, were never heard of again. As a final gesture of rage, Frank had the village leveled to a pile of smoking masonry. When word of the massacre eventually seeped out to a horrified free world, Karl Frank was dubbed the Butcher of Lidice.

Frank, meanwhile, learned that the Czech assassins were holed up in the basement of a church in Prague. After several assaults by SS troops, the resistants were gunned down.

Now Lieutenant Richard Pinder, a British spy, found himself in an incredible situation: he was working as a gardener for the Butcher of Lidice. As cruel as he was, Karl Frank had a sentimental side. He loved to stroll in his garden and caress the flowers, which were blooming profusely. He was delighted with the work of his "French landscape artist," who himself was unable to understand why he had a natural talent as a gardener. Perhaps he had been born with "green fingers," Pinder decided.

If the Briton was to survive, he had to please his boss. It would be suicide to try to flee from Prague and make his way for hundreds of miles through hostile territory. Often he hatched schemes for killing Frank, but all had to be rejected as unworkable.

Helping to relieve Pinder's frustration—being close to the Gestapo chief almost daily and unable to kill him—the Briton managed to make contact with the underground in Prague and passed along information on Frank's habits and itineraries. These tidbits might be helpful to the resistants in "neutralizing" the dreaded Gestapo head. But Frank seemed to lead a charmed existence, and he never ventured away from his heavily guarded mansion without a large bodyguard of SS troops.

When Soviet forces moved into Prague in the spring of 1945, the "French gardener" was among the first to greet the soldiers. Soon, the war was over.

About a year later, the Butcher of Lidice went to the gallows as a war criminal, never aware that he had been rubbing elbows for two years with a British spy who was seeking a chance to kill him.[16]

Part Four

A Sleeping America Awakens

A Plot to Coerce the United States into War

WEARING A CIVILIAN SUIT to disguise his true identity, a U.S. army captain strolled into the Capitol in Washington and made his way to the office of Senator Burton K. Wheeler, a staunch isolationist. The military officer, who used a phony name, left a package for Wheeler, a three-hundred-and-fifty-page War Department report with "Top Secret" stamped on the cover. It was late November 1941.

More than a year earlier in August 1940, Congress was embroiled in an acrimonious debate over the Selective Service and Training Bill, which called for the first peacetime draft in the nation's history. Isolationists were nearly apoplectic. "If you pass this bill," Senator Wheeler thundered, "you accord Hitler his greatest and cheapest victory to date!"

When the measure was passed, Wheeler claimed that Congress had "plowed under huge numbers of American boys."

Although the United States was beginning to build up its armed forces in the months ahead, Wheeler continued his efforts to keep America out of global conflicts. So he, no doubt, was delighted to receive the War Department report from the captain, who said he had been motivated out of concern for the American people and to warn them that President Franklin D. Roosevelt was trying to drag the nation into war against Nazi Germany.

Titled "*Victory Program*," the War Department report forecast U.S. government plans to enter the conflict against Germany, and gave an estimate of the number of troops and equipment needed to launch an offensive against the Third Reich.

Wheeler passed the secret document along to the isolationist *Chicago Tribune*, which splashed it across the front page with blaring headlines. Its story began: "A confidential report prepared by the [U.S. high command] by order of President Roosevelt . . . is a blueprint for engaging the nation in total war."

The *Victory Program* document gained wide circulation in the United States and abroad. A copy was obtained by the German Embassy in Washington, and a summary was radioed to Berlin. Although war leaders in Germany hailed the "fantastic intelligence coup" by operatives in the Reich Embassy, the *Victory Program* was a fraud.

It was hatched by operatives in the British Security Coordination (BSC), a cover name for a secret agency located in New York City's bustling Rockefeller Center. BSC's specified mission was to investigate and take counteraction against German undercover operations in the Western Hemisphere.

The *Victory Program* was concocted out of information already known to German intelligence, along with much misleading data. The primary goal of this hoax was to use isolationist channels, such as Senator Wheeler, as a means of disclosing to Adolf Hitler a "secret plan" of the United States calculated to provoke him into declaring war against the United States. Even if Japan were to launch a heavy assault against American bases in the Pacific, the British— meaning Prime Minister Winston S. Churchill—feared that the United States would still not declare war on Germany.

Wheeler, the apostle of peace, had unknowingly tripped a wire in the minefield of Adolf Hitler's mind.[1]

American Postcards Aid Pearl Harbor Attack

A BRILLIANT SUN, rising majestically over Mount Tantalus, began drenching Pearl Harbor, Hawaii, in its first warming rays. Even for the island of Oahu, this was an uncommonly glorious Sunday morning. It was December 7, 1941 (Honolulu time).

Except for a handful of aircraft carriers, the U.S. Pacific Fleet was roosting drowsily on Battleship Row: seventy combat ships. All had one boiler lighted, but few had enough steam generated to make a quick sortie for the open sea in case of an emergency.

But no emergency was contemplated. Most of the officers and crewmen were deep in slumber following a typical Saturday night shore leave. As a result, dawn found the fleet suffering its full share of hangovers.

Prior to daylight, Captain Misuo Fuchido, who was regarded as one of the most brilliant young officers in the Imperial Japanese Navy, lifted off in his red and yellow airplane from the aircraft carrier *Agaki*, 230 miles due north of Oahu. Fuchido had been chosen to lead the sneak attack on Pearl Harbor. Within fifteen minutes, 183 fighters, bombers, and torpedo planes from six carriers formed up in the dark sky and followed Fuchido toward the target.

As the Japanese armada winged toward America's largest base in the Pacific, the pilots knew the position of virtually all U.S. ships. In the cockpit of each plane was a large panoramic aerial view of Pearl Harbor, divided into small numbered squares. Each pilot or bombardier knew which square was his target and the ship or ships he would find there.

Japanese pilots had before them in their cockpits this approximate view of Battleship Row (foreground) at Pearl Harbor. Blowups were made from an American three-cent postcard. (U.S. Navy)

These photos had been blown up from ordinary postcards made in the United States. A Japanese spy had bought them two months earlier in a Honolulu gift shop. The price? Three cents each.[2]

Urgent Mission: Disguise California

IN THE EARLY WEEKS after Pearl Harbor, the Japanese armed forces seemed to be invincible. Throughout the Pacific, they launched a blitzkrieg that dwarfed anything Adolf Hitler's vaunted juggernaut had achieved in Europe. Within a two-month period of time, the Japanese army seized Guam, Hong Kong, Manila, Singapore, and other locales.

Although the leaders in Washington had no direct knowledge of Japan's future actions, one worried general declared in private: "If the Japs invade California, about all we have to confront them will be a few platoons of Boy Scouts!"

In Tokyo, the Japanese warlords had been laying plans for several years for widespread conquest in the Pacific—and beyond. They focused on mass landings between San Francisco and Los Angeles. First, however, their time-table called for the capture of Midway Island, a tiny dot in the central Pacific held by a small American force, then a leap to Hawaii, eleven hundred miles to the northeast, and seize that weakly defended territory. Using Pearl Harbor as a base, convoys would steam for California and land powerful armies.

During February 1942, U.S. Navy monitors on the West Coast tracked a Japanese submarine skulking outside of San Francisco Bay. A few nights later, another Japanese submarine surfaced off Santa Barbara and fired a few shells at an oil storage facility.

Panic erupted in California. There were constant rumors of looming attacks by Japanese submarines and bombers. Frenzied newspaper stories with blaring headlines urged the people to be prepared for a Japanese invasion.

Now it was clear to the War Department in Washington that the West Coast, especially California, was vulnerable, and every conceivable defensive measure was urgently needed.

On the heels of the "attacks" by the two submarines, an ongoing flood of rumors about Japanese aircraft carriers heading hellbent for California, and wild espionage stories about Japanese spies hiding behind nearly every bush on the coastline, the War Department issued an urgent order to Lieutenant General John L. De Witt, head of the Western Defense Command: carry out passive defense measures for all vital installations along the Pacific Coast.

In essence, General De Witt had been instructed to disguise California. Leading that seemingly impossible endeavor would be Colonel John F. Ohmer, an enthusiastic achiever who was in command of a camouflage training center at March Field, a large military base forty miles east of Los Angeles.

Ohmer was a pioneer in camouflage, deception, and misdirection, techniques utilized for centuries by magicians around the world. During the Battle of Britain in late 1940, when Reichsmarschall Hermann Göring tried to bring England to her knees by a mighty air onslaught, Ohmer visited British airfields and other key installations for a firsthand look at ingenious camouflage and misdirection projects that caused the Luftwaffe to waste thousands of tons of bombs on empty fields.

For many months prior to Pearl Harbor, Ohmer had risked the wrath of his superiors in Washington by campaigning incessantly for the protective cover of American targets, both at home and in the Pacific. Among the detailed plans presented to the War Department was one for "hiding" Wheeler Field, the major air base near Pearl Harbor.

Ohmer's plan was rejected by the higher-ups in Washington. Too costly: $56,210. When the Japanese hit in Hawaii a few months later, Wheeler was nearly blasted off the map. Its warplanes, neatly lined up wingtip-to-wingtip, were blown to smithereens, and scores of Americans were killed. American airpower on Oahu had been virtually wiped out.

Colonel Ohmer agonized after the smoke had cleared in Hawaii. How many lives and airplanes could have been saved at Wheeler Field if he had received approval to use camouflage and misdirection techniques to confuse the Japanese pilots?

Washington order to "disguise California" followed a shell explosion from a Japanese submarine on this ocean pier at Santa Barbara on February 2, 1942. (U.S. Army)

In spite of being slapped down by Washington time and again, in 1940, Ohmer, then a major, and other prophets kept doggedly promoting their cause. Using minimal funds scraped up here and there, a few experiments were conducted on a modest basis at Maxwell Field, Alabama; Eglin Field, Florida; Langley Field and Fort Eustis, Virginia; and Barksdale Field, South Carolina.

A year before Pearl Harbor, negotiations were held with the Goodyear Company to manufacture rubber decoy aircraft of the kind that the British were using so successfully in fending off the German Luftwaffe assaults. Goodyear produced several realistic samples that could be duplicated in large numbers for only $1,000 per "airplane." Ohmer had hoped to sprinkle these dummies around the U.S. air bases in Hawaii, but his plea for funds was rejected by the War Department.

Then, on July 12, 1941, Lieutenant General Walter C. Short, who had recently been assigned to command the Hawaiian Department, responsible for the defense of the islands, fired off an urgent signal to Washington:

> There is a definite need for camouflage treatment of airfields [in Hawaii]. Up to this time no camouflage treatment has been undertaken on any air base.

Again no action was taken on the appeal of Short, who later would be singled out as one of the two scapegoats for the Pearl Harbor disaster, along with the Navy commander in Hawaii, Admiral Husband E. Kimmel.

Now, with the United States at war and the West Coast considered to be vulnerable, Colonel Ohmer went to work to "disguise" California. With him at March Field was an engineer camouflage battalion. His task was made less complex by the proximity of Hollywood and its pool of gifted technicians in the realm of make-believe. From Metro-Goldwyn-Mayer, Disney Studios, Twentieth Century Fox, Paramount, Universal Pictures, and other companies came a stream of scenic designers, painters, art directors, landscape artists, animators, carpenters, lighting experts, and prop men.

The experience of these volunteers and "draftees" ranged from veteran art director Gabriel Scognamillo to neophyte Harry Horner, who later art-designed such blockbuster movies as *Born Yesterday, The Heiress,* and *The Hustler.* None had any military know-how, but they made up for that deficiency with energy and enthusiasm.

Deluged by this flood of creative talent, humdrum March Field soon resembled the back lot of a bustling movie studio in Hollywood. The base became a huge laboratory where techniques, gadgets, and other implements of the magician's craft underwent extensive experimentation to determine how best to "disguise" California.

At March in these early weeks of 1942, it was hard to tell where reality ended and fantasy began. A casual visitor, meandering through the creative area, might come upon a small farm complete with barns, a silo, outbuildings, and a battered pickup truck. This pastoral setting was actually created of lumber and painted on canvas. It covered a large ammunition dump. The creation gained reality when a local farmer agreed to graze his quite live cows near the phony buildings.

Scattered around March Field were decoy aircraft constructed of odd materials such as foliage, cardboard ration boxes, canvas scraps, burlap on chicken wire, discarded packing crates, and flattened tin cans. One Hollywood figure joked that the reason he drank so much beer was so the cans could be used in the project.

None of these makeshift aircraft could withstand routine inspection, but when seen hastily from a racing airplane miles overhead, they proved amazingly realistic.

Colonel Ohmer and his gung-ho Hollywood associates also created fake runways for their "airplanes," mainly by the controlled burning of grassy strips. When seen from above, these "runways" seemed to be the real thing.

Now that this experimentation at March Field into applying Hollywood techniques to the war effort was concluded, Ohmer and his men, working with military personnel and private contractors, applied some form of camouflage and misdirection to thirty-four air bases, including foliage replanting and structural cover. Among them were Hammer, Mills, and Salinas Fields in California; Salem and Portland Air Bases in Oregon; and McChord and Paine Fields in Washington.

At the same time, Ohmer and his magicians were concealing key war factories and assembly plants, likely targets for Japanese aircraft on the West Coast. A California firm, Walker Construction Company, was called on to disguise several huge facilities it had built, including the Douglas Aircraft plant in Long Beach. It would be a prodigious task. Only through the exceptional skills of some of the finest special effects men and other artists and craftsmen in Hollywood could an entire industrial area be camouflaged.

The most ambitious of these many "disappearing acts" was the Lockheed-Vega aircraft plant at Burbank, California. The huge building, together with parking lots holding thousands of employee automobiles, was hidden beneath a complete "suburb."

The sprawling factory was covered by a gigantic canopy of chicken wire, scrim netting, and painted canvas. This vast umbrella was held up by a scaffolding of posts and cables, and the edges sloped to the ground to melt into the landscape.

Then the artists took over. Using tons of paint, they carried genuine local roads and streets up one side of the umbrella, along the top, and down the other slope. Canvas houses were placed along the streets, and hundreds of fake trees and shrubs were "planted."

Creating the vegetation was in itself a unique and challenging task. The fake trees and shrubs were made of chicken wire that had been treated with an adhesive. Then vast amounts of real chicken feathers were attached to these forms to give a leafy texture and spray-painted in tones of green, along with splotches of brown where the vegetation had "died."

Dummy automobiles and trucks, each of which could be carried by two men, were placed at logical points, as were clotheslines filled with laundry.

To keep the thousands of Lockheed-Vega employees toiling beneath the gargantuan umbrella from having breathing problems, many air ducts provided ventilation. These ducts were masked by such standard items as fake, hollowed-out fireplugs.

Maintaining the illusion required intricate timing and planning. The "suburb" had to show signs of normal life and activity. So craftsmen regularly crawled through trap doors that led up to the canopy. Walking about on hidden catwalks, they did necessary maintenance work, moved the parked "automobiles" on occasion, and even "took in" the regular Monday wash from the clotheslines.

Colonel Ohmer was quite delighted with the new "suburb," but he wanted to put it to a test. With a visiting War Department general as a passenger, Ohmer flew a light aircraft out to sea off the California coast after asking the two-star officer to point out the location of the Lockheed-Vega plant.

Turning back toward the California coast and winging over the Santa Susana hills at five thousand feet, many small towns were spread out below. Continuing eastward toward Burbank, the general looked down on yet another

Concealed below this artificial suburb, a remarkable masquerade, was the Lockheed aircraft plant at Burbank. Thousands of workers built warplanes under this vast canopy of dummy houses, streets, shrubs, and lawns. (Lockheed Aircraft Corp.)

pleasant little community with its houses, tidy green lawns, and gently meandering streets. Carefully inspecting the landscape below, the general had no idea that under that suburb thousands of workers were turning out P-38 "Lightning" fighter planes.

Along the Pacific Coast, other airplane factories were given elaborate coverups. In Seattle, the huge Boeing Aircraft complex, sprawled over twenty-six acres, was covered by a complete "town." Also given the vanishing treatment in California were North American Aviation in El Segundo, Vultee in Downey, Northrup in Hawthorne, Consolidated in San Diego, and Douglas in Long Beach.

This enormous creativity and effort to disguise California served a valuable purpose through most of 1942 when Washington feared that a Japanese task force of aircraft carriers might sneak close to the West Coast and launch a "Pearl Harbor" against these crucial plants producing fighter planes and bombers. But with the U.S. Navy's smashing defeat of a Japanese carrier task force at Midway Island, the threat of a serious attack against the West Coast diminished, then vanished.[3]

The Mysterious Camp X

BY DECEMBER 1941, the reign of terror by the Nazi occupiers of Poland had steadily grown in intensity. Two years after Adolf Hitler's legions had seized their country, leaders of the underground Polish Home Army reached a gut-wrenching decision. Knowing that the Germans would retaliate savagely, the Polish patriots would kill in as public a manner as possible the high Nazi officers responsible for the atrocities.

One of the first Germans to be given a death sentence by the Home Army was SS General Franz Kutschera, the brutal commander in Warsaw. In a carefully planned action, nine Poles armed with light machine guns and grenades ambushed Kutschera outside his home, gunned down his bodyguards, and riddled the general with bullets. The bloody corpse lay in the street for Polish civilians to view.

Reichsführer Heinrich Himmler, a one-time chicken farmer and now head of the SS, learned of the assassination of one of his generals, and he, no doubt, attributed it to the random act of a group of Polish "terrorists," as the underground was called by the Germans. He had no way of knowing that the operation had been developed and coordinated by a secret British facility thousands of miles away.

Known as Camp X, it was located along the north shore of Lake Ontario in Canada, about three hundred miles northwest of New York City. These closely guarded acres of farmland were separated from the United States by a stretch of black, cold lake water.

At Camp X secret agents were trained, guerrilla devices and tactics were tested, and Hollywood-like dummy buildings were constructed in imitation of important Nazi hideouts to be assaulted by underground warriors of Allied spies and saboteurs.

Once the Polish Home Army had made the decision to kill General Kutschera, details of his residence, office, habits, and appearance were assembled at Camp X. This included the timetable of the SS general's activities compiled by three teenage Warsaw girls and radioed to British intelligence in London.

Guarding Camp X was a contingent of British Commandos, veterans of raids along the German-held coasts of Europe. Should a hostile individual or group try to infiltrate Camp X along the two narrow land approaches from east and west, the Commandos were under orders to "neutralize" him or them with hat pins, thin copper wire, and other silent weapons so as not to alarm the local inhabitants or draw the unwelcome attention of the region's constabulary.

As time passed, Camp X kept growing. Station M forged documents. One-man submarines and underwater demolition devices were tested in Lake Ontario. Hydra, a powerful transmitter, linked Camp X with British secret service posts around the world.

Camp X leaders recruited experts from both Canada and the United States. They came from all levels of society. Some were wealthy or famous. Others were safecrackers and professional bank robbers whose expertise could not be remotely matched by trained amateurs.

One recruit at Camp X had compiled in peacetime a directory of German business firms, and he could rapidly make associations between bits and pieces of information as though he carried a cross-index in his head. A type-writer expert could duplicate any patented machine in the world. An American conveniently removed from the U.S. Federal Bureau of Investigation's "wanted" list was moved across the border into Canada and contributed his unique talent to the counterfeiting of European currency.

Young men and women of the Travellers Censorship, an undercover operation related to Camp X, watched at the U.S. immigration entrances for clothes bearing the stitching and labels of established European tailors. The sleuths also were looking for pens and pencils manufactured in places in Europe now under German control.

On occasion, an immigrant would be taken to a small cubicle, where his or her suitcases and clothing underwent a systematic search. Most of these bewildered people no doubt thought they had escaped from the Nazi regime in Europe only to be ensnared in a totalitarian government in the United States. However, most of the detainees issued sighs of relief when they received profuse apologies for the delays and were told they could continue on their way. Few, if any, noticed that the Camp X people had removed a small item or two from their belongings.

The United States FBI and other law enforcement agencies cooperated in the scavenger hunt for genuine items with which to equip secret agents to be infiltrated into Nazi-held Europe. One young woman arrived by ship in New York with a wardrobe of high-quality clothes tailored in Berlin. After passing through Customs, she boarded a train for Chicago. When she arrived, the woman was told that her luggage had been lost.

Her anguish over losing her clothing soon after arriving in "the land of the free" was greatly relieved when, to her astonishment, the "railroad" immediately made a cash settlement several times the amount the wardrobe had cost her.

A week later, her clothes were at Camp X and given to a young Jewish woman who had spent the previous several weeks studying the new Reichskanzlei in Berlin. Within a month, this female agent, wearing the clothes "lost" on the train to Chicago, was parachuted into France. Using documents forged at Camp X, she made her way by train to Berlin, where her assignment was to ascertain the daily movements of Adolf Hitler and other top Nazi officials for future assassination efforts.

In early 1941, Allied military planners in London wanted to blow up a port facility in German-occupied France. It was located where only frogmen with explosives could get the job done. However, a former sea captain who lived in the United States had a knowledge of the waters in the targeted area.

A clandestine visit by Camp X agents to the sea captain resulted in his agreement to come to the secret facility and brief the would-be saboteurs about navigational matters at the targeted site. But a problem surfaced. President Franklin D. Roosevelt was projecting a neutral stance in the war in Europe, so

Arrow points to the location of Camp X.

his Immigration Department did its best to keep Camp X recruits from crossing the border into Canada. When the sea captain showed up, he was denied permission to cross over.

Camp X leaders promptly contacted William J. "Wild Bill" Donovan, founder and director of the new U.S. Office of Strategic Services (OSS) in Washington, about the problem. Donovan and Roosevelt had been longtime friends, so the OSS master spy contacted the president. The "door" along the Canadian border was quickly opened, and the immigration officers on duty there conveniently looked the other way when the sea captain moved on into Canada.

Detectives from Scotland Yard, the fabled London Metropolitan Police, were brought to Camp X to teach the fine art of smuggling. Women were reminded that they had one more place of concealment in their bodies than did men, and they should take advantage of the reluctance of some enemy security officers to search that intimate part.

The passage of bits and pieces of equipment across the U.S.–Canada border was almost continuous. Most had to be smuggled. Under the direction of the Scotland Yard sleuths, espionage trainees were given a taste of reality. The would-be agents were sneaked into the United States, then given a cache of illegal drugs that they were told to smuggle into Canada. Some masquerading smugglers were caught; most were not.

Meanwhile, the Scientific Research Section at Camp X developed an amazing array of lethal sabotage devices: explosive loaves of bread, fountain pens that squirted cyanide, artificial logs that would blow up when tossed on a fire, and incendiary cigarettes. An American colonel paying a visit to Camp X looked at the articles and remarked, half in awe: "I don't see anything around here that's safe to even touch!"

Station M at the camp conjured up illusions and laid false trails that could be used one day by agents in some foreign land. Jasper Maskelyne, one of the world's most celebrated magicians in peacetime and now an officer in the British army, spent time at the facility to teach his expertise. Mask, as he was known, was a genius in make-believe.

When J. Edgar Hoover, the renowned chief of the FBI, came to pay a visit, the British conjurer decided to play a good-natured trick on the American sleuth. When standing in a hut, Hoover was astonished to see what appeared to be several German warships on Lake Ontario. Mask had rigged mirrors to produce a magnified effect with toy German warships.

Murder and mayhem were important ingredients in a would-be secret agent's training. A group of hard-nosed, skilled, and experienced British officers, directed by Colonel John S. Wilson, taught brutal techniques. These specialists in unarmed combat were known as "leopards." Recruits were shown how to silently kill an adversary by karate chops or by sticking an ordinary needle into a part of the neck that resulted in almost instant death.

Much of the activity that took place at Camp X would never be entered into an official record, as were so many events by regular military units. Much of what went on there would never be officially admitted. Yet evidence indicates that this secret reservation on the U.S.–Canada frontier played a major role in bringing eventual victory to the Allies.[5]

Probing Secrets of the Atlantikwall

IN EARLY 1942, Adolf Hitler had grown alarmed by the threat to his stolen empire in western Europe by British Commando raids along the English Channel coast. Consequently, in mid-March, he signed Directive 40, decreeing that an Atlantikwall, stretching from the snowy fjords of Norway to the Spanish frontier, be constructed with "fanatic speed."

The führer had spoken, and work got underway on what he conceived to be one of the great engineering feats in history. The fifteen-hundred-mile long barrier to Allied invasion would consist of sixteen thousand concrete and steel structures, immune to bombing and naval gunfire, to protect a continuous belt of weapons commanding the major ports and potential landing beaches.

This monumental project was targeted for completion by May 1, 1943, at which time Hitler and his Oberkommando der Wehrmacht (armed forces high command) expected the Allies might strike in force across the English Channel. Thousands of slave laborers from all over Europe were rushed to the coast, where they would toil around the clock under the direction of the Reich's paramilitary construction branch, the Todt Organization.

In London, Allied intelligence soon became aware of the beehive of activity along the Channel coast and began pressing underground leaders in

Thousands of slave laborers were brought in from throughout Nazi-occupied Europe to work on the Atlantikwall. (National Archives)

Nazi-occupied territory for detailed information. London was especially interested in a 125-mile stretch of the Channel coast extending from the Cap de la Hague at the northern tip of the Cherbourg peninsula eastward to Ouistreham. Only a relative handful of top Allied leaders knew that one day powerful armies would storm ashore along this sector of Normandy.

Consequently, in the fall of 1943, Marcel Girard, a burly, brainy cement salesman and head of the Centurie underground in Normandy, decided to create a detailed master plan of the Wall. Obstacles to Girard's gigantic mapping project seemed insurmountable. For one, the Germans had established a forbidden zone several miles deep along the Normandy coast, and anyone caught inside that region would be executed.

However, Centurie agents, armed with "official" German passes—painstakingly crafted by a Caen housewife—infiltrated the forbidden zone to recruit hundreds of average French men and women to serve as the eyes and ears for the map project. Daily they risked their lives to collect and pass along bits and pieces of information on the Wall to collecting points in Caen.

However, it took more than raw courage and flaming idealism to obtain information on the Wall construction. In many instances, it required tricking the Germans on guard against spies.

Between Cherbourg and Le Havre, one of the most important harbors was Port-en-Bessin, where the Germans based a minesweeper flotilla and five swift, heavily armed E-boats. One of the Centurie agents snooping out secrets there was a husky young fisherman, Leon Cardron, who was well known to the Gestapo in the Port-en-Bessin region—mainly because he was not "right in the head." Almost daily during the long months of Nazi occupation, the Germans saw Cardron strolling about the docks, talking loudly to himself and halting periodically to stare at the sky for long periods of time.

Considered harmless by the German authorities, Cardron periodically obtained their permission to take his trawler from the harbor to ply his trade as a fisherman. Often he became an annoyance to the Germans, who had to chase his boat away when it came too close to shore near Longues, where a battery of large-caliber coastal guns was being installed.

On another occasion, Cardron's trawler stumbled into the center of an offshore area being surveyed for a minefield. Eventually, the German port commander had had enough of this stupid Frenchman and denied him future fishing permits. But Cardron didn't mind. Using an ancient Kodak camera, Cardron had photographed the entire coast from Arromanches to Port-en-Bessin. The fisherman had no way of knowing that one day, invading British forces would build an artificial port (known as Mulberry) off Arromanches or that his pictures would be of great assistance in developing Mulberry.

Not far from Port-en-Bessin, Centurie agents were unable to penetrate the small port of Luc-sur-Mer. The nervous German commandant had slapped a 7:00 P.M. curfew on civilians. This decree seemed to squash any hope of obtaining detailed information on the Wall at Luc-sur-Mer. But people do get sick, so when the local fifty-six-year-old physician, gray-haired Dr. Jacques Sustendal, requested a special permit to travel through the restricted area at any time of the day or night, German authorities issued it.

Certainly the town doctor was what the Germans called "an enlightened Frenchman." He accepted the Nazis as holding the brightest future for France, so he often made calls to aid German military men who had become sick or injured—and refused to accept a fee for his services.

Returning to his office after making a house call, Sustendal quickly wrote down in detail everything he had seen of the Atlantic Wall construction and passed his notes to Centurie agents.

One night late in 1943, the physician was on his way to place his notes in a "drop box," where they would be picked up and shuttled on to Caen by another agent. A German sentry, who did not know the physician, halted him.

While searching the Frenchman's pockets, the guard discovered the incriminating notes.

Two days later, Dr. Jacques Sustendal was shot by the Gestapo. But he had tricked the Germans long enough to provide London with a wealth of specific information about the Wall, data that would save countless lives when Allied assault troops stormed ashore.[6]

Contrivances to Save Jewish Children

FRANCE'S RAILWAYS were bustling with trains pulling cattle cars filled with Jewish men, women, and children. The final destinations were the nightmare concentration camps in Poland—Auschwitz, Belzec, Chelmno, Majdanek, Treblinka, and Sobibor. The Jews would systematically be murdered. It was May 1942, two years after Adolf Hitler's booted legions had brought the vaunted French army to its knees in only forty-two days.

According to country-by-country quotas established by Reichsführer Heinrich Himmler, chief of the Gestapo and commander of the elite Schutzstaffel (SS), France was to send one hundred thousand Jews to Auschwitz during the next three months. It was clear to all in France that Hitler had launched what the Nazi leaders secretly called "the final solution to the Jewish problem."

Many French men and women were moved by religious belief, compassion, or moral conviction to aid the Jews. Large numbers of Jews were warned by notes pushed through their mailboxes, or by anonymous telephone calls that the *grande rafle* (big roundup) was underway. Forewarned, some of the targets were able to go into hiding.

Although their lives were at risk, a group of French citizens led by Joseph Weill, a businessman, set into motion a covert operation to smuggle Jewish children out of France. An elaborate children's rescue network under the aegis of Archbishop Salisge of Toulouse, in southern France, located Catholic homes for many children and placed convents at the disposal of the network helpers for hiding others. Countless children—sometimes entire families—were smuggled from convent to convent at night until they crossed the frontier into the sanctuary of neutral Switzerland.

Georges Loinger, a network volunteer charged with organizing escape routes, set up an ingenious means for crossing the Swiss border at Annemasse, near Geneva. The cover for this machination was a French recreation camp for the children of railway employees. Jewish children also were represented as campers.

Loinger masqueraded as a physical education instructor, and each day, he would escort a number of Jewish children to a nearby soccer field near the

Swiss border. At the end of each match, far fewer "players" returned to the camp than had left it earlier in the day: the others had sneaked across the frontier into Switzerland.

A day later, scores of youngsters would be taken to the field to play another soccer match. This routine continued until all of the Jewish youngsters were in Switzerland.

The mayor of Annemasse pretended to be a collaborator with the Germans, but actually he was an active member of the French underground. He was fully aware of Loinger's scheme and helped mask it when possible.

One day, the Annemasse mayor advised Loinger that the Gestapo had grown suspicious of so many soccer matches taking place. So it became too dangerous for Loinger to escort groups of children across the border. He had to ask for the help of Frenchmen who were professional *passeurs* (escorts), and the network had to pay a certain amount for each child.

To get the needed money, Loinger changed disguises. Dressing as a cyclist, he pedaled into Switzerland on a racing bike and returned with financial contributions. He hid the currency, a good-sized sum, in an extra tire. Although halted by German police a few times, they accepted his story that he was just out for the exercise and permitted him to continue his trek.

The money Loinger picked up in Switzerland was provided by the American Joint Distribution Committee and had been donated by Jews in the United States.

One non-Jewish organization that received funds from the American Joint Distribution Committee was the Christian Fellowship, which worked closely with Archbishop Salisge's children's group. Its ostensible purpose was to provide food and clothing for indigent, non-Jewish foreigners. But its main function was rescuing Jewish families from being shipped to concentration camps.

A founder and moving spirit of the Christian Fellowship was Father Pierre Chaillet, a Jesuit priest from Lyons, in central France. Under the pen name Testis, he also wrote pieces for the underground press in which he told Catholics that it was their duty to try to aid the Jews.

In the fall of 1942, six months after the Christian Fellowship had been launched, a French traitor squealed on the priest and he was arrested. The Germans knew that he had hidden fifty Jewish children, but he refused to disclose their whereabouts. Four months later, with the help of the French underground, Father Chaillet escaped from prison and returned to his base.

During his absence, the Gestapo had arrested his associates. Despite the danger, more daunting than ever, he continued his work. But he was taken into custody again and was released after eating his identity card and giving the Gestapo a phony name and address.

During the time the Germans occupied France, Father Chaillet and his volunteers in the Christian Fellowship saved hundreds of Jewish children from deportation and certain death.[7]

Sneaking a Danish Leader to London

FORTY-TWO-YEAR-OLD EIGIL BORCH-JOHANSEN, the wealthy owner of a fleet of ships, was highly unpopular among fellow Danes. It was clear to them that he was feathering his own nest and increasing his riches by eagerly dealing with the German occupiers. His ships made regular runs to Swedish ports, so he had almost daily contact with German officials, whom he treated with courtesy. They, in turn, regarded him as a friend of the Third Reich.

In the spring of 1942, twenty-four-year-old Christian Michael Rotboll, a former lieutenant in the Danish army, clandestinely contacted Borch-Johansen, despite the ship magnate's reputation as a Nazi sympathizer. Hidden near the rendezvous site were two of Rotboll's heavily armed resistants. If treachery was involved and the Gestapo showed up, Borch-Johansen was to be riddled with bullets on the spot.

Rotboll was taking a calculated risk in setting up the meeting. The Special Operations Executive (SOE) in London had instructed him to find a prominent and well-respected leader to be smuggled to London and head the Free Danish Council there.

Rotboll cautiously asked Borch-Johansen for his help in getting the chosen Dane, Christian Moller, out of Denmark and to England. Moller was a former cabinet minister. The shipping line owner immediately agreed to try the hazardous task.

Within a week, Moller, his wife, and their young son were brought to the coast at Limfjorden, individually by automobile, under a veil of night. On arrival, each was whisked aboard one of Borch-Johansen's coasters, chosen because of its relative speed for the dash to Gothenburg in neighboring Sweden, a neutral nation.

Borch-Johansen knew that there would be the ongoing danger of the coaster being halted for inspection by German patrol boats, whose crews were on the lookout for Danish resistants being sneaked into Sweden. So with the help of a few trusted workmen, the Moller family made the trip in a specially built secret compartment. If Germans were to board the coaster, they would find nothing incriminating.

At Gothenburg, the Mollers were taken in tow by Albert Christensen, who was masquerading as a British vice consul, but was actually the top SOE operative in Sweden. A month later, the three Danish refugees reached London, and Christian Moller was promptly elected chairman of the Free Danish Council.

The announcement by the BBC (British Broadcasting Corporation) of Moller's "escape" from Denmark and the creation of a Danish government-in-exile triggered an enormous surge of pride in his home country, which had been under the Nazi yoke for two years.

In the streets of Copenhagen, Danes began openly displaying small badges on their jackets or blouses bearing the letters "SDU," initials for the popular slogan *Smid den ud* (throw them out). These letters popped up on the sides of many buildings. Audiences in movie theaters greeted the frequent appearance of Adolf Hitler in newsreels with catcalls of, "Who is that bastard?"

There were often clever retorts by the Danes in the theaters when a newsreel showed a Luftwaffe flight. The German commentator would say: "These one hundred bombers are on their way to attack London." A bull-throated Dane in the audience would shout: "And two hundred of them returned safely to their base!"

During the last half of 1942, sabotage was occurring far more frequently, and German authorities became increasingly concerned. Reports (spread by the Danish underground) of the mass parachuting of British spies and saboteurs into Denmark made the occupiers more and more jittery.

Getting into the rejuvenated spirit of the Danish people, streetcar conductors in Copenhagen would announce: "All British spies change here."[8]

An "Insane" Man in
U.S. Navy Post

EVEN THE INSIDERS in Washington, D.C., were largely unaware of a hush-hush agency code named Op-16-W. It was the Special Warfare Branch of the Office of Naval Intelligence (ONI) and dealt mainly with psychological warfare. It had been created in 1942, a few months after the Pearl Harbor disaster, the brainchild of Lieutenant Commander Cecil H. Coggins.

Coggins seemed to have a curious background for the task. A slender, crew-cut man who was all business and filled with energy and enthusiasm, he had been a naval surgeon specializing in obstetrics. However, he had been an espionage buff all of his adult life.

Soon after launching into his program of largely uncharted waters, Coggins read a book, *German Psychological Warfare*, by Ladislas Farago. Learning that the author was serving as director of research for a civilian agency, the Committee for National Morale, in New York City, Coggins was determined to recruit the man with the offbeat ideas.

A few days later, Coggins walked into Farago's office unannounced and outlined the elaborate scheme he had hatched to assault the enemy's morale. He invited Farago to become his chief of research and general idea man.

Farago, always eager for a challenge, was deeply interested. But there were heavy obstacles standing in the way. He said he doubted if the U.S. Navy would accept him because he had been in the country for less than five years and was still a citizen of Hungary. Moreover, Hungary had declared war on the United States, so Farago's status was that of an enemy alien.

"Never mind about all that," Coggins declared. "I'll fix everything."

Typically self-confident, Coggins even instructed the new recruit to be in Washington on a certain day. "Go straight from Union Station to the Fairfax Hotel," he said. "Don't register. Go directly to Room 307 and enter without knocking. The door will be unlocked. Be there at five P.M. sharp. See you in Washington!"

Back in the nation's capital, Coggins went about "fixing everything." Administratively, an enemy alien could not be accepted into the ONI, so Farago would come aboard as a "secret agent."

Farago's draft status was 1-A (eligible for immediate induction), but Coggins contacted the recruit's New York draft board, identified himself as a physician, and explained that Ladislas Farago had suffered a severe nervous breakdown and had to be committed to a mental hospital.

Farago was reclassified 4-F (insane) and he would remain in that category until he reached his thirty-eighth birthday in September 1944, when he ceased to be eligible for the draft. During those two years, Farago may have been the only certified demented person on active duty with the U.S. Navy.

After his rendezvous with ONI agents at the Fairfax Hotel in 1942, Farago was assigned an office in a makeshift wooden building near the Lincoln Memorial, a structure that had survived since World War I—but barely. Op-16-W occupied three rooms and was flanked by Op-16-Z, whose job was to interrogate prisoners of war, examine and exploit captured documents, study intercepted secret radio messages, and perform odd jobs in cerebral espionage. "Z," as the organization was called, would furnish Commander Coggins, Farago, and others in Op-16-W with the ammunition for its covert activities.

One of Op-16-W's most pressing assignments was to launch a psychological assault on the crews and officers of some 180 German U-boats that were prowling the Atlantic and inflicting enormous carnage on Allied shipping. The task would be difficult. At this stage of the war, early 1943, the U-boat service had become a favorite of the German homefront and the morale of officers and crews was high.

Coggins's ingenious operatives created a wide array of schemes and devices, including concocting rumors distributed among U-boat crews by secret agents and the preparation of leaflets. While interrogating sailors captured when a German ship was sunk, "Z" officers came upon a peculiar brochure. It was a guide to the whorehouses of Bordeaux, a major port in southwest France occupied by the Germans and home base of the ship. The document was turned over to Coggins.

The brochure went into considerable detail: a map of the city indicating the locations of the brothels and identifying them by the name of the star "performer" in each—Maison Mimi (House Mimi), Maison Fifi, and the like. It also listed the specialties of the women in each place. Also itemized were the nearest prophylactic stations where the sailors could obtain condoms or treatments. Like most "products" in wartime Europe, a ration card was attached to each brochure entitling a sailor to one daily visit to the brothel of his choice.

Op-16-W nostrils smelled a propaganda bonanza. Five million copies of the brochure were printed just like the originals, even duplicating the poor-grade paper on which they were produced. These reproductions were scattered about Germany by U.S. Air Force planes flying regular bombing missions.

Only one addition had been made to the brochures. Printed in flaming red letters on the back page was: "German women! Be grateful to your führer for taking such good care of your husbands and boyfriends!"[9]

A German Deception Masterpiece

EARLY IN THE MORNING of June 1, 1942, a lumbering German transport plane carrying Adolf Hitler glided to a landing on a sunswept airstrip near Poltava, the headquarters of Field Marshal Fedor von Bock on the southern sector of the long battlefront in the Soviet Union. The führer was in high good spirits, as he sensed Josef Stalin's Red Army was about to be crushed only a year after Hitler had sent his Wehrmacht plunging into Russia in Operation Barbarossa.

Hitler told Bock that he had come to discuss Operation Blau (Blue), a mighty offensive the führer himself had conceived and designed to administer the *coup de grace* to Stalin's armed forces. Far from "discussing" the plan, Hitler conducted a two-hour monologue with Bock able to inject only an occasional word or two.

Hitler was not an imposing figure. Fifty-four-years of age, he was of medium build, and his straight, jet-black hair was draped down over his forehead. During his entire manhood, he had worn a brush mustache. Those who came in close contact with him—detractors as well as admirers—agreed that he had a hypnotic cast to his eyes, which often influenced others to do his bidding without question.

Now, however, Field Marshal von Bock, one of the Wehrmacht's most successful battle commanders, expressed concern about the reserve forces that Stalin was concentrating behind the front to protect the oil-rich Caucasus, the primary objective of Operation Blau.

Hitler flushed with anger. Even field marshals didn't bluntly question the führer's grand strategic designs. "And what do these reserves consist of, Field Marshal von Bock?" Hitler snapped. "Stupid cotton pickers from Kazakhstan, Mongolian half-apes from East Siberia, who will run away at the first sight of a Stuka [dive bomber]. I tell you, Bock, we have them by their coattails!"

On his return flight to Germany, Hitler was still angry about Bock's "timidity." He confided to an aide that he planned to retire the field marshal. "He is simply too old-fashioned to take part in our future plans."

Although many German generals referred to Hitler derisively as "that Bohemian corporal," after the führer's rank in four years of combat in World War I, others begrudgingly pointed out that the Nazi leader had an amazing grasp of large-scale military operations.

Now Hitler launched a sophisticated subterfuge to direct the attention of Josef Stalin and his generals from the Caucasus by planting clues that the Wehrmacht's primary target for its summer offensive would be Moscow, a thousand miles to the north of the oil fields in front of Field Marshal Günther Hans von Kluge's Army Group Center.

Josef Goebbels, the Nazi propaganda genius, who had total control of all German media, ordered false stories to be published that indicated the führer was eager to capture Moscow. Admiral Wilhelm Canaris, the white-haired spymaster who headed the Abwehr (the intelligence branch of the armed forces), had his thousands of secret agents around the world whisper fraudulent rumors in the neutral capitals of Lisbon, Madrid, Stockholm, and elsewhere, rumors that were a cinch to reach Stalin's ear in Moscow.

Meanwhile, Field Marshal von Kluge, who was responsible for the phony assault on Moscow, undertook a series of misdirection attacks that would appear to be preliminaries to the all-out offensive.

Kluge's machinations were code named Operation *Kreml* (Kremlin). A bogus directive ordering his commanders to prepare for an early offensive against Moscow was drawn up over Kluge's signature. The document was broadcast to his commanders over a frequency known to be monitored by the Soviets.

The Luftwaffe greatly accelerated reconnaissance flights over Moscow. Kluge's commanders distributed maps of the Moscow region and held conferences to discuss the purported looming offensive to seize the Soviet capital. Kluge's panzer units staged convincing preparations. Only a handful of top officers in Army Group Center were aware that these massive overtures to a major offensive were merely window dressing to mask Hitler's true goal—the Caucasus.

At the same time, Hitler focused on keeping preparations for Operation Blau shrouded in secrecy. Field commanders were forbidden to commit their battle orders to writing—and dire consequences, even execution, would befall any violators of this stern edict. Only the smallest amount of oral orders could be conveyed to subordinates.

As time neared for Field Marshal von Bock to launch his massive drive to seize the Caucasus oil fields to fuel the thirsty German war machine, the führer's complicated deception scheme seemed to be hoodwinking Stalin and his generals. Intercepted radio messages and reports from German moles in Moscow indicated that the Soviet leaders felt that their capital would be the target.

Now one of the führer's most talented commanders, Lieutenant General Georg Stumme, leader of a panzer corps in General Friedrich von Paulus's Sixth Army in the south, failed to strictly follow Hitler's secret orders for Blau and nearly blew the lid off the sham. When one of Stumme's divisional commanders was given oral instructions as directed by Hitler, the subordinate pleaded for "just a few words on paper to refresh my memory." Stumme relented and dictated about a page of terse notes outlining the corps' role in Blau. Then Stumme sent copies to each division headquarters.

Two days later, this slight bending of Hitler's instructions took a serious turn. On June 19, Major Joachim Reichel, the operations chief of the 23rd Panzer Division, lifted off in a Storch light observation plane to scout the terrain where the division's regiments would be deployed. He carried with him General Stumme's typed instructions and also a map the major had made denoting the locations of the corps' divisions and their initial objectives.

Somehow, the pilot of the Storch became disoriented and it strayed over Soviet territory. A bullet struck a vulnerable point, and the plane went down some three miles behind Soviet lines.

That evening, Stumme was holding a lavish and raucous dinner party for his staff and top officers in the corps. Word arrived that Major Reichel was missing and was thought to have crash-landed in enemy territory. The general had no way of knowing that he himself had contributed to what now could be a major security breach, one that would unmask Operation Blau.

Soon Stumme learned that Reichel had been carrying the telltale documents. But the general was more worried about the major. If he were alive and captured, Red Army interrogators were masters at extracting secrets from reluctant prisoners, and the enemy would find out everything Reichel knew about the forthcoming offensive to capture the Caucasus.

Adolf Hitler was spending a few days at his Alpine retreat in Bavaria when the shock waves from the episode reached him. He was furious, not so much at Major Reichel, but at the security violation perpetrated by one of his experienced generals.

The führer threw one of his most violent tantrums. The blunder was yet another example of disloyalty by the old officers' corps—"a case of outright disobedience to clear-cut orders."

Hitler was especially irate because just that morning, he had been reading reports from the Abwehr that indicated Josef Stalin had swallowed the deception scenario hook, line, hammer, and sickle.

A hastily convened court-martial pronounced General Stumme and his chief of staff guilty of excessive disclosure of secret orders and sentenced them to long prison terms.

Curiously, the presiding officer at the court-martial, Reichsmarschall Hermann Göring, the number-two man in the Nazi pecking order, persuaded Hitler to grant clemency, pointing out that the homefront would be jolted to learn that one of Germany's most successful and astute generals had pulled such a boneheaded caper. Stumme, who was known as Fireball because of his enormous energy and red face, and his chief of staff were shunted off to North Africa, where they served with distinction against the British.

After extensive consultation with his military leaders, Hitler ordered Blau to proceed as planned. The führer had no way of knowing at the time that the Soviets had recovered Major Reichel's documents and rushed them up the chain of command until they reached Stalin in the Kremlin. The Soviet leader studied the maps and Stumme's notes, which told of the German intention to strike toward the Caucasus.

Because the entire operational plan for Blau was so large and complex, Stalin, seeing only a fragment of it, decided that the Germans had planted the document to lull him into withdrawing forces from the Moscow front and rushing them to the south. So the Soviet dictator dismissed Reichel's paper as a "big trumped-up piece of work by slick German intelligence people" and sent reinforcements to the Moscow region.

Operation Blau kicked off at dawn on June 28. The Soviets were taken totally by surprise. German forces surged forward for several hundred miles before getting bogged down in the formidable Caucasus Mountains after overrunning many of the precious oil fields.[10]

A Deluge of Phony Food Coupons

As DID MANY OTHER ADVERSARIES in the war, Nazi Germany produced and distributed food ration coupons for the civilian population. That necessity triggered a devious campaign by skilled British forgers working in their shops tucked among the houses of London. It was the spring of 1942.

To disrupt the typically efficient German food rationing system and to cause chaos among officials in the Reich, millions of fraudulent food ration coupons were printed. These forgeries had a ready-made delivery apparatus. Almost nightly, Royal Air Force bombers flew over Germany, and it was a simple matter to toss out a deluge of the bogus coupons.

It soon became apparent that the ploy was a resounding success. German leaders appeared on Radio Berlin to issue dire threats against those who were aware that they were using the forgeries.

"Those who draw rations to which they are not entitled are playing a game that may prove very dangerous for them," one official warned in a broadcast.

As the war extended into years, food rationing became even tighter. So many Germans did "play the game," and large numbers of them reportedly were given long prison terms and a few others were executed.[11]

Impersonating a Submarine Fleet

IN JUNE 1942, Major Jasper Maskelyne, a famous British magician and illusionist in peacetime, was posted near Cairo, Egypt, when he was ordered to report to Admiral Andrew C. Cunningham, Royal Navy commander in the Mediterranean. Cunningham had a daunting mission: protecting British convoys in his section of a thirty-five-hundred-mile line of communication between Gibraltar at the mouth of the Mediterranean in the west to Egypt and the Middle East.

Known in the service as "ABC" Cunningham, the admiral had a gargantuan problem. Four months earlier, the "impregnable fortress of Singapore," the British Empire's "Gibraltar of the East," had fallen, and seventy thousand soldiers had been captured by the Japanese. That catastrophe was compounded when the Japanese sank two British battleships, *Prince of Wales* and *Repulse*, after which the Royal Navy lost two cruisers and the aircraft carrier *Hermes* in the Indian Ocean.

As a result of these calamities, the Royal Navy was so weakened in the Pacific that Cunningham was ordered to rush warships from the Mediterranean fleet to the Far East. This left the admiral without enough strength to confront the quite real threat of convoy attacks by the fast, modern ships of the Italian Navy.

Cunningham felt that a large fleet of submarines based along the Mediterranean coast of North Africa might inhibit the Italian fleet from launching major operations. There was one hitch to the idea: only a few submarines were available. So the admiral asked Jasper Maskelyne to pull the proverbial rabbit out of his conjuror's hat—make submarines magically appear.

Although Maskelyne was fond of saying that he could produce minor miracles, he was taken aback by the enormity and complexity of the task he had been handed. He was to create a fleet of dummy submarines, full-sized, able to float like the real things, but also able to be folded up by a few men, travel in a truck for many miles to a new harbor, and "launched" again that night.

This is more staggering than anything the great Houdini had ever done, Maskelyne told his assistants, but he and his Magic Gang of specialists in deceit and camouflage plunged into the job. Using oil drums, canvas, pipes, cables, and paint—plus the remains of several bombed railroad cars—they managed to fashion a full-scale British submarine 258 feet long and 27 feet high. The dummy contained the normal armament of deck guns, plus an anchor.

Built on a secluded Egyptian beach, the remarkable creation was floated on railroad ties. It was so realistic that British pilots began reporting the mysterious appearance of a submarine offshore.

Four such dummy submarines were built and floated. Later, one of the decoys received the highest accolade for creativity: It was attacked and sunk by a flight of Luftwaffe warplanes.[12]

The "Phantom Field Marshal"

FIELD MARSHAL MORITZ ALBERT FRIEDRICH FEDOR VON BOCK was a Prussian of the old school—tall, slender, fine-featured, and vigorous. After Bock played a key role in the Wehrmacht campaign to conquer France in an incredible six weeks in 1940, Adolf Hitler was so delighted with the sixty-year-old Bock that he promoted him to field marshal.

In Operation Barbarossa, the invasion of the Soviet Union launched in mid-1941, Bock was given command of Army Group Center. In only three weeks, Bock's force charged ahead four hundred and fifty miles. Hitler announced publicly that the battered Soviet army was incapable of further resistance.

Dubbed Der Sterber (one who preaches death) by his not too adoring troops, Bock assured Hitler that only one final lunge was needed to end the war in the East. But autumn rains created a quagmire of mud, and Red Army reinforcements were rushed up. Bock's "victory offensive" bogged down on December 1, 1941—five months after Barbarossa had kicked off.

Fedor von Bock, the "Phantom Field Marshal." (Author's collection)

Having expected a swift conquering of the Soviet Union, Hitler began souring on his generals, most of whom, he felt, had not carried out his strategic instructions. The führer especially developed a "distinct antipathy for Field Marshal von Bock," in the words of an aide. Consequently, on July 13, 1942, Bock was relieved of his command.

As though a lowly corporal were being stripped of his rank, Bock was told to turn over his post to General Maximilian Maria Joseph von Weichs, a tall, lean cavalryman whose horn-rimmed spectacles made him look more like a priest or an accountant than one of the Wehrmacht's most capable officers.

Firing Fedor von Bock had to be done in the utmost secrecy. Such was his great prestige and reputation that the führer directed a unique subterfuge be created to hide from the German people the fact that he had fired the field marshal he had spent the past three years praising.

Bock became the "phantom commander" of his army group on the Eastern Front. For months, Propaganda Minister Josef Goebbels, who controlled all communications outlets in the Third Reich, saw to it that stories and photographs of Bock appeared in the press as if he were still in command in Russia. But the field marshal would never see action again. He was killed with his wife and daughter when Allied planes strafed his automobile on a road near his home in Hamburg.[14]

German Soldiers Help
a Woman "Terrorist"

LILLE, A LARGE FRENCH INDUSTRIAL CITY, lies 130 miles northeast of Paris near Belgium. The whole economy of this densely populated region was earmarked to support the German war effort. High Nazi Party officials were put in charge of every industrial plant and a horde of SS troops, field police, and Gestapo agents swarmed around the area.

Despite this phalanx of German operatives, the people of Lille remained truculent and unyielding. Despite their hatred for anything German, they had to survive, and the only way in which a living could be made was by working in one of Lille's many factories, most of which were producing goods and supplies for the German Wehrmacht.

In mid-1942, Michel Trotobas, half English and half French, had been parachuted into the Lille region to take charge of the underground network. He had spent most of his youth in northern France, so he knew the area intimately. Now he was clamoring to blow up several large factories, but that would require bringing in large amounts of explosives, a major problem. Because of the presence of so many armed Germans, it was impossible to find safe airplane landing places or parachute drop zones in the Lille region.

However, Trotobas (code-named Sylvestre) conquered that obstacle. At considerable risk—French informers were everywhere—he recruited a large number of *routiers* (long-distance truck drivers). They drove their big rigs back and forth on the N-17 highway, linking the industrial north with Paris. Mainly, they carried material for the Germans. However, the routiers' cargo often included containers filled with explosives for the underground, with armed German guards seated in the cabs to protect the shipments from French "terrorists."

Explosives earmarked for Michel Trotobas in Lille were parachuted into dark pastures in the vicinity of Meaux, some thirty miles east of Paris. Underground warriors collected the bundles of explosives and put them in a truck. The cargo was driven to Paris, where they were stashed in a small private garage owned by a resistant in the Montmartre district.

Trucks and a few smaller vans were stolen from German motor parks, and new number plates were attached to them. One of the most capable of the van drivers was a young, attractive French woman code-named Brigitte. One day, she was driving from Paris toward Lille when her vehicle began to sputter as she was navigating a steep hill. The van reached the top of the rise; then the engine stopped.

Brigitte was in deep trouble. She knew she could not try to walk to a commercial garage because all the French garages were forbidden to give service to civilians. The van was loaded with plastic explosives and detonators, so she didn't dare leave it and search for help. The cargo was concealed under a tarpaulin.

While briefly mulling over her predicament, she noticed a German depot at the bottom of the hill. Climbing out, she began to push the van. Just then, two Germans who, by their garb, she rightly guessed were mechanics returning to the depot emerged from a small cafe. She smiled at them; they smiled back.

Now Brigitte realized that her survival depended upon performing a bluff. So when the two Germans offered to push the van, she welcomed their suggestion with a flirtatious smile.

Brigitte climbed behind the steering wheel, and her two new "friends" pushed the vehicle to the front gate of the depot. "It's all right, Fritz," one man called to the sentry.

Inside the depot, Brigitte coolly turned on her charm. "Do you think you can repair the engine?" she asked the two mechanics. "I'm in a hurry to get to a hospital. It badly needs the medical supplies in the back."

At the slightest sign of friendship from a French civilian, most Germans in the occupying force responded enthusiastically. So in moments, nearly every mechanic in the depot came up to see if they could help.

Brigitte remained in the van while several Germans tinkered with the engine. After what seemed to her to be an interminable length of time, the repairs were completed. She started the engine, and it hummed merrily.

"I shall write and thank your commanding officer," Brigitte called out as she drove away.

"Now mind you, don't go carrying any of those explosives they say the terrorists are sneaking into Lille," one German shouted.

Everyone roared with laughter, none more so than the woman "terrorist."[15]

Escaping Captivity by a Ruse

BLOND, CLEVER EDITH BONNESSEN joined the resistance in the early days after Adolf Hitler sent his war machine to conquer tiny Denmark in one day in the spring of 1940. Code-named Lotte, the thirtyish housewife was typical of the Danish women who acted as couriers and radio operators, hid spies and escapees, tended to the wounded and injured, and participated in sabotage ventures.

In mid-1942, Bonnessen became the personal aide to Duus Hansen, who was one of Britain's Special Operations Executive's most successful and brilliant agents. He provided SOE in London with an almost continuous commentary of events in Denmark. For two years, Lotte did virtually all of the exacting and tedious cipher work for the radio messages Hansen sent to Stockholm in neutral Sweden and to London.

Hansen's radio transmitter was located in a Copenhagen textile company of which he was an executive, a job that helped provide cover for his espionage activities. Curiously, perhaps, the Gestapo, which constantly was on the lookout for clandestine radio transmitters, never suspected the textile firm.

One day, Lotte went to Hansen's business firm just as she had done hundreds of times before without drawing suspicions from the Germans. A parcel she carried with her contained radio transmitter crystals that had been parachuted into a field outside Copenhagen during the night.

It was Lotte's misfortune that the Gestapo chose that same morning to raid the textile firm. She and several others were hauled off to the Shellhus (Shell House), which the Gestapo had taken over from the famous oil company. The cellar was used as a torture chamber.

After background checking and a considerable amount of physical abuse, the textile firm's employees were released. But incriminating evidence had been found on the woman agent: The package of crystals bearing the inscription "For Lotte" was found in her purse.

For nearly two years, the Gestapo had been searching for a key female underground member called Lotte, but they had been unable to either locate her or determine her real identity. Now, a Gestapo agent dashed out of the interrogation room waving the parcel and shouting exuberantly: "We've got Lotte!"

Calm and collected as always, Lotte protested that she was only a house-wife, that she was not involved in "politics," and that she knew nothing about any Danish underground operation. Her protests were in vain, as she knew they would be.

After a few hours of grilling in which Lotte was repeatedly slapped and punched, she was left in the room with a lone Gestapo agent. It soon became evident to her that he was quite drunk, and he began making sexual advances to the attractive young woman. A consummate actress, she gave the German the impression that she would agree to his physical demands. But first, she explained, she wanted to go to the lavatory.

In his hazy state of mind, the German agreed and pointed to one of the two doors in the room. He had mistaken the lavatory door for one leading into the corridor, and moments later, Lotte found herself alone there.

With typical presence of mind, Lotte walked along the corridor and down the steps, passing several German officers who had not been involved in her arrest or grilling. She smiled and wished them a good morning; they reciprocated in kind.

Reaching the large hall at the main exit of the building, she saw that it was guarded by two SS soldiers. Pausing briefly and pretending to inspect the seam in her hosiery, she saw that a pass was needed by civilians to get by the sentries and out of the Shellhus.

Now she backed off and began a tour of the building. In one office, she took some files off a desk, put them under one arm, and assumed the role of a secretary for the Germans. Then she returned to the front door hall and fell into step right behind two SS colonels. Nearing the guards at the front door, Lotte felt her heart beating furiously. It was now or never. If her ruse was detected, no doubt she would be brutally beaten and then executed.

As the two German colonels reached the front door, the guards snapped to attention, correctly staring directly to their front. Lotte strolled on past and out of the building, but parted from her two "escorts" when they climbed into their car. After the colonels had closed the doors and could not hear her, Lotte, for the benefit of the SS sentries at the Shellhus, waved as their car drove off and called out, "I'll see you this afternoon."

Lotte strolled rapidly away and soon was lost in the usual swarm of Copenhagen civilians on their way to work or to shop. Only later would she learn from a mole planted in the Shellhus that the Germans had conducted a frantic, room-by-room search for the female terrorist who had simply vanished.

Now Edith Bonnessen was well known to the Gestapo, which was conducting a search for her. In September 1944, she was spirited out of Copenhagen to refuge in Sweden.[16]

The Grand Mufti's Rejected Report

FRANZ SEUBERT, a colonel in the German Abwehr but now garbed in civilian clothes and masquerading as a Munich businessman, was in Rome in mid-July 1942. Under highly clandestine conditions, he conferred with Haj Amin al-Husseini, the Grand Mufti of Jerusalem, who was violently anti-British.

Since 1938, the Grand Mufti had been a friend of Admiral Wilhelm Canaris, chief of the Abwehr. They had met in Baghdad when German intrigues against British influence in the Middle East were raging. After the collapse of an anti-British uprising, the Mufti had fled to Rome, where he accepted the protection offered by Italian dictator Benito Mussolini. There the Mufti continued his Middle East rabble-rousings, which, presumably, would be of benefit to Italy and to Germany.

Now, in the covert meeting in Rome, Colonel Seubert, a hardened veteran of the cloak-and-dagger wars, nearly had his breath taken away by what the Grand Mufti showed him: a highly detailed report of a looming invasion of French Northwest Africa by the Americans and British.

The Allied landings were scheduled for early November, with nine American divisions sailing from the United States and five from the British Isles.

Seubert knew that the blockbuster information would be promptly rejected by Admiral Canaris—and by Adolf Hitler himself—unless the source of the report was known to them. Despite the pleas of the Abwehr officer, the Mufti refused to disclose his source. Finally, he gave in when Seubert assured him that this information would be disclosed only to Canaris.

Again, Seubert was startled: the source was Muhammed V, the Sultan of Morocco, the nation's political and military leader. Rumor had it that the sultan had graduated under an alias from Oxford University in England. Whatever may have been the case, he was now anti-British, although he had kept a facade of being friendly to the United Kingdom and to the United States.

Seubert rushed back to Berlin and excitedly showed the Mufti's report to Canaris. In turn, the Abwehr chief rushed to put it before Field Marshal Wilhelm Keitel. A ponderous, humorless man, Keitel was sort of a Wehrmacht administrator at the highest level who did not, in the strictest sense of the meaning, intervene in field operations. As chief of staff of the Oberkommando der Wehrmacht (high command), he had been at Hitler's elbow and ear since the war began.

True to the agreement with the Mufti, Canaris did not disclose the report's source to Keitel, who was known behind his back to many top German generals as "Blockhead." Keitel scurried to Adolf Hitler with the report, and both men ridiculed it.

Hitler was especially bitter: "Canaris is a fool!" he snapped to Keitel. "He swallows everything the Americans feed him!"

As it developed, Hitler and Keitel were the "fools." Because of an elaborate British deception scheme, the two men had become convinced that the Allies would strike next at either Sicily or Sardinia, two islands in the Mediterranean.

Just past midnight on November 8, 1942, Operation Torch, an Anglo-American invasion of the French colonies of Morocco and Algeria, struck at three places along one thousand miles of North African coastline. Surprise was almost total. The entire invasion, including the date, unfolded precisely as the Sultan of Morocco had disclosed through the Grand Mufti of Jerusalem. Two days after the landings, a ceasefire between the invaders and the armed forces of the Vichy French government was called.

In mid-January 1943, just over two months after the Torch landings, President Franklin D. Roosevelt and Prime Minister Winston S. Churchill held a conference in Casablanca, French Morocco, to discuss future strategy. Two nights before the American leader was to depart for home, he played host to a lavish banquet for "my good friend the Sultan of Morocco," the man who could have turned Torch into a bloody debacle for the Americans and British had Adolf Hitler not rejected his detailed intelligence report.[17]

British Magicians Hoodwink Rommel

ALTHOUGH BESET BY A GARGANTUAN STOCKPILE of mind-boggling problems that required his presence in London, British Prime Minister Winston S. Churchill landed in his private aircraft in Cairo, Egypt, to give his Eighth Army in the North African desert "the biggest shake-up in our modern history." It was mid-August 1942.

A cunning German general, Erwin Johannes Eugen Rommel, had just administered a crushing defeat to the British, driving them hundreds of miles eastward across the desert wastes of Libya back to the hamlet of El Alamein near the Egyptian border, not far from Cairo.

A virtual unknown in the Fatherland only a year earlier, before his arrival in North Africa, Rommel now was one of the most celebrated figures in the Third Reich. He became the darling of the Nazi news media after his smashing victories in North Africa, and a grateful Adolf Hitler elevated him to field marshal, the youngest of that rank in German history.

As promised, Prime Minister Churchill sacked the Middle East commander, General Claude Auchinleck, and General Neil Ritchie, leader of the decimated and defeated Eighth Army. The new leader in the Middle East would be General Harold R. L. G. Alexander. A relatively unknown general back home, Bernard Law Montgomery, would command the Eighth Army.

Before flying back to London, Churchill, waving a long cigar for emphasis, barked at his new commanders: "I don't want the Desert Fox [Rommel] chased into a hole—I want him *killed*!"

Churchill had appointed Bernard Montgomery to the key post because of the general's supreme self-assurance. There was good reason for Montgomery's optimism. Although much of the world felt that Rommel was about to charge into Egypt, capture Cairo, and then seize the Suez Canal (Britain's lifeline to its interests in the Middle East), Montgomery knew that the Desert Fox was finally vulnerable.

Through the miracle of Ultra, code name for an ingenious British device that intercepted and broke the "unbreakable" code used by the Germans in sending radio messages, Montgomery discovered that Rommel had reached El Alamein with an exhausted army that had only twelve serviceable tanks remaining. At the same time, tanks, guns, and troops were pouring into Cairo for Montgomery under strict secrecy.

Subterfuge and illusions would play a major prelude to Montgomery launching his all-out offensive, code-named Lightfoot. During September and the first weeks of October, a group of German agents captured in the Middle East and "turned" by the British were orchestrated to convince Rommel in radio messages that Montgomery would not be able to start an offensive before late November. Actually, the British general intended to strike on the night of the October full moon, the 23rd.

Montgomery, a shrewd tactician and the master of the set-piece battle, knew he was confronted by a major problem that defied solution. The El Alamein front stretched forty miles from the shore of the Mediterranean Sea southward to the Qattara Depression, which was an enormous, impassable sea of sand. Montgomery, therefore, could not skirt around Rommel's flank in the south. So the only method of attack would be a frontal assault somewhere along the forty-mile sector—and Rommel knew this.

Montgomery would attack in the north. But success would depend on the British creating one of history's greatest battlefield masquerades to confound and confuse the crafty Desert Fox. The problem was tremendous in scope. The desert in the El Alamein region was flat, made of hard sand with a few stone outcroppings and camel scrub. Nearly all of this terrain was visible from German positions.

In mid-September, Colonel Francis W. "Freddie" de Guingand, Montgomery's able chief of staff, summoned Colonel Dudley Clarke, an expert in unorthodox warfare and clandestinity. Clarke had surrounded himself with a diversified team that included a music hall conjurer, a movie scenario writer, an artist, an intelligence expert, a banker, a chemist, and a nobleman or two.

Meeting in de Guingand's caravan near the Mediterranean shore, Clarke was briefed on Montgomery's attack plan and on Bertram, code name for the role to be played by Clarke and his deception artists.

Flat terrain made it especially difficult for British "magicians" to "hide" Montgomery's army at El Alamein. (National Archives)

"Well, there it is," de Guingand said. "You must conceal one hundred and fifty thousand men with a thousand guns and a thousand tanks on a plain as flat and as hard as a billiard table — and the Germans must not even gain a hint about it, although they will be watching every movement, listening for every noise, charting every vehicle and tank track."

Clarke, who loved a seemingly impossible challenge, was momentarily silent, struck by the enormity of the task he had been handed. "You can't do it, of course," de Guingand exclaimed. "But you bloody well got to!"

After leaving the caravan, Clarke hurried to confer with Major Jasper Maskelyne, a well-known conjurer who had traveled throughout Europe with his family's theatrical company in peacetime, and Lieutenant Colonel Geoffrey Barkas, a camouflage expert and former movie producer. Their task was daunting: hoodwinking the craftiest and shrewdest of all of Adolf Hitler's generals.

Working in a dusty room in the ramshackle El Alamein railroad station, the three sleight-of-hand experts came up with a theme in only two hours. The only way to "hide" Montgomery's large force, they concluded, was to move it forward under camouflage so gradually that the Germans' sharpest eyes and camera lenses would fail to perceive the shifts.

Now began the remarkable feats of illusion. Major Barkas and his men started with the six thousand tons of supplies in the north that had to be concealed within five miles of the German front line. Crucial among these supplies were huge quantities of tank fuel.

Two of Barkas's principal assistants, Captain Michael Ayrton and Lieutenant Brian Robb, knew that close to the El Alamein railroad station were one hundred sections of slit trenches lined with masonry. The excavations had been there for over a year, and most certainly would be regarded by the Germans as part of the furniture of the battlefield.

By experimentation, it was found that if each wall of the trenches was given an extra facing of "masonry," in the form of fuel cans, the shape of the internal shadows remained unchanged when seen from the air. Under the cover of darkness, two thousand tons of fuel cans were neatly layered along the walls of the ready-made trenches, where they would be immediately available for use when Lightfoot kicked off.

As a test, the Royal Air Force was asked to send observation planes aloft to find the secret fuel dump, but the airmen were unable to locate it. The internal shadows of the trenches had remained unchanged.

Now Barkas and his aides created a masterpiece to conceal the vast amount of food, ammunition, and other stores. During three nights, four thousand tons of supplies were brought forward and stacked in such a way that when covered with camouflage nets, they resembled the shapes of ordinary three-ton trucks.

Scattered about the area in the same manner that genuine trucks would be dispersed, the illusions were all that the battlefield magicians could hope for. Seen through the air or viewed through binoculars from a distant rise in the ground, the supplies looked like camouflaged transport vehicles of no combat significance.

Next came a more difficult task. General Montgomery planned to launch Lightfoot with a thunderous barrage from some one thousand artillery pieces in the north, so the guns had to be concealed under the noses of the vigilant Germans. Compounding the problem was the fact that both a gun and its prime mover (towing device) had distinctive shapes.

First, dummies of some twelve hundred trucks were taken forward at night, and each was placed where artillery officers wanted the guns to be situated. By backing up the prime movers and the guns, it was possible to get both under the bogus trucks. In one night alone, three thousand pieces of equipment—guns, limbers, and movers—were in place and camouflaged. To the Germans, twelve hundred harmless trucks scattered about the desert was not an uncommon sight.

As Zero Day grew closer, Barkas and his assistants were facing their greatest challenge: how to conceal the forward movement of two entire armored divisions. These outfits would have to be concentrated twice: first in the rear staging area, and then, just before the attack, in forward positions facing German lines.

About two weeks before Zero Day, the divisions' soft-skinned vehicles—genuine trucks and the like—were driven into the forward area quite openly.

Sunshield enclosing British tank makes it look like a truck from the air. (National Archives)

The idea was to get the Germans to become accustomed to seeing the vehicle concentrations; when the British seemed to be doing nothing further, the watchers might relax their vigilance. That is precisely what happened. The Germans concluded that these trucks were merely bringing up food and supplies to the British infantry already in defensive positions.

In the meantime, more than seven hundred large wood and canvas hulls, known as Sunshields, were rapidly built in Cairo and moved into position near no-man's-land. These hollow objects resembled harmless British ten-ton trucks. When time for the assault neared, Montgomery's tanks, self-propelled guns, and armored cars would move up at night and go into hiding inside the hollow Sunshields.

Meanwhile, the genuine British armor was concentrated some sixty miles from the lines and was purposely left partly exposed. The magicians wanted Rommel's reconnaissance pilots to observe the heavy armor far to the rear, where it would be no immediate threat.

Coordinating this enormous secret shift of armor required painstaking planning and timing. Each of the Sunshields had a serial number and was earmarked for a particular tank or other armored vehicle. The crew of each armored vehicle was also given a corresponding serial number. Over many nights, one man from each crew was taken forward to see where his own Sunshield was located.

While these remarkable ruses were taking place in the north, other magicians under Captain Phillip Cornish and Lieutenant Sidney Robinson were performing their conjuring acts some thirty miles to the south. The keystone of this deception rested on the fact that the Germans knew of the continuous need for fresh drinking water in the sunbaked desert. An existing pipeline was already in place, running southward for several miles from a point behind El Alamein. In classic Houdini fashion, the magicians decided to misdirect Rommel's attention by continuing this water conduit southward in dummy form.

Knowing that the Germans were monitoring the progress of the bogus pipeline, a trench was dug in normal fashion for five miles at a time, and a dummy pipeline, constructed from used four-gallon fuel cans, was laid alongside the excavation's parapet. Then, in the night, the phony pipeline was moved forward while the trench was filled and an extension trench started.

The rate of progress was timed precisely to the rate at which a real water pipeline would be built. And, hopefully, the Germans would draw the conclusion that it would not be completed until forty-eight hours after Zero Day, about which they knew nothing. This scheme was designed to deceive the Germans even more about the time of the attack.

To give the false water pipeline credence, three dummy pump houses, overhead tanks, and can-filling stations were built. Genuine vehicle traffic was diverted to the twenty-mile-long project to inject life into fiction.

It would have been obvious to Rommel that an assault could not be launched in the south without a huge supply of food, fuel, ammunition, and other stores. So at the southern end of the phony pipeline, a large patch of desert (code-named Brian) was developed into a supply dump. Seven hundred stacks of empty boxes and other containers were brought in, creating the illusion that nine thousand tons of war stores were in position.

Then the magicians and their helpers moved in three and a half regiments of artillery—telegraph poles put in gunpits and covered haphazardly by camouflage netting. The idea was for the Germans to know that these guns were there.

Now the entire masquerade to decoy Rommel about Montgomery's true intentions had been completed without serious mishap. All that was visible in the north was a heavy concentration of dummy trucks. Yet the British 1st and 10th Armored divisions lay there under the Sunshields, silently, coiled, ready to spring. There was heavy wireless communication—all of it phony—but it was coming from the south.

Now Ultra disclosed that Rommel had been hoodwinked by the machinations. For perhaps the only time in his scintillating career, he committed a major blunder. Not knowing where Montgomery would hit, he split his armor to cover both the north and the south sectors. Then, assured by his intelligence officer that the British could not attack for at least a month, Rommel left for Germany to undergo badly needed medical treatment.

On the evening of October 23, 1942, as a boiling sun settled into the western horizon, it was quiet along the El Alamein front. At German head-quarters west of Tel-el-Eisa, there was no indication that the British would strike. General Georg Stumme, who was in command during Rommel's absence, was dining leisurely with his staff officers.

At precisely 9:45 P.M., a gigantic roar rolled across the desert and the eastern sky lit up as though it were daylight. Montgomery had unleashed his hidden artillery. Lightfoot had begun. The armor crews, who had been waiting all day under the blast-furnace sun, knocked the Sunshields aside and hundreds of tanks rumbled toward and through German lines.

The great northern offensive had taken the Germans by total surprise. Adding to the confusion, the commander of the 21st Panzer Division tele-phoned Stumme to state that the British had also launched a major assault in the south. Actually, a few artillery pieces of General Marie Pierre Joseph François Koenig's Free French Brigade had been camouflaged along with the dummy guns. They opened fire to inhibit the Germans from rushing troops from the southern sector to the northern one.

On the afternoon of November 5, after Field Marshal Rommel's hurried return, his battered army was in full retreat. Its vehicles and troops jammed the narrow coastal road for sixty miles west of El Alamein. The British magicians had contributed mightily to the eventual destruction of German and Italian forces in North Africa.[18]

Part Five

Turning of the Tide

A Danish Spy Preaches
to the Germans

FOR NEARLY SIX MONTHS, Paul Johannesen, a peacetime sailor in the Danish merchant navy, had been in regular touch with cloak-and-dagger agencies in London from his radio post in a house in a suburb of Copenhagen. When he had parachuted from a British airplane in April 1942, he had landed in a tall tree two miles from where an underground reception committee had been waiting for him. The spy was painfully injured, but he managed to extricate himself from the top of the tree and dodge German patrols as he made his way to Copenhagen. There he made contact with resistance warriors.

On the night of September 4, a German direction-finding van located Johannesen's transmitter. A contingent of German field police and soldiers surrounded the house. When the door of the Dane's room was burst open, he fired a pistol, killing the first man and wounding two or three others.

Knowing that he was trapped, Johannesen dashed into an adjoining room and swallowed a cyanide pill that most secret agents in Europe carried. He was dead in minutes.

Abwehr officers conducted a diligent search of Johannesen's room and discovered materials that pointed to Mogens Hammer, who had been the first Dane to parachute into his native land. He had jumped "blind" on December 27, 1941.

Hammer was a free spirit, one who marched to his own drummer. These traits were not suitable for a secret agent. He was connected with the production and distribution of clandestine newspapers, which left him more vulnerable to detection and capture by the Gestapo.

Through moles in the Copenhagen police department, Hammer learned that his identity was known and the Gestapo was on the lookout for him. His controllers in London directed him to leave Denmark and return to England, but he ignored the order.

Now he became a master of disguises, and he seemed to relish thumbing his nose at the German sleuths. Often he donned the garb of a Protestant parson, including the backward collar. His role-playing had been so believable that on one occasion, at the request of German military officers, he preached at an impressive Nazi military service.

One day, the "parson" learned that the Gestapo had penetrated his disguise and was hot on his trail. Despite his bravado, Hammer realized that his arrest was almost a cinch. So he obtained the use of a kajak (canoe) and, with another Danish resistant on the lam, paddled across the Sund to neutral Sweden. A week later, the "Reverend" Mogens Hammer arrived in London.[1]

Japan Wants Lethal Gas on England

GENERAL HIROSHI OSHIMA, a gifted soldier and skilled diplomat, was the Japanese ambassador to Germany during most of the war, and he often met with the high and the mighty in the Nazi regime to exchange top-secret information. Affable and astute, Oshima had no way of knowing that he had become a vast clearinghouse of intelligence for the Americans and British.

Years before the United States was bombed into global conflict at Pearl Harbor on December 7, 1941, the warlords in Tokyo had been preparing for vast conquests and to drive the Americans and British—"white devils," they were called—from the Pacific. Consequently, the brightest Japanese officers, including Oshima, were assigned as military attachés to embassies around the world. Their orders were to painstakingly keep Tokyo informed daily of events in their regions.

After war broke out, these dedicated Japanese attachés flooded Imperial General Headquarters in Tokyo with both blockbuster and trivial reports. None of the Japanese involved in the global intelligence apparatus were aware that their day-to-day reports were being read within twenty-four to forty-eight hours in Washington, D.C., and in London.

One of the war's best-kept secrets was that in the spring of 1941, six months before Pearl Harbor, U.S. army and navy cryptologists had broken the Japanese secret code, and technicians in Hawaii and Washington were eavesdropping on the wireless messages. "Magic" was the cover name that U.S. intelligence used to protect the source and circulation of the inside information from within the highest councils in Tokyo.

Security was so tight in the Magic operation that only ten officials in Washington (and a few in London) received the daily intelligence summaries. On the covert list were President Franklin D. Roosevelt and his military advisor, Admiral William D. Leahy; Secretary of War Henry L. Stimson; Army Chief of Staff George C. Marshall; the Chief of Naval Operations, Admiral Ernest B. King; Secretary of State Cordell Hull; Secretary of the Navy Frank Knox; and three key intelligence officers.

Each day, a military officer would deliver the Magic summary to the designated person on the list. After reading the text, the recipient was required to return his copy to the courier. No reproductions of the contents were allowed,

Japanese Ambassador Hiroshi Oshima unwittingly provided Americans with summaries of Adolf Hitler's plans and viewpoints. German Foreign Minister Joachim von Ribbentrop is at right. (National Archives)

nor could the recipient take notes. The retrieved copies were taken to a designated branch in the War Department and immediately destroyed.

A careful record was kept of those who received and read each Magic summary. Also, what was the time of day when the official had been handed the document? What was the time of day that it was returned to the courier? When did the summary get back to the special branch, and to whom was it given and at what time? Who was present when the document was burned? What were the names of the two officers who had been specifically assigned the task of witnessing the destruction of the summary?

As the highest-ranking Japanese official in Berlin, General Oshima held regular discussions with top Nazi leaders, including Adolf Hitler himself on occasion. Oshima transmitted the most important intelligence to Imperial General Headquarters in Tokyo over a high-speed radioteleprinter link in a code the Japanese thought was unbreakable.

On September 17, 1942, while General Dwight D. Eisenhower was putting the final touches on Operation Torch, an Anglo-American invasion of Northwest Africa set for early November, Ambassador Oshima was engaged in a wide-ranging discussion with German Foreign Minister Joachim von Ribbentrop, who was one of the most intense schemers and plotters among a group of experts in the Nazi hierarchy.

Oshima told Ribbentrop (who had added the "von" when he rose up the Nazi totem pole) that it was crucial for Egypt to be cut off from England by the German army and for Japanese forces to isolate India. "They are the two greatest mainstays of England and the United States," Oshima declared.

Ribbentrop, a former wine salesman and one of the most pompous among Hitler's aides, where the competition for that designation was fierce, listened without comment as Oshima lectured him on how Germany and Japan could win the war by the end of 1944.

Although the Wehrmacht was making steady progress in the war against the Soviet Union, German efforts should be accelerated to bring the Red Army to its knees no later than the spring of 1943, Oshima said. After the Soviet Union had been crushed, Hitler should launch immediate plans to invade and conquer the British Isles no later than the summer of 1944.

The only way Britain could be brought to heel was through an invasion, the Japanese ambassador declared. "Only with England in your [German] control can we [Tokyo] make the British accept our terms at the surrender conference," Oshima added.

Then the Japanese general briefed Ribbentrop on how England could be rapidly conquered. Collect the equipment (such as landing barges and supply vessels) needed for the operation. Vigorously train amphibious assault troops and airborne forces. Even Ribbentrop, perhaps, was startled by Oshima's next gratuitous piece of advice: precede the invasion with the heavy use of lethal gas on British defensive positions, airfields, and civilian populations.

Although the use of lethal (poison) gas would be a gross violation of the rules of civilized warfare as laid down by the Geneva Convention, the proposal was not rejected. The foreign minister told Oshima that he was flying to Hitler's headquarters behind the Eastern Front the next day, and that he would take up the subject with the führer.

After Ribbentrop's return to Berlin two days later, Oshima met with him again. "The führer is considering various ways to bring the war to a successful conclusion," the German said, thereby neatly skirting Tokyo's suggestion that the Wehrmacht unleash poison gas in an invasion of England.

Apparently, the Japanese ambassador sensed the reason for the führer's evasiveness. Twenty-four hours later, he reported to Tokyo that Germany's mammoth end-the-war offensive in Russia "seems to have bogged down."

Perhaps as much as anyone outside the Allied camp, Oshima played a major role in the eventual *defeat* of Germany and Japan. His intercepted and decoded reports to Tokyo throughout the war were equivalent to contributions by a dozen or more active spies.

After the war, a general in the Pentagon quipped: "The Allies should pin a high decoration on Hiroshi Oshima."[2]

General Eisenhower's Furious Wife

IN THE FALL OF 1942, tension gripped the headquarters of General Dwight D. Eisenhower on London's Grosvenor Square (called Eisenhowerplatz by wags).

An Anglo-American invasion of French Northwest Africa was scheduled for early November and the one-time Kansas farm boy, known as Ike, would command the operation, code-named Torch.

For weeks, presumably well-meaning old army friends had been bombarding Eisenhower with tales of the failure of allied coalitions going back to the days of the Greeks, five hundred years before Christ. It was whispered in his ear that any general placed in his position would be an ideal scapegoat should Torch meet with disaster.

These were difficult times for the supreme commander, who was putting in eighteen-hour days. Often he nibbled on a sandwich for lunch at his desk. Much of the time he spent refereeing lower-level disputes and explaining to London society lionesses why he could not attend their parties.

As D-Day for Torch drew closer, Allied officers in London responsible for the security of the operation were confronted by a seemingly unsolvable problem of major proportions. Eisenhower had been highly visible as he dashed around London and the British Isles. Now that he was about to depart for his battle headquarters deep inside the Rock of Gibraltar at the entrance to the Mediterranean Sea to take command of Torch, how could his sudden absence from England be covered? Nazi spies were sure to note his disappearance, and Adolf Hitler would suspect that a major Allied operation was looming.

Word was leaked to two U.S. reporters that Eisenhower was secretly returning to Washington for a series of consultations. The next day, the *Washington Post* carried a page-one story that the general had been called back and was now in the capital. Actually, he was at Gibraltar.

At a news conference in the White House that afternoon, President Franklin D. Roosevelt was bombarded with questions about the reason for Eisenhower being in Washington. The cagey chief executive replied that for him to "mention the movement of army officers would only aid the enemy."

Some fifty reporters left the White House convinced that Eisenhower was in Washington and, as intended, they published their conclusions all over the United States—and in England.

The *ruse de guerre* (war trick) had been a smashing success. But Eisenhower personally was left with a vexing problem, one he could not disclose. His wife, Mamie, sitting out the war in Washington, no doubt had been furious to read and hear on the radio that her husband was in the city and hadn't even telephoned her.[3]

The Gestapo Tricks British Spymaster

BRITISH MAJOR FRANCIS A. SUTTILL adjusted his parachute straps as his Royal Air Force plane neared his drop zone in German-occupied France. Code-named Prosper, he was being sent on a crucial mission. Because Operation

Torch, the Allied landings in northwest Africa, was imminent, it was felt by leaders of the Special Operations Executive (SOE) in London that it must have a Paris-area clandestine organization under direct control of British authorities. It was October 2, 1942.

Suttill had been handed a tall order: Torch was only a month away and he had been given instructions to set up his *réseau* (network) in central, northern, and eastern France. SOE chieftains had promised that a good-sized number of officers, radio operators, and couriers would soon follow.

Suttill had the qualifications for his difficult task. He had lived for many years in Lille, France, where he was managing director of a large textile business and, at one time, was president of the Lille Chamber of Commerce. He had also been an international attorney, and when war broke out, he received a British army commission and completed a seven-month course at SOE Special Training schools.

Now, in the early hours of blackness before dawn, Major Suttill bailed out of his airplane into a pasture and was met by men and women of the French resistance. Soon he was ensconced in a farmer's house concealed in a thick woods.

Suttill, as expected, proved to be a whirlwind. With an enormous expenditure of energy, diplomacy, leadership, and cunning, he established some sixty réseaux and groups, from Le Mans and Angers in the west to Orléans, the Sologne, and Tours in the south, and to Troyes, Chalons and St. Quentin in the east.

London had provided Prosper with a fake identity that permitted him to travel widely without arousing the suspicion of the Gestapo. His forged documents had the name of François Desprée, a salesman of agriculture products. Paris, however, was his base.

Prosper would have ten thousand clandestines working for him, but among them were German double agents, and eventually the Gestapo and the Abwehr began competing to capture the notorious master spy.

Prosper's own sense of security was often lacking. Going against SOE rules that forbid agents in the field to even speak to one another in public, he sometimes dined in popular French restaurants with his entire staff—an unwise move in a climate where informers abounded, some of whom would sell out their grandmothers for a pack of cigarettes.

Like many in the espionage fraternity, Prosper had a need to demonstrate his bravado. On one occasion, he got in the spotlight at a packed Montmartre nightclub to show the audience how a Sten submachine gun worked.

On another occasion, the peacetime lawyer presumably wanted to flaunt his identity to German authorities in Paris after two veteran members of the resistance, Germaine Tambour and her sister, Madeleine, were arrested on Good Friday, April 22, 1943. Prosper's usually sound judgment may have been

Major Francis Suttill (Prosper).
Executed by the Germans.
(Author's collection)

clouded by the fact that these middle-aged women had been his first contacts when he had arrived in Paris in October 1942.

Disregarding his own security, he made contact with a V-man (as the Germans called French traitors who cooperated with them) and through him made an offer to two SD (SS intelligence) officers of francs equivalent to $24,000 (some $250,000 in the year 2001).

Word got back to Prosper that the Germans agreed to his proposal, that the Tambour sisters would be let out of a van that would stop at a specified point while taking the prisoners from Gestapo headquarters to Fresnes prison at night. There the women would be handed over to Prosper's men.

The two Germans in the van did halt when the vehicle was driving through a quiet residential neighborhood. But Prosper was appalled to learn that the women picked up were not the Tambour sisters, but two elderly whores who, apparently, thought they had found new customers.

Prosper, a cool-headed operator in most instances, had hoodwinked large numbers of Germans. But now, he himself had become the victim of a Gestapo trick.[4]

London's Devious "Shadow Warrior"

ONE OF THE MOST PECULIAR JOBS in the Allied camp in Europe during the war was that of a Briton prominent in literature and broadcasting in peacetime who sat all day in an office at the Special Operations Executive headquarters on Baker Street in London. The task of this "shadow warrior" was to invent "sibs" (so-called from the Latin *sibilare*, to hiss).

These sibs (rumors) were designed to approach the German mind through elaborate fictions, calculated to throw the enemy off its guard, to lower its morale by appealing to the selfish, individual motives of the German military men and the *herrenvolk* (citizens) in the homeland. Hopefully, this activity would drive a wedge between the Nazi leaders and the military, in France and the Low Countries, and the civilians in the Reich.

The Briton in London charged with creating dangerous rumors would think of what the German soldiers liked least to believe about their own situation and about conditions in the Fatherland where most had wives or families.

By spreading rumors in a French port that all the prostitutes (of which there was no shortage) had a venereal disease and that a man could have the disease for two months without obvious symptoms, the "sib master" succeeded in having all the German soldiers there confined to barracks for four weeks. The troops became almost mutinous.

Other sibs focused on such matters as the virtue of wives and girlfriends left alone in Germany for a long period of time. Not to worry, the rumors floated through the Wehrmacht in France: the Nazi party leaders were personally making certain that the young women did not lack male company.

A related sib had it that wives of German soldiers serving in other countries were expected to put in a certain number of hours weekly at posh brothels set up for officers of the elite Schutzstaffel (SS). It was a duty Adolf Hitler expected the women to perform.

The rumor campaign attacked morale from any conceivable angle: nothing was too low if it hurt the Germans. Word went out that Germany was having a food shortage, and that the sausage supplied to Wehrmacht cooks was actually dehydrated mule brains.

Before D-Day in Normandy in June 1944, sibs were circulated in neutral embassies around the world that animal blood was going to be used for transfusions in Heer (army) field hospitals. It was also widely circulated that two entire trainloads of ammunition bound for Normandy had to be returned to Germany because it was found to be the wrong size.

Another rumor campaign aimed at the morale of the Feldgrau (field gray, the typical German soldier) in France was that they were expected to be sacrificed by the Oberkommando der Wehrmacht (high command) when the Allies struck across the English Channel because ammunition supplies were desperately short in France. Hitler and his generals, so went the sib, did not intend to put up any real resistance against the invading Allies; the important thing was for the invaders to get ashore over the bodies of the Feldgrau before the Russians arrived.

When the sibs reached German soldiers, many told their loved ones about them in letters back home. In this way, the sibs gained added circulation throughout the Third Reich.[6]

Jim, the Talented Forger

THERE WAS A WAR ON. A global war. The bloodiest war in history. So the U.S. Office of Strategic Services (OSS), like cloak-and-dagger outfits everywhere, was not too picky about the character (or lack of it) and morals (if any) of those recruited to do its dirty work.

Among those with no known scruples who toiled for the OSS was a very pleasant, soft-spoken man in his forties known in the Documentation Branch, where he performed his magic, only as "Jim the Penman."

Jim was an expert in his field—forging names. His biggest mistake was a few years earlier, when he counterfeited the signature of a high U.S. Treasury official on engraved papers that almost—but not quite—resembled government bonds. For his indiscretion, he became a guest at a federal penitentiary.

When it became clear to the still-green OSS in late 1942 that duplicating enemy signatures was one of the surest ways to gain an objective through trickery, Jim was let out of prison and found himself being escorted to the OSS headquarters in Washington.

Experts—that is, those in the criminal community—swore that Jim was the most talented signature duplicator who ever lived. It had not been his failure in this field, but rather the paper texture that had landed him behind bars.

However, the OSS men were skeptical: he couldn't be that infallible. So Jim had a high-ranking official write his signature—"just the way you would on a check"—on a ruled tablet of paper. Then Jim studied the writing for about two minutes.

Arrayed in front of him were twenty pens of all shapes and sizes—instruments of his "profession"—along with several bottles of ink of various shades. Finally, he selected a pen, dipped it into one of the ink containers, and began dashing off signatures, one on each of the ruled lines above and below the authentic signature.

Now Jim turned to the OSS man and said, "I'll bet you a dollar you can't pick out your own handwriting."

"You're on!" the other fired back, whipping out a dollar bill from his pocket. Any idiot could recognize his own signature. When the list of signatures was shown to him, the official had to concede defeat.

With a large, infectious grin, Jim pocketed the bill with the whimsical remark: "There's a fortune to be made in just writing people's names!" Then he gave an exaggerated wink.

Jim the Penman was put to work. He would never know the precise use made of his incredible skill, but he did know that somehow he was helping to defeat Germany. That was good enough for him.

Jim was a sensitive artist, so word was passed around headquarters to refer to his products as "duplications" and never as "forgeries." It had become obvious that he was bursting with pride over what he was achieving for his country, and he did not have Secret Service or FBI agents on his tail.

With a copy of a genuine signature to study, Jim would write down the name on a document with gusto. Any hesitation or retracing or patching the forgery would be fatal flaws, ones that would be quickly discovered by German or Japanese technicians. Names like Adolf Hitler, Benito Mussolini, Marshal Henri Pétain, Heinrich Himmler, and Hermann Göring were familiar jobs for Jim the Penman.

Like a great athlete performing at his best in crucial games, Jim was at top form when forging almost illegible signatures. Gestapo chief and SS head Himmler had one of the most hard-to-read signatures, but Jim dashed off the "duplications" one after the other on fifty SS identification cards.

After the war was over in 1945, OSS officials tried to get some sort of official recognition for Jim the Penman. No response was ever received; clearly Washington shied away from awarding citations to a convicted forger—even one who played such a major role in tricking the enemy.[7]

The Lady Journalist Was a Spy

HELSINKI, THE CAPITAL OF FINLAND, was gripped by Arctic cold when Therese Bonney arrived in the city on a reportorial assignment for *Colliers*, a large-circulation magazine in the United States. It was December 12, 1942.

Three years earlier, Bonney, as a freelance writer, had been in Finland to cover the war between the Soviet Union and the tiny Scandinavian country. During the four months of that brutal conflict, she had established a close relationship with Field Marshal Baron von Mannerheim, the Finnish strongman, because of her sympathetic stories in American newspapers.

After gaining the admiration of most of the free world because of the Finnish army's battling the Soviets to a standstill, overpowering numbers of Russian soldiers and a much stronger air force had caused the Finns to surrender on March 12, 1940.

When Adolf Hitler's mighty Wehrmacht invaded Russia on June 22, 1941, Mannerheim, seeking to protect his nation from eventual destruction, associated Finland with the Third Reich, not as an ally, but as a "co-belligerent."

Actually, Therese Bonney was using the *Colliers* assignment as a cover. She was an agent of the Office of Strategic Services (OSS) and had been sent to Finland with instructions to persuade her old friend, Baron von Mannerheim, to abandon his nation's role as a co-belligerent of Nazi Germany.

On reaching Helsinki, Bonney immediately was tailed by Gestapo agents, of which there was no shortage in Finland. Nonetheless, she arranged a covert meeting with Mannerheim, who greeted her warmly. Although she failed to

An American woman spy tried to talk Baron Carl von Mannerheim, a Finnish leader, into abandoning his support of Adolf Hitler. (National Archives)

convince him to break openly with Adolf Hitler, she did obtain a wealth of intelligence about Finland's military organization and Nazi plans for pursuing the war against the Soviet Union.

On her way back to Washington, D.C., to report to OSS headquarters on her secret mission, she decided to pay a short visit to the U.S. Embassy in neighboring Stockholm, Sweden, a neutral nation saturated with spies from many countries. In Stockholm and other neutral capitals in Europe, most American diplomats looked on OSS secret operations as some sort of satanic mumbo-jumbo. OSS agents working under diplomatic cover in embassies usually met with strong resistance by the tradition-bound, staid professionals of the State Department.

Arriving at the embassy in Stockholm, Bonney called on a State Department official of long acquaintance. She disclosed nothing of her connection with the OSS, but subtly asked her friend his opinion of that clandestine organization. Glancing around as though there were a spy hiding in the room, the diplomat confided: "I can always smell an OSS agent. We never give them any help!"[8]

America's Black Propaganda Experts

WHEN THE U.S. OFFICE OF STRATEGIC SERVICES (OSS) (then called the Coordinator of Information) was created less than a year before World War II broke out, its founder, William J. "Wild Bill" Donovan, began recruiting many of the nation's foremost brains. Among the most devious thinkers were those in the Morale Operations Division (MO).

The MO consisted mainly of skilled professionals in the mass communications field—journalists, Hollywood screenwriters, advertising and public relations experts, and authors. They cranked out "black"—or covert—propaganda, and their work had so infuriated the Nazis that propaganda chief Josef Goebbels sneeringly lampooned them as "fifty professors, twenty monkeys, ten goats, and twelve guinea pigs."

Using names culled from German newspapers smuggled out of the country, the OSS black propaganda experts mailed fake "official" death notices to the families of Wehrmacht soldiers known to be at the fighting fronts.

MO had become adept at spreading frightening rumors throughout Germany. One rumor that gained widespread currency in the Reich was that the Allies had developed a bomb that sucked oxygen out of the air and caused massive—and agonizing—deaths by suffocation. A tiny outbreak of bubonic plague in German-occupied Rotterdam inspired another MO hoax, the planting of a rumor that the outbreak had been triggered by a new Allied secret weapon—a germ-carrying rocket.

One macabre scheme was implemented by OSS agents while a bloody seesaw battle was in progress. They planted fake newspaper clippings in the uniforms of dead German soldiers. When Germans found the corpse, they would be likely to read the phony clipping. It was a pronouncement from SS chief Heinrich Himmler that any German wife of child-bearing age who had not had a baby during the previous two years would have to report for duty to an SS "breeding farm."[9]

A "Water Donkey" Subterfuge

SINCE ADOLF HITLER had declared war on the United States four days after the Japanese sneak attack had virtually wiped out the Pacific Fleet at Pearl Harbor, the Atlantic Ocean had been a vast and bloody battleground of unprecedented violence. Although the Western Allies—mainly the British—had taken a heavy toll of German U-boats in the first forty months of the war, Admiral Karl Doenitz, commander of the submarine service, began the year 1943 with about four hundred U-boats available, compared to the fifty-seven he had had at the outbreak of war in September 1939.

A *dummy U-boat conning tower filled with explosives was intended to blow up Allied warships on impact.* (Author's collection)

During 1942, German naval forces, mostly U-boats, had sunk 1,665 Allied ships, mainly cargo vessels, on the North Atlantic sea lanes, along which flowed from the United States to England the men and materials for a contemplated cross-Channel invasion of Normandy in mid-1944. So crucial was the struggle on the ocean to the eventual outcome of the war that British Prime Minister Winston S. Churchill labeled it "The Battle of the Atlantic."

At his headquarters in Berlin's Hotel-am-Steinplatz, Admiral Doenitz continually tracked the deadly clashes in the North Atlantic. Aware that both sides were evenly matched at the beginning of 1943, Doenitz prodded German scientists to develop a device or weapon that would provide his U-boats with an edge and turn the Battle of the Atlantic in favor of Germany.

The German scientists came up with a floating subterfuge that they were convinced would take a devastating toll on Allied ships. It was called a *Wasseresel* (Water Donkey), and its centerpiece was a decoy conning tower, a raised structure on the deck of a submarine used as an observation post and as an entrance to the vessel. Packed with high explosives, the bogus conning tower would be towed along the surface at the end of a long cable by a genuine submerged U-boat.

British and American warships escorting large convoys would mistake the bogus conning tower for the real thing—or so the inventors hoped—and ram the decoy. The ensuing explosion would sink the Allied vessel.

Under heavy pressure from Adolf Hitler, who as supreme commander of the German armed forces called all the shots, several Water Donkeys were built. Dubious U-boat skippers and crews put to sea with the devices, convinced that the heavy encumbrances would result in a disaster—for the U-boats. None of the skippers was eager to be delayed by two heavy cables and a dummy conning tower while being chased by Allied cruisers hurling depth charges.

Admiral Doenitz began receiving reports that the Water Donkeys were "accidentally lost at sea" soon after the U-boats left port for the Atlantic battleground.[11]

Strange Role for a Copenhagen Hotel

FLEMMING BRUUN MUUS was a husky, outgoing Dane who laughed heartily and had an almost constant zest for new—and dangerous—adventures. For years, he had been tramping about the world as a prospector, an engineer, and a sailor, and now he was manager for the Elder Dempster Shipping Line in Liberia, "in the darkest Africa," he would explain.

In 1940, Muus, then thirty-three years of age, learned that the Germans had invaded and conquered his tiny homeland in only a matter of hours. He promptly fired off telegrams to Danish embassies in Washington and London, volunteering for any kind of service against the Third Reich.

For a year and a half, Muus heard nothing in response to his telegrams. When he learned that Danes were forming a legion in England, he took off for Britain in a roundabout way to avoid German warships and patrols and finally reached Liverpool on April 1, 1942.

After interrogation by British intelligence officers who recognized his leadership qualities, desire, energy, and grasp of several foreign languages, he was trained by the Special Operations Executive (SOE). Then, in February 1943, Royal Navy Commander Ralph Hollingworth, head of the Danish Section of SOE, summoned Muus.

"The man who is presently our leader in Denmark is being recalled," Hollingworth stated. "I want you to accept the leadership of the SOE circuits there." He went on to explain that the SOE's leader in Denmark had done a terrific job, but that the Gestapo was hot on his trail.

There was a short pause as the enormity of his task promised to overwhelm Muus. Then he replied: "Yes, sir, I will."

Hollingworth sent the Dane to the SOE "makeover shop," where he was given an entirely new identity. Flemming Bruun Muus vanished, replaced by Carl Moeller, a salesman in Copenhagen. His British shirts were given a tag bearing the name of a well-known Copenhagen store. On his jacket, bought on London's Regent Street, was sewn the name of a popular Danish tailor.

Masked by the veil of night on March 12, 1943, Muus and three other agents took off in a British aircraft from a secluded airfield north of London, and three hours later, they parachuted into Denmark. They took refuge in a safe house, and after daylight, Muus set out for Copenhagen. There he made contact with resistance leaders whose names he had been given in London and told to memorize.

Carl Moeller (Muus), a man of action, quickly took over the reins of the SOE apparatus in Denmark. His first order of business was to establish a headquarters that would be reasonably secure from detection by the Gestapo. His choice was a masterpiece of masquerades. His elderly aunt in Copenhagen, Gudrun Zahle, resided in a private hotel, the Damenhotellet, which had provided accommodations strictly for women for nearly a century. Every German spybuster in Denmark knew that the proprietress adamantly refused to let any male—including the king, some would say—even step inside the front door.

Muus had a gifted tongue, and he persuaded the aged hotel owner, Else de Neergaard, to allow him to use the premises as headquarters for clandestine operations in Denmark.

It was not long before Auntie Gudrun and hotel owner Else were themselves eagerly immersed in cloak-and-dagger operations. "Carl Moeller," the traveling salesman, had become the only resident male guest at the Damen Hotel.[12]

War among London's Spy Chiefs

NOT ALL THE INTRIGUE, hoaxes, and deceptions involving cloak-and-dagger agencies of the Allies were aimed at the Germans, Italians, and their satellites. In the spring of 1943, a rousing squabble between the espionage agencies was raging in London.

America's Office of Strategic Services (OSS) was less than two years old. The British, steeped in a tradition of centuries of clandestine operations and with four years of practical experience under their belts in the current war, looked on the OSS officers who were now flooding London with disdain. The "newcomers from the Colonies" were regarded as fresh and innocent inductees from high-brow finishing schools into the no-holds-barred arena of intelligence and dirty tricks. There was considerable merit to the British point of view.

Chief of the OSS in London was tall, handsome David K. E. Bruce, the multimillionaire son of a U.S. senator. Married to steel baron Andrew Mellon's daughter, who was known as "the world's richest woman," the forty-four-year-old Bruce surrounded himself with other bluebloods.

Bruce and his bluebloods were received warmly in London's exclusive social clubs, but at OSS headquarters in Grosvenor Square, they milled around in bewilderment. Only a short time earlier, they had been engaged in tranquil civilian pursuits. Now they found themselves executives in a dark and sinister "corporation" whose principal assets were fraud, intrigue, deceit, skullduggery, and occasional mayhem.

In January 1943, David Bruce and the chief of Britain's Special Operations Executive (SOE), Charles Hambro, had reached an agreement—on paper—that the secret agencies of the two allies would cooperate in supporting the European underground. But a practical consolidation could not be created instantaneously by signatures on a scrap of paper. So the seasoned officers in British intelligence and the SOE found it difficult—even impossible—to treat the green Americans as equals.

In Washington, D.C., meanwhile, Major General William J. "Wild Bill" Donovan, who had founded OSS as a colonel back in mid-1941, had grown angry about what he considered to be a condescending attitude by the British toward his OSS greenhorns. He ordered Colonel Bruce to compete with the British by establishing OSS's own espionage network in German-occupied Europe.

Donovan's order triggered an uproar. Most vocal in opposition to a full partnership with the OSS was Claude Dansey, the acid-tongued, irascible, but brilliant assistant chief of MI-6, the British secret service responsible for overseas operations. Dansey had long been critical of anything American. He nearly broke out with apoplexy when he learned that the OSS upstarts were courting Major André Dewavrin (code-named Colonel Passy after a famous Paris subway station), who was commander of the Bureau Central de Renseignement et d'Action (BCRA), Charles de Gaulle's secret service based in London.

Six-foot-eight-inch de Gaulle had been a relatively obscure general in 1940 when he led a French division in the futile fight against Adolf Hitler's blitzkrieg. He eluded capture and escaped to England, where he proclaimed himself head of the Free French and called on his countrymen to continue the struggle against the Nazi oppressors.

One of de Gaulle's first actions on reaching London was to direct the twenty-eight-year-old Colonel Passy, who also had escaped to England, to organize an espionage network in France to help pave the way for the Allies' (and de Gaulle's) eventual return to the Continent.

Claude Dansey had been working closely with the BCRA and considered de Gaulle's agency to be his private preserve for obtaining intelligence from German-occupied Europe. For their part, David Bruce and Dr. William Maddox, who had taught international affairs at Princeton and Harvard and was now head of Bruce's Secret Intelligence (SI), were deeply impressed by the mountains of raw intelligence turned over to the OSS from Colonel Passy's spy network.

Although Colonel Passy had long had a harmonious relationship with Claude Dansey at MI-6, for two years the Frenchman had been feuding with Charles Hambro's SOE. Passy had violently protested the SOE policy of having its own French Section operating espionage networks in Europe. He argued that all French cloak-and-dagger activities should be conducted by one agency—his.

Meanwhile, the fledgling OSS was starving for information from inside occupied Europe. David Bruce was convinced that the only way for his late-blooming spy operation to obtain intelligence was through a typical American free enterprise approach: buy it from existing espionage networks.

Consequently, Bruce offered huge sums of money to the underground in France in exchange for intelligence. But first, Bruce felt it prudent to obtain the approval of de Gaulle's BCRA in London.

Far from giving his blessing, Colonel Passy was outraged and curtly rejected the American proposal, arguing that French resistance groups should not accept money from a foreign power, albeit an ally. The BCRA chief was convinced that the entire matter was a devious plot cooked up by the powers-that-be in Washington, D.C.—mainly President Franklin D. Roosevelt—to undermine General de Gaulle's Free French apparatus. Roosevelt and de Gaulle had become staunch enemies, although ostensibly cooperating in the war effort.

Colonel Passy, no doubt parroting the view of de Gaulle, was convinced that Roosevelt's goal was to aid the cause of French General Henri-Honoré Giraud, a bitter rival of de Gaulle. Giraud, who had performed an incredible escape from towering Colditz Castle in Germany where he was being held prisoner several months earlier, was considered to be de Gaulle's principal rival to lead France after her eventual liberation.

Now Wild Bill Donovan, David Bruce, and other OSS leaders became furious at de Gaulle. They denied any partisan interest in who would govern France one day, and they stressed that their only concern was wiping out Adolf Hitler and his Nazi clique.

Soon word of the generous money offered by the Americans reached the BCRA underground leaders in France, and a violent difference of opinion erupted among them. One resistant leader, François de Benouville, argued vehemently that thousands of young Frenchmen had fled to the mountains and forests to continue the fight in groups called the Maquis. These freedom fighters could be armed only with the aide of OSS money, de Benouville declared.

Then Jean Moulin, a diminutive, dark Frenchman of outstanding intellect, energy, and charm, leaped into the intramural skirmishing among the resistants in France. Code-named Max, Moulin was General de Gaulle's personal representative to the French underground networks. He encouraged the resistance to break off all contacts with the OSS.

However, the controversy over accepting American money in exchange for intelligence continued to simmer, although the Maquis warriors continued to harass and wreak havoc upon the German occupiers. Finally, in a move of reconciliation and by diligent effort, Moulin organized a coordinating committee in which all eight major French resistance movements would be represented without surrendering their separate identities.

On May 27, 1943, Moulin presided over the first joint session of the Conseil National de la Résistance (Council of National Resistance) at 48 Rue du Four in Paris. Several of the Maquis leaders agreed to accept OSS money, but Communist leaders refused to have anything to do with the "Yankee capitalists."[13]

A Cat Bombardier

FOR MONTHS, THE BRITISH ADMIRALTY was haunted by the knowledge that the mighty German battleship *Tirpitz* was anchored beside the towering black mountains along Alta Fjord in northern Norway. This formidable warship posed an ongoing threat to what the Allies called the Murmansk run, in which convoys carrying tanks, airplanes, and other accoutrements of war to the Soviet Union sailed north of Norway and anchored above the Arctic Circle at Murmansk. This critical lifeline to Russia was only a short distance from Alta Fjord, the lair of the *Tirpitz*.

With the arrival of spring 1943, the British Admiralty had come up with numerous schemes to destroy the *Tirpitz*, but all had to be rejected. The warship could not be attacked by surface vessels, for its anchorage was considered to be impenetrable. Nor could heavy bombers hit the holed-up battleship, because it was beyond the range of British and U.S. aircraft then available.

Meanwhile, the frustration of the British Admiralty over wiping out the *Tirpitz* had reached the headquarters of the Office of Strategic Services (OSS) in Washington. One day, Stanley P. Lovell, a noted chemist and holder of scores of patents, received a visit from a man who described himself as an expert on felines.

Lovell was the director of research and development for the OSS, an operation known to insiders as the Dirty Tricks Department. As was his practice, he listened to the feline authority's scheme, because no trick that would inflict damage to an enemy was ruled out automatically.

Lovell's attention was seized within moments when the visitor declared that he had a trick to destroy the *Tirpitz*. The centerpiece in the scheme would be a cat. A cat always lands on her feet, and a cat hates water, the man reminded Lovell. So his idea was to parachute a feline, feet down, in a harness below a bomb with a mechanism set so that the animal's every move would guide the vanes of the free-falling bomb.

The cat-guided bomb would be dropped above the *Tirpitz*. When she spotted the hated water and the one piece of dry ground (the battleship), she would steer the explosive to the *Tirpitz* and become a heroine in the free world—although a quite dead one.

But how would the cat get above the *Tirpitz*? By trickery. The German gunners protecting the ship were on the lookout for approaching heavy bombers, but they would pay no attention to a light, unmarked aircraft, which presumably would be one of their own. So the cat would be dropped from this plane over the target.

Stanley Lovell was receptive to any ingenious scheme, but he viewed the cat project as totally unworkable. However, a U.S. senator, who was head of the powerful Appropriations Committee that dealt out funds to the OSS, had learned of the feline project and was an enthusiastic supporter of it. No argument from the OSS could squelch the senator's fervor. So a trial run had to be made at a small airfield outside Washington. A cat in a harness was dropped and became unconscious and, therefore, ineffective in the first fifty feet of the fall, so she had no control over the bomb's direction.

Only then did the senator lose his enthusiasm. The cat bombardier project was quietly buried.[14]

A Plot to Kidnap the Pope

MOMENTOUS EVENTS WERE UNFOLDING in the Mediterranean region in mid-1943. A large Anglo-American force invaded Sicily, an island at the toe of the Italian boot, on July 10 and overran that key outpost of Adolf Hitler's Festung Europa (Fortress Europe) in a lightning thirty-eight-day campaign.

That disaster broke the back of an already demoralized Italian military establishment and civilian population. On July 25, mild King Victor Emmanuel III summarily dismissed Hitler's crony, bombastic Benito Mussolini, as premier, a post he had held for twenty-one years. The monarch had the deposed leader arrested and locked up at an undisclosed locale.

King Victor promptly appointed Marshal Pietro Badoglio premier and ordered him to form a new government, whose secret mission was to obtain an armistice from the Western Allies.

In Berlin, Hitler was furious. King Victor, he exclaimed, had betrayed him. The führer sent Admiral Wilhelm Canaris, chief of the Abwehr, to Rome to analyze the situation and report back to Hitler.

Canaris, a ringleader in the Schwarze Kapelle (Black Orchestra), a secret German group bent on getting rid of Adolf Hitler and the Nazi regime, met for two days in early August with General Cesare Amé, Italy's chief intelligence officer. The two men were old friends. They issued a joint memorandum of the meeting in which Italy pledged to stand beside her ally, Nazi Germany. Privately, in long walks through a Rome forest where bugs would not be planted, the intelligence officers agreed that Italy would drop out of the war—and soon.

While Canaris and Amé were engaged in their machinations, thirty-two-year-old Brigadeführer (SS Major General) Walter Schellenberg, chief of the Sicherheitsdienst (intelligence service), was hatching wild ideas about the

"Italian situation." Bright and intelligent, he constantly sought ever more power, and pulling off some ingenious caper to help the führer might catapult him still higher up the Nazi pecking order.

Schellenberg began planning an escapade that was sure to trigger worldwide attention. He would send a platoon of SS troops in civilian clothes into Rome with orders to kidnap Pope Pius XII, spiritual leader of about three hundred and fifty million Catholics in both warring camps. After being abducted, the pope would be spirited to Berlin and an announcement would be made that he was being held "for security reasons."

No doubt Schellenberg, who had divorced his first wife and married a woman high in Berlin society, felt that Hitler would be deeply impressed by the plot to kidnap the pope. Berlin insiders knew that the führer had long hated the Catholic leader. Back in 1937, when he had been a cardinal named Eugenio Pacelli, the future pope had publicly condemned the Nazi regime.

After Pacelli had been elected pope on March 2, 1939, there was much fear among his confidants that Hitler might instigate his assassination. There was even speculation that Pius XII might have to take refuge in the United States. President Franklin D. Roosevelt, a Protestant, and the new pope had been friends since 1936.

Hitler's fury against the Vatican in general and Pius XII in particular grew even more intense in 1940 when Roosevelt broke a seventy-year tradition by sending Myron Taylor as U.S. representative to the Vatican. At the same time, the pope had snubbed the führer's emissary, Joachim von Ribbentrop, a onetime wine salesman skilled in "coersive diplomacy" (veiled threats).

Now Admiral Canaris learned about the plot Schellenberg was cooking up to abduct the pope, and he sent an urgent warning to his friend, General Amé, in Rome. Presumably, Amé tipped off Vatican security. No doubt word reached Berlin that Italian authorities were aware of the kidnap caper, so Schellenberg's scheme to impress Adolf Hitler was quietly dropped.[15]

Capturing an Island by Deceit

ON JULY 24, 1943, two weeks after Allied forces had cracked open Adolf Hitler's Festung Europa (Fortress Europe) by invading Sicily, Colonel James M. Gavin's U.S. 505th Parachute Infantry Regiment was approaching the western port of Trapani. Gavin had orders to seize the town, through which supplies could be brought in by sea to U.S. forces in the western half of the triangular-shaped island.

Known to his men as "Slim Jim," the thirty-five-year-old Gavin expected a bloody battle. Intelligence disclosed that some five thousand heavily armed Italians were holding the key port. On the eastern outskirts of the town, the paratroopers were suddenly pounded by artillery and raked by small arms fire from a twenty-five-hundred-foot mountain that guarded the approaches to the town.

Admiral Alberto Manfredi, the commander of the garrison in Trapani, knew that most of Sicily had been occupied by the Allied invaders. His honor satisfied by the minimal resistance (only one American was slightly wounded), he surrendered the port and its five thousand defenders.

Lying a few miles off Trapani were the Egadi Islands, which were held by Italian units. On the Egadies were several batteries of large coast and field artillery guns that could play havoc with Allied vessels trying to enter Trapani harbor.

Major General Matthew B. Ridgway, the U.S. 82nd Airborne Division commander, decided that the islands—Favignana, Marittimo, and Levanzo—had to be neutralized and their big guns silenced. An amphibious assault by his paratroopers could result in heavy casualties, so he called in Lieutenant Ivan F. Woods, a tall young Texan, and handed him a daunting mission: take a small group of paratroopers, sneak onto the tiny islands, and negotiate a peaceful surrender with the Italian commander.

"How many of the enemy are there on the islands?" Woods asked.

"G-2 [intelligence] doesn't know," Ridgway replied.

"Where are they located?"

"G-2 doesn't know that, either."

Woods saluted and said, "We'll get the job done somehow, General." After taking a few steps, Woods spun around and asked, "By the way, sir, where do we hook up with the navy craft to take us to the islands?"

Casually, Ridgway responded, "None is available. You'll have to scrape up your own boat."

Hastily, Lieutenant Woods rounded up twenty-eight paratroopers and hurried to the Trapani docks. There, after ten minutes of heavy haggling with a native fisherman, he secured the rental of a battered, leaking wood boat barely twenty feet in length. For an added fee, the Sicilian agreed to operate the vessel.

Woods, his paratroopers, and the fisherman crammed into the boat, and a course was set for the nearest island of Levanzo. Landing at the docks, the Americans leaped out with weapons at the ready, anticipating a volley of small arms and machine-gun fire. Woods and his men scoured the small piece of land and found no Italian troops.

Back into the vessel scrambled the paratroopers, and the Sicilian skipper headed for the next island, Marittimo. The craft tilted and threatened to capsize when one side or the other held too many men. At Marittimo, the landing procedure was repeated, and again, there was no sign of the enemy.

"Okay, head for the big island," Woods ordered the Sicilian, who was now grumbling about the mission being much longer than he had anticipated. Clearly, Favignana held the enemy force, Woods surmised. The looming showdown would be there. Woods and his men were ready to do battle, possibly against a force much larger than that of the Americans.

Woods and his troopers, with Tommy guns and rifles poised for immediate action, edged up to the rickety wooden dock at Favignana. The only sounds were the gentle lapping of the surf on the beach and the monotonous throbbing of the wheezing old boat motor.

"Shut off that damned engine!" a nervous GI called out in a stage whisper.

Clambering onto the dock, Woods and his men moved cautiously down the only street of the tiny town. Interrogating a few natives through an interpreter, Woods learned that the headquarters of the Italian garrison was in a farmhouse a mile out of town.

"Ask how many Eytie soldiers there are," Woods instructed his interpreter.

"Hundreds of them," was the reply.

In approach-march formation and with weapons at the ready, the twenty-nine Americans headed for the farmhouse. Nearing the enemy headquarters without being fired on, the troopers spotted an Italian officer emerging from the structure. Cautiously, Woods and two of his men, one an interpreter, went forward to meet him.

The Italian colonel identified himself as commander of the Favignana garrison and explained that he had been out of communication with mainland Sicily for several days, so he presumed the island had fallen to the Allies.

Woods assured the Italian that this indeed was the case, and he urged the colonel to surrender his force to avoid further bloodshed. "My patrol is just the advance guard of our paratrooper regiment," Woods lied. "If you do not surrender, we will have to bring down heavy air attacks and naval shelling on you, then launch a ground assault."

Actually, Woods had neither air nor naval support available, but he reasoned that the Italian colonel did not know these facts.

"With the mainland [Sicily] gone, I see no reason for my men and I to die for a lost cause," the Italian declared. The American heartily agreed.

Woods did not know that four battalions of 75-millimeter guns and four batteries of 152-millimeter coastal guns were zeroed in on Trapani harbor.

Now the Italian's concern turned to his own soldiers' honor. He said he would surrender the garrison only to an American officer of senior rank. This left Woods in a dilemma: either he and his paratroopers might have to fight a much larger enemy force, or he could go back to Sicily and secure a high-ranking officer to accept the Favignana surrender. Woods chose the latter course.

Leaving his troopers near the farmhouse with orders to "be on the alert but don't do anything to provoke the Eyties," Woods took the fishing boat back to Trapani, rushed to 82nd Airborne headquarters, and briefed General Ridgway on the "Mexican standoff" between twenty-eight paratroopers and several hundred Italian troops. He asked for a senior officer to return with him to assuage the Italian colonel's honor and to accept his surrender.

"Hell, I'll go," Ridgway declared, strapping on his .45 Colt. He and Woods climbed into the same native vessel and arrived at the Favignana dock. The two Americans marched briskly to the farmhouse, where the Italian colonel came forward to meet them. Spotting the two stars of a major general's rank on Ridgway's collar, a fleeting trace of relief swept across the colonel's face. His soldier's honor would remain unsullied.

Smartly saluting, the Italian handed Ridgway his ceremonial sword, indicating an honorable surrender to a worthy foe. The general returned the salute, accepted the steel blade, and after a brief conversation departed for Trapani.

Lieutenant Woods and his troopers set about disarming the Italian garrison. A head count disclosed that four hundred and thirty-seven enemy soldiers had surrendered. Returning the POWs to Trapani was a tedious and time-consuming task. The wheezing, huffing old fishing boat shuttled hordes of Italians from Favignana to Sicily for the next several hours.

Woods accompanied the last group of prisoners. As the boat chugged along, there was a loud explosion and the craft seemed to rise slightly out of the water. It had struck a floating mine. There were gasps of concern from the Italian POWs, and Woods pondered if all on board were destined for a grave on the bottom of the Mediterranean Sea. However, the rickety boat was more sturdy than it appeared. Despite its initial shudders, it putt-putted into Trapani harbor.

His potentially hazardous secret commission accomplished without the loss of a man, Woods had a curious thought: having survived the heavy fighting in the Sicily campaign, it would have been ironic had he perished by drowning in a leaking Italian fishing boat.[16]

"Fishermen" Blow Up Key Canal

CAPTAIN GUSTAVE BIELER, a burly Canadian giant from Montreal, parachuted from a Royal Air Force plane outside Paris on a moonlit night in mid-November 1942. The dark ground rushed up and he crashed with enormous impact. The underground warriors on hand to meet the spy knew that he had been seriously injured.

Loading Bieler into the back of a truck, the resistants drove him to a hospital in Paris, where he was admitted under an assumed name. No doubt the doctors and nurses knew the full story, but when they were told he had been injured in a vehicle accident, they dutifully entered that fact on their records, knowing that the Gestapo occasionally dropped by in search of maimed or ill spies.

For three months, Bieler remained a patient at the hospital. Several times, he could see Gestapo agents walking along the corridor. But when the Canadian was discharged, he promptly became a whirlwind in carrying out his

Captain Gustave Bieler (Guy). Executed by the Germans. (Author's collection)

mission: creating a *réseau* (network) in the St. Quentin region, about a hundred miles northeast of Paris.

Under the code name Guy, Bieler and his French helpers blew up railroad tracks and destroyed signal boxes and repair sheds between St. Quentin and Valenciennes in France and other cities in Belgium. Guy and his men also cut the main rail line between Paris and Cologne, Germany—thirteen times.

Along with being an important railroad center, St. Quentin lies at the heart of the waterway system of northeast France. Several canals pass by, and they were used extensively by the Germans to transport war materials by barge to their forces in southern France.

The lock gates around St. Quentin were hit often by British bombers, but within a few days after being damaged, industrious German engineers, using forced French labor, repaired them. So in the spring of 1943, the British chiefs of staff listed the canal system around St. Quentin as a top-priority sabotage target. Gustave Bieler was ordered to disrupt the German barge traffic.

Bold and cagey as he was, Bieler secretly felt that the mission was impossible. The canals were closely guarded by German soldiers, so outsiders could not get anywhere near the key locks without being detected—or shot. But the Canadian was determined to make the effort.

Bieler was known to the Germans in the region, and the Gestapo was on the lookout for him. It would have been suicide for him, and resulted in the destruction of the mission, if he tried to do the perilous task. So it was assigned to his chief helper, André Cordelette, a farmer, who gave Bieler his house to operate his radio and to store explosives (hidden under hay in a barn).

Cordelette was a most unlikely figure to be an espionage agent. Frail, soft-spoken, and middle-aged, he took strength from Bieler's enthusiasm. So, as expected, he promptly agreed to the sabotage job to destroy the St. Quentin locks. Two other resistants would go with him.

Typically, Bieler decided to elaborate on London's instructions. He would not only blow the locks, but would try to destroy loaded barges as well. There was only one way to achieve these goals: the sharp-eyed German sentries would have to be fooled. So Bieler hatched a scheme.

Cordelette and his two helpers would be disguised as a fishing party—a slightly drunken one. They were armed with fishing poles, picnic baskets, and several half-empty wine bottles.

Climbing into a small boat on which explosives were concealed under a canvas, the three saboteurs began paddling along a canal, bound for the key lock. As the carefree party neared the first German soldiers at a machine-gun post, the resistants talked raucously, waved, shouted friendly greetings to the sentries, and brandished the wine bottles. The Germans, no doubt happy to receive such a warm accolade from Frenchmen, grinned and waved back.

Reaching the targeted gate, Cordelette placed an underwater charge with a time-lapse mechanism; then his boat leisurely edged along a line of barges filled with materials for the German Wehrmacht. Explosive limpet charges were placed on the barges just below the waterline and out of sight. These charges had timers attached to them.

That night, the region was rocked by a series of loud explosions. Dawn would find perhaps thirty barges and a key canal lock in ruins.

In December, Gustave Bieler and his radio operator, Yolande Beekman (code-named Mariette), a young British woman, were seated together at the Café Moulin Brulé in St. Quentin, casually sipping wine. Suddenly two Gestapo cars screeched to a halt and several Germans rushed in. The two spies had been betrayed.

Two weeks later, Bieler and Beekman were executed.[17]

Part Six

The Allies' Road to Victory

Cat-and-Mouse Duel
with the Gestapo

ADMIRAL WILHELM CANARIS, the Third Reich's master spy who controlled thousands of Abwehr secret agents around the world, was seated behind the mammoth mahogany desk in his office at 76-78 Tirpitzufer, overlooking the beautiful chestnuts of Berlin's Tiergarten. Two stern-faced visitors were escorted into his cavernous domain: Gestapo Commissioner Hans Sonderegger and Dr. Manfred Roeder, an army investigator. It was April 5, 1943.

Canaris remained impassive, but no doubt he knew this was the beginning of the end of the Schwarze Kapelle (Black Orchestra), a conspiracy of prominent German military men and government and civic leaders whose goal was to "eliminate" Adolf Hitler and his Nazi regime. Canaris had long been one of the conspirators.

The inquisitors immediately charged that Hans von Dohnanyi, a lawyer who was a deputy in the Abwehr, along with his brother-in-law, Dietrich Bonhoeffer, a theologian, were engaged in an espionage plot with the British secret service to overthrow the German führer.

These blockbuster allegations were accurate. Dohnanyi had been active in the Schwarze Kapelle; Bonhoeffer had made several trips to neutral capitals in Europe to gain support for the conspiracy.

Specifically, Dohnanyi was accused of taking bribes to smuggle Jews from Germany into neutral Switzerland. Indeed, there had been an undercover project (code-named Operation 7) that had been sneaking Jews across the frontier for more than a year. Canaris himself had conceived the plan, and Dohnanyi masterminded the exfiltration of Jews disguised as Abwehr agents.

Now Roeder demanded the right to search Dohnanyi's office safe. Canaris protested, but agreed when it would appear that the Abwehr operatives were concealing incriminating documents. When the safe was being searched, Canaris, Dohnanyi, and Colonel Hans Oster, the number-two man in the Abwehr and a leader in the Schwarze Kapelle, looked on in silence.

Finally, Roeder had all the contents piled on a desk, and he began to examine several slips of paper known within the spy agency as "playing cards." These cards contained information about secret missions. One of them, which

Dohnanyi spotted before Roeder did, gave instructions for Bonhoeffer to go to the Vatican in Rome.

Aware that this "playing card" could be the death warrant for Canaris, Oster, and himself, the quick-witted Dohnanyi snatched it from the desk and slipped it to the Abwehr chief, telling the two investigators that it told of a super-secret mission then in progress and should be seen by no unauthorized person.

Canaris, in turn, gave the card to Oster, who tried to sneak it into his coat pocket. Sonderegger saw the move and called out to Roeder, who demanded loudly that the card be given to him. Oster denied he was hiding anything, but Roeder reached over and snatched the incriminating card from Oster's pocket.

Roeder found even more damning evidence in the safe, including documents linking both Dohnanyi and Bonhoeffer to a conspiracy against the Nazi regime. Roeder announced that Canaris's three associates were under arrest. Canaris protested violently, to no avail. Dohnanyi was hauled off to the German army prison at 64 Lehterstrasse in Berlin, and Oster was taken to Dresden and put under house arrest surrounded by an armed guard. Pastor Bonhoeffer was put in solitary confinement in a filthy cell at Tigel Prison.

A few days later, Bonhoeffer, handcuffed and shackled by ankle chains, was dragged before a hearing of the Reichskriegsgericht (Reich War Court). A highly cerebral man, the pastor wove an intricate camouflage over his secret activities as an Abwehr agent. This duel raged, off and on, for eighteen months. No evidence surfaced linking Bonhoeffer to a conspiracy.

Seeking to protect both himself and the Schwarze Kapelle, Wilhelm Canaris, a shrewd operator, tried to steer the focus of the investigation of Hans von Dohnanyi away from conspiracy and toward fraud. However, Roeder insisted that Dohnanyi was guilty of high treason, a capital offense. Dohnanyi, an able attorney, declared that all of his activities were simply ordinary Abwehr operational matters in the best interest of the Third Reich.

Dohnanyi thwarted Roeder at every turn. He "proved" that Bonhoeffer's numerous trips to neutral capitals (on behalf of the Schwarze Kapelle) were actually counterespionage missions to discern the "mood of the enemy."

Even Roeder's charge that Dohnanyi had profited financially from Operation 7 sputtered and died for lack of evidence.

Now the wily Canaris made his move. He visited Field Marshal Wilhelm Keitel, a hulking figure who had been at Adolf Hitler's elbow since the beginning of the war as his Wehrmacht chief of staff. Most in the German officer corps regarded the monocled field marshal as a stooge for the führer, and he was called (behind his back) *Lakaitel*, making a pun on *Lakai*, which is pronounced "lackey."

Projecting outrage, the Abwehr chief complained to Keitel that Roeder's main goal was to smear the good name of the Heer (army) by proving treason against a dedicated high official in the Abwehr. Keitel acted promptly: he fired the bewildered Roeder from the investigation and appointed in his place a far less ambitious officer.

Dohnanyi appeared to be safe for the present time, but he was kept in jail, where he developed an inflammation of the veins in both legs, an exceedingly painful affliction. Probably through the behind-the-scenes machinations of Schwarze Kapelle conspirators, he was transferred to the medical clinic of Professor Sauerbruch, a noted German surgeon—and a member of the anti-Hitler conspiracy.

Manfred Roeder, meanwhile, had refused to get his teeth out of the conspiracy investigation. Roeder barged into Professor Sauerbruch's office and demanded that the "prisoner," who was no longer under army jurisdiction, be handed over to him. The surgeon declared that Dohnanyi was afflicted with a life-threatening ailment and could not be moved.

Vowing to return with armed guards, Roeder stomped out of the clinic. Presumably, unknown conspirators again took a hand in the situation. Roeder was banished to the Wehrmacht's version of Siberia—he was assigned to the Balkans in the judge advocate's office.

Roeder was out of the picture, but not the Gestapo. Reichsführer Heinrich Himmler, chief of the Gestapo and SS, lusted for even more power. He hoped to destroy the Abwehr and fold its global operation into the Gestapo. On January 22, 1944, an SS physician with an ambulance unexpectedly appeared at the Sauerbruch clinic.

No doubt a mole in the clinic had tipped off the Gestapo that Professor Sauerbruch would not be present. So the SS doctor examined Dohnanyi in his patient room, and had three of Himmler's men, disguised as civilian ambulance drivers, take the ailing man to an SS clinic. There he was "examined" by Professor Max de Crinis, who had been a psychologist at Berlin Hospital before the war. He declared that Dohnanyi would be able to testify before SS interrogators in ten days.

Dohnanyi now knew that he would have to resort to trickery if he—and the Schwarze Kapelle—were to survive. He managed to smuggle a letter out of the prison clinic to his wife. Pointing out that he would have to gain time, he said that he had to make sure that he was physically unfit to stand trial. He planned to achieve that goal by developing a heavy attack of dysentery.

Dohnanyi instructed her to go to the Koch Institute, a medical center, and obtain a culture, presumably from an associate there who was sympathetic to the Schwarze Kapelle. Then, he wrote his wife, she was to wrap up some food in which the culture had been inserted and place it in a red cloth. When he received the package in his clinic room, he would know that it would contain the ingredients for causing a dysentery attack that would put him in a legitimate hospital.

Frau von Dohnanyi, at the risk of her life, followed her husband's instructions and got the bundle to him. But the culture failed to work.

In another letter, he told his wife to repeat the process, only this time to obtain a diphtheria culture. Again she succeeded. Two days later, her husband broke out with a serious case of the illness. For many days, the ploy kept him from being interrogated and out of court.

Eventually, the Gestapo, presumably acting under orders from on high, carried the gravely ill Dohnanyi to a vacant tract near the SS clinic and shot him to death. Murdered with him was his brother-in-law, Dietrich Bonhoeffer.[1]

Hedy Lamarr Creates Panic

BY THE SUMMER OF 1943, the U.S. Office of Strategic Services had begun to come of age. Only two years earlier, it had been started from scratch with seven people and its founder and director, William J. Donovan, who had acquired the nickname "Wild Bill" when a football player at Columbia University.

Donovan personally had recruited hundreds of agents, including a large number of mild-mannered men whom he affectionately called "my gray hairs." They were assigned to the Research and Development Division—inventors, scientists, geographers, psychologists, and anthropologists. Their job was to conjure up unorthodox and devious weapons, gadgets, and schemes to trick, undermine, and befuddle the enemy.

One especially innovative gadget developed by the R&D Division was known as Hedy, after the beautiful and sultry Hollywood movie star Hedy Lamarr. It had been conceived after an OSS agent told about being trapped in the fashionable Adlon Hotel in Berlin. "I would have given anything had I been able to create panic in the crowded lobby," the agent exclaimed. Luckily, he had managed to escape.

R&D's answer to the spy's suggestion was Hedy, so-named because the young officers in the Washington OSS headquarters pointed out that Hedy Lamarr triggered panic among the men wherever she went.

Hedy was a firecracker device which, when a small wire loop was pulled, sounded precisely like a falling bomb and then ended with a deafening bang. It was harmless, but by activating Hedy, a spy could have a chance to escape in the wake of the turmoil created.

On August 28, 1943, Stanley P. Lovell, the R&D chief, was asked to demonstrate several of his group's devices before the Joint Chiefs of Staff at the new Pentagon across the Potomac River from Washington. He showed several fiendish devices, then began explaining the need and use for Hedy Lamarr. Unnoticed by the galaxy of brass, he activated a Hedy and casually dropped "her" into a nearby metal wastebasket while continuing to speak.

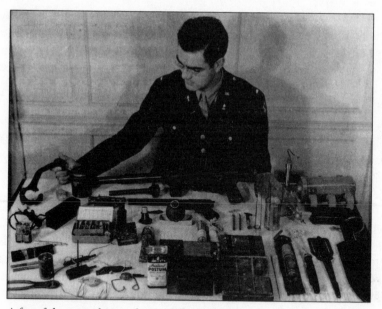

A few of the many devious devices Office of Strategic Services scientists developed for secret agents. (National Archives)

Rudely, Hedy interrupted the speaker and began shrieking and howling with an ear-piercing wail. Then—*BAANNGG!* Generals and admirals began clawing and scrambling to get out of the room's single door.

Curiously, Lovell was never again asked to put on a demonstration for the august Joint Chiefs of Staff. But a large number of Hedys were sent abroad where, Lovell would learn, they did indeed save the lives of some trapped spies when the would-be captors were tricked by a device named after a Hollywood star.[2]

A Bluff Saves an Underground Chief

ON A DARK NIGHT in late August 1943, Roger Landes, code-named Aristide, bailed out of an airplane near the major port of Bordeaux, in southwestern France. He landed hard in a pasture, shucked his chute harness, rolled the chute into a ball, and hid it in thick foliage.

Landes found himself alone in German-occupied France. The underground reception committee that was supposed to be waiting for him was not there. So stealthily he made his way into Bordeaux, where his London controller in the French Section of the Special Operations Executive had ordered him to replace the leader of the *réseau* (resistance network).

A thin man of medium height in his late thirties, Landes was a British subject of French origin (he had an English father, but was born in France). He spoke French more fluently than he did English.

Aristide, as he would be addressed exclusively by *réseau* members (few actually knew his real name), found a room on the Quai des Chartrons, above a *tabac* (tobacco store) where his comings and goings would be largely unnoticed.

Soon he set up his radio in an empty house at Quatre Pavillons, only a few hundred yards from a major German headquarters. There was method to his seeming madness—he concluded that the Germans would not be looking for a resistance transmitter on their own doorstep.

There was only one small problem. Quatre Pavillons was on a hill and transmissions to London were excellent most of the time—except that Aristide's radio frequency and that in the German headquarters set occasionally clashed and interfered with each other. However, both the underground chief and the German operators in the headquarters worked around the occasional inconvenience.

Aristide's network was a large one, spread over many square miles in the Bordeaux region. Consequently, he had to rely heavily on couriers to get his orders and information to subchiefs.

Many of the couriers were young women, who generally were able to move about with far greater freedom than could men. These women knew they faced perils and could expect no mercy from the Gestapo if captured. Coolness and courage were their common denominators.

On August 15, 1944, a year after Aristide took charge at Bordeaux, Allied forces stormed ashore in southern France in the co-called second D-Day. They were to drive north for three hundred miles and link up with the Normandy armies that had broken out of their bridgehead.

Two days after the Allied force landed along the Mediterranean coast, Aristide was in the town of Sisteron briefing a group of saboteurs. It seemed to be just another of hundreds of similar sessions that he had held during the past year. Moments after he stepped out of the building, he was pounced on by three Gestapo agents. His luck had run out.

Witnessing Aristide's capture was a young Polish woman code-named Christine, who was his courier and had been rushing to catch up with him when he was taken. She followed at a discreet distance as the network leader was marched to the local Gestapo headquarters and hustled inside.

With typical calmness, Christine analyzed the situation. There would be no time to round up resistance men in the area and storm the Gestapo station. By that time, the Germans would probably discover that their dragnet had landed a large fish, and they would rush the secret agent out of town.

There was only one hope to save Aristide, Christine concluded. She would try to free him through a bluff. If it failed, both she and Aristide were

Major Roger Landes (Aristide).
Escaped captivity. (Author's
collection)

doomed. She walked up to the headquarters and went inside, where she approached a German lieutenant at a desk.

"Are you in charge here?" she demanded.

"You can tell me what you want," the German replied.

"My business is with the commandant," the woman said. "I have important information for him."

Now the German showed anger. "The commandant's busy. I can take a message."

"I must see the man in charge in person. If you don't let me see him, your superior officers in Berlin will hold you personally responsible. It is to his advantage to hear me."

The German frowned, but rose and went into the inner office. Through the open door, Christine could see Aristide sitting in a chair with a Gestapo man on either side of him. The captive saw her, but gave no sign of recognition.

Moments later, a German colonel burst out of his office, his face livid. Who was this impudent French woman demanding to see him? "Well, speak up," he barked. "I'm a busy man."

"What I have to say, I must say to you alone," Christine said. The chief nodded and the lieutenant left the room.

"I am here to speak to you on behalf of the Maquis [resistance forces]," she replied in a confident tone.

The colonel was flabbergasted. "What? What?" he snapped.

"You heard right," Christine exclaimed. "You have a prisoner in your office. I demand that you give him up!"

"Are you mad?" the German shouted.

"Not at all. In only a few hours, the Americans will be here. Our Maquisards have informed me that they are on all sides of you, and you can never escape," she lied.

The German looked shocked. Christine could tell that in the confused military situation, he had no idea where the advancing American forces were located. Actually, they were some fifty miles from Sisteron.

"When they arrive, I have a most interesting story to tell them," she added. "That you, Colonel Wessels, have arrested and tortured an innocent civilian, one who has done no wrong."

Anticipating that he might eliminate that problem by "eliminating" this woman, Christine pointed out that should she fail to return, her comrades in the resistance would tell the story to the Americans.

Christine and her comrades knew that Wessels had been guilty of torturing and executing numerous members of the Maquis. But now he turned into a mild-mannered man. "Bring the prisoner out," he yelled.

"You are free to go," the Gestapo chief told Aristide. The resistance leader stared at Christine and blinked. He could not believe his ears.

"Come on," the courier said to Aristide. The colonel followed them down the corridor to the front door, instructing the guards to let the couple pass.

Before going out the door, the subdued German said, "When the Americans arrive, you will tell them what I have done?"

"Oh, yes," Christine replied. "We'll be sure to tell them *everything* you've done!"[3]

A Stowaway Lands on a Hostile Beach

EARLY ON THE MORNING of September 10, 1943, U.S. Lieutenant General Mark W. Clark climbed down a rope ladder on the USS *Ancon* and into a small assault boat that took him ashore near Salerno, Italy. A day earlier, assault units of Clark's U.S. and British Fifth Army had invaded Adolf Hitler's Festung Europa (Fortress Europe).

After a bloody fight at the shoreline along the Gulf of Salerno, Clark's force pushed inland. But Field Marshal Albert Kesselring, one of the Wehrmacht's most able battle leaders, rushed reinforcements from all over Italy to the invasion site, and a furious clash raged.

Now Clark was landing to inspect the situation for himself. Walking along the sandy beach with his long strides, he heard the insistent barking of a dog. Looking around he saw, much to his amazement, the source of the canine uproar—the general's beloved German shepherd.

Named Mike, although a female, the animal had been given to Clark by a sergeant several months earlier. Since that time, Mike had been the general's almost constant companion.

On leaving Algiers, North Africa, several days before the Salerno invasion, Clark had bid goodbye to his pet. There were strict regulations against taking dogs on navy ships. But Sergeant Chaney, Clark's orderly, engaged in a mild subterfuge. He put a tag on Mike's collar and turned her over to two Salerno-bound soldiers before they boarded their ship. All this was accomplished without the general's knowledge.

The tag was inscribed by Chaney to be subtly intimidating in tone. It read: "This is General Mark Clark's dog. She is going to Salerno."

As no reasonably rational officer in Fifth Army had any desire to assume the responsibility for ejecting the commanding general's pet from the ship, Mike went ashore at hotly contested Salerno, reportedly at H-Hour plus 18. There, with shot and shell all around, she had the time of her life, leaping up and down on the beach and dashing hither and yon.

General Clark was as delighted over this unexpected reunion with Mike as was the dog with her master. He realized, however, that her hyperactivity would be a distracting influence to those involved in shoreline functions. So with a gentle pat on Mike's head, the commanding general ordered that, in essence, she was to be confined to quarters until further notice. She was put inside a small shack on the beach.

Later, it was reported, Sergeant Chaney quipped to pals about how he had pulled off the caper: "Mike came ashore masquerading as a second lieutenant."[4]

Sardine Treats for U-Boat Crews

SOON AFTER ADOLF HITLER sent his powerful German Wehrmacht to take over peaceful Norway on April 9, 1940, a notorious collaborator, Vidkun Quisling, became the most hated man in the nation when he founded Nasjonal Samling (NS), the Norwegian Nazi party.

During the early winter of 1940, Norwegian patriots began organizing an underground network of spies extending along the southern coast from Oslo on the east to the major port of Stavanger, some two hundred miles to the southwest. In the months ahead, the Norwegian resistance became perhaps the most efficient, ruthless, and deadly of all underground organizations in Europe.

Being a resistance warrior was only a part-time endeavor. Norwegians still had to make a living to feed their families. As had been the case for centuries, fishing was an occupation in which many of the resistants engaged. Consequently, it was an especially brutal shock to the underground men and women

A German U-boat crew, such as this one, may have been in for a surprise when the men consumed a sardines "treat." (National Archives)

when the Nazi headquarters in Oslo ordered the entire sardine catch to be turned over to the German occupiers.

Norway's underground had one of the most efficient intelligence services in Europe, including one member who worked undercover in German headquarters. So it was soon learned by underground leaders that the choicest of the sardine supply was earmarked for Saint-Nazaire in western France, home base for U-boat wolfpacks prowling the Atlantic Ocean to sink Allied ships bringing crucial supplies to England. Presumably, the sardines were going to be a treat for the submarine crews to take along on their extended missions.

Leaders in the Norwegian underground contacted British cloak-and-dagger officials in London and asked for the largest shipment of croton oil they could put together. Croton oil is a powerful purgative.

Before the sardine shipment was handed over to the Germans, the resistance men doused the batch earmarked for Saint-Nazaire with liberal doses of croton oil. Its acrid taste would be masked by the fishy tang of the sardines. The liquid was substituted for the oils normally used.

As with most subversive acts, the Norwegians never found out precisely what was the result of their caper. But they had reason to believe that there was considerable turmoil (and, therefore, lack of efficiency) on U-boats sailing from Saint-Nazaire to prowl beneath the Atlantic.[5]

Heists by the "Oslo Gang"

GUNNAR SONSTEBY, who fit the traditional role of a mild-mannered accountant (which indeed he had been in peacetime in Norway), was a man of many

People of all ages served in the Norwegian underground.
This boy flees from site of an explosion at a German
facility. (National Archives)

disguises and aliases. Joining the Norwegian resistance soon after the German Wehrmacht crushed his homeland in early 1940, Sonsteby was variously known as Broch, Erling, Field, Kjakan, and Number 24. He well may have been the slickest and most efficient secret agent in Norway—and there were many in that category.

Sonsteby put together a team of industrious and eager young men who proudly called themselves the Oslo Gang. Their exploits were mind-boggling. They bombed the Oslo Gestapo headquarters, attacked an SS barracks, wiped out a Luftwaffe facility, and blew up an armaments factory, among many other escapades.

Late in 1943, the Germans announced the compulsary mobilization of labor to be sent to the Third Reich, and eighty thousand engineers, fitters, and technicians were ordered to report. To keep track of Norwegians in those categories, the Germans used tabulating machines.

Sonsteby learned that the only firm in Norway that had these machines was the Norsk Watson Company. In broad daylight, the Oslo Gang charged into the office and destroyed the machines, saving thousands of men from deportation.

Vidkun Quisling, the Norwegian traitor who was the puppet head of the government, had his Department of Justice and the Nazi-controlled police in Oslo keep meticulous records on those who collaborated with him. Sonsteby wanted these records to bring what came to be known as the "quislings" to justice after the war. He knew that plans had already been made by Quisling to destroy these archives at the proper time.

Aided by moles in the Department of Justice and the police force who secretly were resistants, Sonsteby secured genuine passes for entering their two buildings. He and several others in the Oslo Gang donned the uniforms and insignia of high police officials, also secured by the moles.

At the Department of Justice, Sonsteby presented a forged order from Gruppenführer (SS General) Heinrich Fehlis, head of the Gestapo in Norway, authorizing the delivery of all records concerning Norwegian collaborators. No one in the department felt inclined to challenge a lawful order from on high, so the employees, at Sonsteby's order, pitched in to help load two tons of materials into a waiting van (on which the Oslo Gang had painted the words "Property of the SS").

After the van had been driven away, Sonsteby and the others, still masquerading as high police brass, strolled into the headquarters of the Oslo police force. Perhaps the officer on duty was suspicious, and he said that he had no keys to the safe containing the files about activities of the Norwegian quislings that Sonsteby demanded be turned over to him.

Striding arrogantly around the office, Sonsteby loudly berated the police official for his negligence, then ordered the safe to be removed from the building. The heavy load was trundled down the corridor and outside into a German van that the resistants had stolen earlier that night.

Norway was the only German-occupied country in Western Europe to liberate herself. A few days after the Oslo Gang pulled off their capers, General Nikolaus von Falkenhorst, the German commander in Norway, surrendered on May 4, 1945. The records confiscated by Gunnar Sonsteby's Oslo Gang provided all the evidence that was needed to convict Vidkun Quisling and other Norwegian traitors and German war criminals at trials that were held soon after the liberation.[6]

Fashion Model Unmasks German Spy

TWENTY-ONE-YEAR-OLD ALINE GRIFFITH, a shapely brunette who had been a model for Hattie Carnegie, the world-famous designer of fashionable women's hats in New York City, arrived in Europe on the Pan American Clipper, a large flying boat. On New Year's Eve 1943, she strode to the registration desk at the ornate Palace Hotel in Madrid. No one in the lobby would have suspected that she was a spy—and on her first mission.

Back in September, Griffith had joined the Office of Strategic Services (OSS) in New York, stating that she was anxious for a job that would help the war effort. A brother was aboard a submarine in the Pacific; another brother was a fighter pilot based in England.

A week later, the fashion model began her espionage training in a rambling old house thirty miles outside Washington, D.C. She was given the code name Tiger and warned not to disclose her true name to others in the school, known as the Farm.

Along with twenty-eight men, she completed a rigorous mental and phys-ical course designed to convert civilians into effective cloak-and-dagger opera-tives. Then she was escorted into a room to meet with an OSS official who identified himself only by his code name, Jupiter.

"The mission you have been selected for is vital," the man said in almost a whisper. "A contact inside the Gestapo in Berlin has informed us that a crack Nazi agent has been sent to Madrid with the task of uncovering Allied plans for our invasion of southern France, code-named Anvil. It is scheduled to hit in late June, about two weeks after the invasion of Normandy." (Later the code name for the southern France invasion would be changed to Dragoon, and the landings would take place in mid-August 1944).

Jupiter added that the mole in Berlin had provided the names of four people in Madrid, one of whom, the agent believed, was the head of an espi-onage network operating in neutral Spain. "All of these suspects move in inter-national high-society circles, so we believe you can fit right into that group," he told the young woman.

Tiger's cover would be as an employee of an oil mission of the United States, a legitimate business organization whose manager in Madrid was secretly cooperating with the OSS.

Now, after having reached Madrid, Tiger reported for work at the oil mis-sion, where she was contacted by an OSS agent code-named Mozart who had an office there. He told her that he was the only one in Madrid who knew of her precise mission to unmask the Gestapo spy. Her task had been given the code name Bullfight.

Then Mozart handed Tiger a piece of paper and told her to memorize the names of the four suspects identified by the mole in Berlin: Prince Niko-laus Lilienthal, a Czech citizen who was a friend of Reichsführer Heinrich Himmler, the notorious chief of the Gestapo; Countess Gloria von Fürsten-berg, a friend of top Gestapo leaders in Germany who was living expensively in Madrid with no known means of financial support; Ramón Serrano-Suner, the brother-in-law of Spanish dictator Generalissimo Francisco Franco and a friend of Adolf Hitler; and Hans Lazaar, press attaché at the German Embassy in Madrid.

Vivacious, well-educated, and stylishly dressed, Tiger was rapidly accepted into Madrid's society whirl. She was invited to lavish balls and dinners, meet-ing the crème de la crème of the Spanish upper class and influential persons from Germany, Italy, and other nations.

Tiger felt like a full-fledged spy involved in a deadly game of wits. In her purse, she carried a small Beretta pistol and a cigarette lighter that was actually a camera. Also in her handbag were some "L" pills that were poisonous. If trapped, she could bite into a pill and be dead in seconds. The intelligence she gathered was sent to Washington on a high-powered transmitter operated by OSS men in the attic of the U.S. Embassy in Madrid.

In late July 1944, with the Allies ashore in Normandy and time running out to unmask the Nazi agent whose mission was to uncover the date and place of the pending invasion of southern France, Tiger received a telephone call from an OSS agent code-named Edmundo, with whom she had been working. In an excited tone, he asked if he could pick her up at midnight for a highly important task.

Several hours later, the two agents were driving through the deserted streets of Madrid. Edmundo halted the car before a building at 14 Calle Hermosilia. Only now did he make a comment about the trip. Someone had given him a tip. Both climbed out of the automobile and pulled out their pistols. The street was enveloped by darkness.

In seconds, Edmundo picked the front door lock, and the pair crept silently down a long, dark hallway, then up rickety stairs to the third floor. A thin crack of light seeped from the bottom of a closed door. Again the lock-picking. Edmundo slowly turned the knob and both agents burst inside. Two figures moved. "Halt or I'll shoot!" Edmundo called out.

Tiger caught sight of a familiar figure—Countess Gloria von Fürstenberg. She stood there, petrified. Next to her was her radio operator. In the corner was a huge transmitter, one capable of reaching Berlin.

Caught red-handed, the countess admitted that she was sending messages on the pending Allied invasion of southern France to the Gestapo in the German capital. "I had to do it," she weeped, "to earn money to feed and clothe my children."

"Such a devoted mother," Edmundo snarled, knowing that she had been living in style. "It tugs at my heartstrings."

Both the countess and the radio operator were taken into "protective custody," where they would remain until the Dragoon invasion.

A few days after the countess was unmasked, Tiger received another shock. Edmundo told her that an OSS agent code-named Pierre, a handsome, engaging young man with whom she had socialized and worked, was actually a double agent in the pay of the Abwehr. Edmundo disclosed that he had known the Spaniard was a double agent, so during the past three weeks he had fed him bits and pieces of information that indicated the southern France invasion would hit at the port of Marseilles.

Then Edmundo had arranged to parachute Pierre outside Marseilles with the ostensible mission of informing the French underground of the site of the Allied landings, knowing that Pierre would also pass that crucial information to the Abwehr in Berlin. Pierre would soon learn that he had been a dupe: Dragoon struck not at Marseilles, but along the French Riviera, far to the east, where the German defenders had been taken by total surprise.[7]

A Trojan Horse Ploy

ON THE MORNING OF JANUARY 14, 1944, Abwehr Major Hermann Sandel arrived at his office on Sophien Terrace in Hamburg and was handed an urgent message:

Hoerte, dass Eisenhower am 16, Januar in England eintreffen wird
(Heard that Eisenhower will arrive in England on January 16).

The sender of the signal was A.3725, Sandel's most productive spy in England, the young Dutchman Hans Hansen. This was Hansen's 935th message to Hamburg since the summer of 1940, when he had parachuted at night near Salisbury. Miraculously, perhaps, A.3725 had avoided capture, remained at large, and was sending a stream of intelligence over his Afu radio.

Good old A.3725. He had come through again. Major Sandel put this crucial intelligence on the G-Schreiber, the direct-line teletype, for distribution to Group 1 at Belinda, code name for Abwehr headquarters in Berlin.

Sandel had been hoodwinked—again. Hans Hansen had been captured soon after his arrival and "turned"—given a choice of being hanged or sending finely orchestrated intelligence bulletins back to Hamburg. The signal to Major Sandel that Eisenhower (code-named Overlord) was arriving in London to take charge of the invasion of Normandy was calculated to strengthen Hansen's credibility with the Abwehr. What harm could result from it? Two days later, Adolf Hitler and the entire world would be let in on the "secret."

From the moment Supreme Commander Eisenhower had stepped off Bayonet, his private railroad coach that had whisked him to London, Operation Overlord began to dominate every aspect of the war against Nazi Germany. Despite having one of the most enormous strike forces that history had known, the cross-Channel assault would be a highly dangerous endeavor—almost a gamble.

Unless Hitler and his generals could be bamboozled about the date and place of the Normandy landings, the Allies could suffer a bloody debacle from which they might never recover. So the game of grand illusion began. A nebulous smokescreen was put up, behind which the Germans were allowed to suspect feverish preparations for an invasion somewhere in Western Europe. The goal was to keep the Germans confused and cause them to spread their forces along a two-thousand-mile front, from Norway in the north all the way to the Spanish border in the south.

In March 1944, Allied deception artists sprang a Trojan Horse machination on the Germans. According to ancient Greek legends, a war between Troy and the Greeks continued for ten years outside the walls of the city of Troy. Then the Greeks thought of a way to enter the city. They built a large wooden

Original Trojan Horse.
U.S. "Trojan Horse," B-29
bomber. (U.S. Air Force)

horse, told the Trojans that it was a gift for the goddess Athena and sailed away. At night, the Trojans opened a huge gate, and brought in the horse. Out of it leaped a group of Greek soldiers, who opened the gate. Meanwhile, the Greek fleet returned and the soldiers charged through the opening and captured Troy.

The modern-day Trojan horse, a brand-new B-29 Superfortress bomber, was flown from the United States to Bovington Airfield in England. The huge plane had a wingspan forty feet wider, was twenty-five feet longer, and was twice as heavy as the B-17 Flying Fortresses and B-24 Liberators the U.S. Eighth Air Force, based in England, was using on bombing missions.

Although the B-29 long-range bombers were being built in the United States for missions against the Japanese in the Pacific, the sudden appearance of the Superfortress in England was to coerce German intelligence into believing that the monster planes that could reach almost any point in Europe were to be used against the Third Reich.

Allied deception artists went through a rigamarole of appearing to be hiding the huge airplane. But to make certain that its presence reached Berlin, the Spanish military attaché in London, who was known to send regular reports to German intelligence through Madrid, was told about the B-29 by a "drunk" British officer at a reception.

At a time when the Germans could have been concentrating on realistic measures to thwart a looming Allied invasion, the Trojan Horse with wings resulted in much reshuffling of German air defenses and a great deal of wasteful activity trying to learn more about this new Allied threat to Hitler's stolen empire.[8]

A Cherbourg Priest Plays Kickball

ONE OF THE MOST EFFICIENT and bold underground *réseaux* (networks) in France was Centurie, covering 125 miles of the English Channel coast in Normandy. The spy apparatus consisted mostly of amateur agents—farmers, housewives, doctors, lawyers, truck drivers, plumbers, train conductors, mechanics, government officials, merchants, secretaries, and policemen.

No one in Centurie had an inkling that one day, powerful Allied forces would storm ashore at five Normandy beaches. Most of the spies risked their lives and were sustained in their endeavors by religious faith and a fierce resolve to rid their beloved France of the German oppressors—the hated Boche.

Likewise, Centurie's spies had no way of knowing that the Allied high command in London regarded Cherbourg in Normandy as the most important port in the world. Unless the Americans landing at Utah, the closest beach, twenty-five miles to the south, could rapidly capture Cherbourg to bring in reinforcements, guns, tanks, artillery, ammunition, vehicles, and fuel, the Allies would be in danger of withering on the vine and being cut to pieces by German panzers converging on the Normandy beachhead.

In Berlin, Adolf Hitler was fully aware that a major port near the landing beaches was crucial to the Allies, so he designated each port along the English Channel a fortress and ordered their commanders to fight to the last man and the last bullet if need be.

Although the Germans and the French sensed that time was nearing for the great invasion, life had to go on in Cherbourg. One morning in March 1944, several German sentries looked on casually as a black-cassocked Catholic priest enthusiastically engaged in an impromptu game of kickball with eight or ten youngsters a short distance from the waterfront. There was much laughter and shouting. The boys were happy to have a revered priest playing ball with them in the street.

Whatever his ecclesiastical talents, the perspiring priest obviously was not skilled at kickball. He drew back his foot and gave the oval a terrific—and errant—boot. The ball sailed past the youngsters and headed directly for a concrete-enclosed gun position some forty yards away.

"I'll get it!" the man of the cloth shouted, apparently embarrassed that he had performed so ineptly. He chased the ball all the way to the gun position, where it had rolled. Now the German guards, who had been lulled into inattention, suddenly realized that an unathorized person was trotting into the large-caliber gun position in pursuit of an errant ball.

"*Verboten! Verboten!*" the alarmed Feldgrau yelled as they ran after the priest, frantically waving their arms.

By this time, the clergyman had reached the ball. After pausing to presumably catch his breath, he picked up the oval and started back with it, apologizing profusely for unwittingly intruding into a forbidden area.

Minutes later, the priest concluded his strenuous athletic activity and began to walk away. He was approached by two strangers in civilian garb and took them to be French, but he could not be certain. They might be German agents. One of the strangers said to the man in the flowing black robe, "We know you're not a priest."

"Why, I don't know what you're talking about," the kickball player replied. "Of course I'm a priest."

"Look, we don't know who you are, but you're not a priest. You'd better get the hell out of here before the Gestapo grabs you!"

A flash of concern spread across the face of the man with the backward white collar. Indeed he was masquerading as a priest. He was a Centurie agent whose assigned perilous task had been to get a closer look at the German gun position and report the caliber of the weapon and its firing direction.

Before rapidly departing, the "priest" was curious. "Tell me, how did you *know* I'm not a priest?" he inquired of the two strangers.

Pointing toward his feet, one of the men replied, "Because those bright red socks of yours stick out like two beacons in the night!"[9]

History's Most Incredible Impersonation

OPERATION OVERLORD, the cross-Channel invasion of Normandy, would be launched in a few weeks. The mighty endeavor was backed by the industrial muscle of the United States and Great Britain. For two years, the sharpest military minds had been developing the plan. Yet pessimism was rampant in London's stately Grosvenor Square, the location of Supreme Headquarters, Allied Expeditionary Force (SHAEF).

Fifty-four-year-old Supreme Commander Dwight D. Eisenhower, who had been an obscure American staff colonel in Texas less than three years earlier, told a friend in the Pentagon by a scrambler telephone, "This will not be just another battle. All the chips will be on the table!"

As March turned into April 1944 and the lush meadows of England were putting on their finest greenery, Prime Minister Winston S. Churchill, the British Bulldog, exclaimed in a moment of gloom, "Why are we trying to do *this*?"

Churchill's closest military confidant, Field Marshal Alan Brooke, whose courage had been legendary in World War I when he earned a chestful of medals, scrawled in his diary: "I am very uneasy about this whole operation. At the best, it will come very short of expectations. At its worst, it well may be the most ghastly disaster of the whole war."

British Lieutenant General Frederick E. Morgan, who had laid the groundwork for the Overlord plan, held an equally dark view: "If the Germans have even a forty-eight-hour advance notice of the time and place of the [Normandy] landings, we could suffer a monstrous defeat!"

Seven weeks before Overlord was scheduled to be launched in the first week of June, British Lieutenant Colonel J. V. B. Jervis-Reid, second in command of SHAEF's Special Means Committee (whose mission was to deceive the Germans), was perusing the *News Chronicle* when he spotted a head-and-shoulders photo of a man in army uniform wearing a beret. The caption stated: "You're wrong! His name is Lieutenant Clifton James."

James was a dead ringer for British General Bernard L. Montgomery, who would be in command of ground forces for Overlord. The striking resemblance hatched in Jervis-Reid's nimble mind a scheme that could play a major role in grossly misleading the Germans about Overlord.

James prided himself on being "history's oldest lieutenant." He had been a stage actor for twenty-five years before volunteering his services as an entertainer when the war had broken out. Instead of being assigned to that logical function, James was given a commission in the Royal Army Pay Corps, where, by his own admission, he was a "royal misfit."

Late one morning, the telephone rang at the desk of Lieutenant James in the Pay Corps office in Leicester, England. "This is Colonel Niven of the Army Kinematograph section," a pleasant voice said. "Would you be interested in making some army films?"

James immediately recognized the voice of the caller: the celebrated British and Hollywood movie actor David Niven. "Yes, sir!" James almost shouted. "I most certainly would."

"Good," Niven responded. "Come to London for a screen test as soon as you can."

James replaced the receiver. He was elated. Now maybe the army was going to correct its mistake in assigning him to the Pay Corps.

That was the beginning of one of history's most incredible impersonations, one that conceivably would bamboozle Adolf Hitler and save countless Allied lives on D-Day in Normandy.

Upon reporting to a designated building in London, James was taken in tow by British cloak-and-dagger agents. Soon he received the jolt of his life: he had been chosen to act as a double for the folk hero General Bernard Montgomery.

On closer scrutiny, it appeared that the impersonation, code-named Copperhead, would have to be scrapped. Montgomery was a teetotaler, and James, it was found, had periodic bouts with John Barleycorn and lost nearly all of them. Moreover, there was a sharp personality gulf between the general and the lieutenant. Montgomery was arrogant and self-assured; James, despite his quarter-century on the stage, came across as meek, uncertain, even introverted.

However, after lengthy discussions, SHAEF's Special Means Committee decided to pursue the project. Perhaps the specter of piles of Allied bodies sprawled on Normandy beaches reminded them of the crucial need to mislead the Germans on the time and place of the invasion.

Clifton James (masquerading as Montgomery) would be paraded around Gibraltar, the British Crown Colony at the entrance to the Mediterranean Sea, and Algiers, in North Africa. The scheme was to pile up credible evidence that Monty—who had already been widely trumpeted as the ground forces leader for Overlord—had left his post in England for a different part of the world. The machination was to imply to German intelligence that a cross-Channel invasion was not imminent, or even to suggest that the preparation for a Normandy invasion was a gigantic hoax and that the Allies would land in southern France, five hundred miles away.

James promptly broke out with a severe case of stage fright. He had been a teenage private in World War I and had retained a schoolboy fear of senior officers. Now he was to impersonate the most popular British general of them all.

The first move was to separate Clifton James from both his bottle and his wife. Then, hour after hour, the need for total secrecy was pounded into his head by his stage managers. Any action that might betray him as a Monty double could jeopardize Overlord. James became even more jittery, and he was leery of talking to anyone—even his coaches.

"You should look on all this as a play in which you are starring for the benefit of Adolf Hitler and his generals," James was told. "We have to hoodwink the German high command."

In the days ahead, James was tutored relentlessly for his role of a lifetime. Endlessly, it seemed, James studied newspaper photographs and watched newsreels of the general. Officers drilled him in hundreds of details of the impersonation, including Monty's idiosyncrasies, of which there was no shortage.

Finally, as a sort of graduation test, the Pay Corps lieutenant was assigned to Montgomery's staff in the guise of an Intelligence Corps sergeant, and for several days he watched the general like a hawk, trying to catch his fleeting expressions, his characteristic walk with hands clasped behind his back, and the way he pinched his cheek when thinking. James was finally convinced that he could impersonate Monty as far as voice, gestures, and mannerisms went. Fortunately for the masquerade, both men had the same relatively short, wiry build.

Next, the Pay Corps officer was taken to Myer and Mortimer, military tailors in London, and was outfitted in an elegant battle dress with the scarlet gorgets of the Imperial General Staff, epaulets holding a general's crossed swords, five rows of decorations and ribbons, a black beret, a gold chain and fob, and a few handkerchiefs with the initials BLM. A makeup artist, sworn to secrecy, trimmed James's mustache a shade, brushed up his eyebrows to make them bristle like Montgomery's, and applied a touch of hair color to his temples to make them appear slightly more gray. The Copperhead controllers beamed over the finished product. The likeness between General Bernard Montgomery and Clifton James was amazing.

One haunting specter gripped the coaches: since Monty never drank or smoked or even permitted others to do so in his presence, what if James were to get hold of a bottle before his public debut as Montgomery and come out reeling and reeking of alcohol?

Meanwhile, far to the south, Copperhead agents were busy planting rumors around the Mediterranean that Montgomery might be coming to take command of an invasion of Southern France.

At 6:30 P.M. on May 25, 1944, the curtain rose on the Copperhead stage show. Clifton James donned his general's battle dress and black beret with its Armored Corps badge. Followed by a real brigadier, two real captains, and two phony aides, James strolled briskly out the door of headquarters to his waiting Rolls-Royce, which was flying Monty's pennant.

A large crowd had gathered, and a rousing cheer echoed across the landscape. James flashed the brilliant Monty smile and the famous Monty salute. Shouts of "Good old Monty!" rang out. Paced by two motorcycle policemen and trailed by three cars with assorted military functionaries, the Rolls drove through the streets of London, where cheers and shouts greeted the legendary general.

At Northolt airport there were more crowds. Undercover men strolled through the gathering and passed remarks that the general was bound for North Africa. The imposter boarded Prime Minister Winston Churchill's private airplane and, moments later, took off on the overnight flight to Gibraltar.

Neither of James's "aides" was aware that he had concealed a pint flask of gin in his handbag. After those on board had settled in for the night, James went to the toilet in the rear of the plane. Later, an escort missed him and hurried to the rear—just in time to find James swigging the bottle. The flask was empty.

When the airplane was but two hours from Gibraltar, James was still inebriated. If he arrived in that condition, the entire stratagem would be blown.

Actor Clifton James (right) hoodwinked the Germans with his impersonation of General Bernard Montgomery (left). (National Archives)

So a crash program was initiated to sober him up. Treatments included forcing him to vomit and holding his face to the icy slipstream coming through the plughole in a cabin window. Then James was slapped, massaged, and finally stripped naked and doused with cold water.

When the aircraft landed at Gibraltar, "General Montgomery" was sober. After brief welcoming ceremonies and a review of the guard of honor, James was driven through the streets of Gibraltar town while throngs of civilians watched the procession. There were more crowds at Governor House, where Ralph Eastwood, governor-general of Gibraltar and an old friend of Montgomery, smiled and held out his hand: "Hello, Monty, it's good to see you again." Eastwood had been briefed on just enough of Copperhead to put on a convincing act. Inside Governor House, General Eastwood stared in astonishment at James. "I can't get over it!" he exclaimed. "You *are* Monty!"

That evening, Eastwood gave a small party and introduced "Montgomery" to a pair of prominent Spanish bankers, one of whom was known to have contact with German intelligence. "General Montgomery," a talkative chap, twice let slip remarks about "Plan 303," presumably code for a pending invasion of southern France. Each time, General Eastwood, playing his role to the hilt, tugged gently at James's sleeve, and he abruptly changed the subject.

The two Copperhead "aides" hovered over James like mother hens, alert to make certain that he did not reach for the cocktails that servants were carrying around the room on trays. That night, searching James's luggage for alcoholic contraband, they locked him in his bedroom and stood guard outside the door.

"Montgomery's" departure from Gibraltar was much like his arrival. Bayonets flashed in the sun and a flight of Spitfires zoomed low overhead, dipping their wings in salute.

In order to buy time for a sizeable crowd to gather, the scenario called for the prime minister's airplane to develop a minor engine gremlin. Eastwood and James went to the airport restaurant for a cup of tea and within earshot of Spanish employees, "Montgomery" began talking once more about the mysterious Plan 303. When the pair departed, James had left behind a handkerchief embroidered with the initials BLM.

Within a few hours after James had reached Gibraltar, German intelligence in Berlin knew of his presence. Orders were flashed to German agents throughout the Mediterranean: "At all costs, find nature of Plan 303."

When James's airplane touched down at Maison Blanche airfield in Algiers, he was greeted by hulking British General Henry M. "Jumbo" Wilson, Allied commander in the Mediterranean. After the usual pomp and circumstance attendant to the arrival of a distinguished warrior, James was driven to the ornate St. George Hotel and ensconced in a plush suite once occupied by General Dwight Eisenhower when Algiers had been his headquarters.

For the next few days, there were official receptions, guards of honor, pep talks to troops, and cheering crowds of civilian spectators—no doubt with German agents among them. James's car sped to and fro as though he were heading to urgent meetings. British intelligence reported that the Algiers region was buzzing with talk about the presence of the famous General Montgomery.

Suddenly, "Montgomery" vanished from the Mediterranean. His job was done—and Copperhead coaches did not want to stretch their luck. Dressed in his lieutenant's uniform, James was smuggled out the back door of Jumbo Wilson's headquarters at night, flown to Cairo, put up in a small room under guard, and kept there until the Normandy invasion.

When Lieutenant Clifton James finally returned to his regular job in the Royal Army Pay Corps, colleagues speculated that he had been off on a five-week drunk.[10]

"Black Radio" Blackmails Germans

ENGLAND WAS GRIPPED by invasion fever. Supreme Allied Commander Dwight D. Eisenhower had at his beck and call the mightiest ground, sea, and air force ever assembled. More than half of his three million soldiers were American, while British and Canadian troops jointly totaled one million. It was late May 1944. The cross-Channel assault against Normandy was less than two weeks away.

Only a few hundred miles away in the Paris suburb of Saint-Germain, aging Feldmarschall Karl Rudolf Gerd von Rundstedt, Oberbefehlshaber Westen (supreme commander in the West), was poring over air reconnaissance photos and reports that disclosed heavy night road traffic in southern England across from Normandy. It seemed clear to the man known in Germany as "the Last of the Prussians" that the Allies would strike soon.

Meanwhile, German counterintelligence officers in the West filed a report that stated that a bogus radio station known as Soldatensender Calais was causing considerable unrest and confusion among German servicemen along the English Channel by broadcasting about the military situation and conditions in the Fatherland.

Every night at 6:00 P.M., with a roll of drums and a blaring of trumpets, a boisterous German march would burst from radio sets tuned to the station. Then, in crisp German, an announcer would say: "Here is the Soldiers' Radio Calais, broadcasting on wavebands 360 meters 410 and 492 meters. We bring news and music for comrades in the command areas West."

Soldatensender Calais (so named because it ostensibly was broadcast from the German-occupied French port of Calais on the English Channel) actually was based outside London. It was the brainchild of thirty-five-year-old Sefton "Tom" Delmer, who had spent several years in Germany as a bureau chief for a British newspaper before the war. He spoke fluent German and had interviewed most of the Nazi bigwigs.

The objective of the black radio operation was to subtly taunt and subvert the German fighting men and the homefront, to make them disillusioned with the Nazi regime.

Soldatensender Calais was a component of the black propaganda campaign conceived and orchestrated by Great Britain's Political Warfare Executive (PWE), a clandestine group that was based at Bush House in London and at Woburn Abbey, a large estate in the English countryside.

What especially disturbed the German command in the West was the fact that Soldatensender Calais was broadcasting verbatim accounts actually sent out by the official German news service over Radio Deutschland in Munich. The fact that the black radio outlet was scooping the Germans on their own newscasts strengthened the British operation's credibility with its audience.

When Great Britain had declared war on Adolf Hitler's regime on September 3, 1939, the London correspondent of an official German newspaper departed from England in such a hurry that he had left behind his Hellschreiber (teleprinter). Unaware that the British had the Hellschreiber, Josef Goebbels, Hitler's propaganda genius, continued using the machine to send news throughout Germany and the countries it had overrun. So Sefton Delmer was able to receive the German news agency's bulletins at the same time as did German radio stations and newspapers. Because Delmer's staff was quicker—

and speed was important—Soldatensender Calais was usually able to broadcast the pirated news first, often giving its own desired slant.

Delmer acquired much of his information for Soldatensender Calais from prisoners of war, the German newspapers, Allied intelligence, and undercover sources, along with Royal Air Force photographic reconnaissance flights of the damage inflicted by bombing raids on Reich cities.

It was crucial, Delmer knew, for the broadcast information to anxious German soldiers manning the ramparts along the English Channel to be extremely accurate. Should the servicemen find that their neighborhoods had not been severely damaged as claimed, Soldatensender Calais would suffer a credibility loss.

So meticulous were the black radio reports on the damage to German cities that even the streets where carnage had occurred were named. This incredible achievement was made possible by high-flying RAF Mosquito planes taking photographs almost as soon as a bombing mission was completed. These prints were rushed to Delmer at his studio, where a special team of experts used stereoscopic viewers and shelves full of maps and Baedeker street guides of European cities to analyze the bomb damage.

Not all the Soldatensender Calais broadcasts were aimed at the Wehrmacht and the Reich homefront. Delmer decided that businessmen in neutral nations who continued to cash in by trading with Germany would make excellent targets. British undercover agents in Stockholm learned that a Swedish firm was smuggling ball bearings into Germany. Ball bearings were crucial to a modern mechanized military force.

Delmer obtained exhaustive details about the Swedish firm from the Ministry of Economic Warfare. Then his broadcasts, which were picked up all over western Europe, zeroed in on the firm and named its top officials. The comments were caustic and obscene. A few weeks later, Delmer received an urgent bulletin at his desk: the Swedish firm had informed Berlin that it could no longer do business with the Third Reich.

"Blackmail by black radio!" Delmer chortled.

Perhaps the Soldatensender Calais broadcasts "softened" the morale of the German forces defending Normandy. But after the Allied invasion struck on June 6, 1944, the radio station had its most productive era.

On June 11, the genuine nephew of General Werner von Fritsch, former commander in chief of the German army who had been railroaded from his job in disgrace by Adolf Hitler, spoke on the air with the intonations of a proper Prussian aristocrat. He had fled Nazi Germany and was now a member of Delmer's team.

"Fellow Germans," the younger Fritsch said, "this is an epitaph and a warning. An epitaph for the comrades of our division that was cut off on the beaches of Ouistreham and Arromanches [in Normandy], who were left in the lurch by Adolf Hitler and hammered to death.

"Only a couple of men made it back to tell the tale. What these comrades have to tell us must be a warning to everyone. It is a warning to all those who may be lying in an outpost somewhere along the [Normandy] beaches, or are stationed somewhere up on a hill. And as you lie there you may get the order, 'Hold on, reinforcements are on the way to you.' The reinforcements will not come. Nothing is being done about sending reinforcements, because all of you men have been written off—written off as dead and lost."

Intelligence reaching London indicated that the black radio broadcasts were having an impact on German forces in the West. "Officers must tell their men about the [station's] pack of lies," a Wehrmacht report stated. "German soldiers must remain untouched by it. We are too pure spiritually to be concerned with such dirt."

Because of such widespread and angry reaction to the broadcast of Soldatensender Calais, it seemed logical to conclude that the station had a large audience in the German armed forces, and that it played its part in the ultimate Allied victory.[11]

A Nazi Campaign
to Defeat Roosevelt

SHORTLY BEFORE 3:00 P.M., the new heavy cruiser *Baltimore* churned into sight of Hawaii's majestic Diamond Head. The sleek warship was bringing President Franklin D. Roosevelt to a crucial meeting with his two top commanders in the Pacific, General Douglas MacArthur and Admiral Chester Nimitz, to settle a dispute on the future strategic course to defeat Japan. It was July 26, 1944.

Roosevelt's six-thousand-mile safari from Washington, D.C., was not viewed with approval by some of his military brass, notably Admiral Ernest B. King, the chief of naval operations, whom the president called the Big Bear for his large frame and gruff disposition.

Noting that Roosevelt had left most of his top generals and admirals behind in the capital and taken along only a speechwriter and a "publicist," King labeled the trip a political stunt to help Roosevelt's November election campaign, a grueling trek to impress on the voters that he was the commander in chief and on top of matters in the war.

After the *Baltimore* docked, General MacArthur, accused by some for his "theatrics," arrived late and stood up in his limousine to acknowledge the cheers of the thousands of Hawaiians who had turned out for the historic meeting with Roosevelt.

After the famed general had walked regally up the gangplank, he strode over to the seated Roosevelt, who had been crippled by polio at thirty-nine years of age. The two men had not seen one another in seven years, since before the war, and MacArthur held the president in low regard. But they beamed at one another and shook hands warmly.

"It's good to see you, Doug!" Roosevelt exclaimed. Few were ever that familiar with the general. Presumably, it was a subtle means of reminding his commander in the Southwest Pacific that a "boss" has the right to call an "employee" by his first name.

"Thank you, Mr. President," MacArthur replied. "It's good to see you, too!"

Later, MacArthur asked Roosevelt what he thought of his chances in the approaching November election against Republican Thomas E. Dewey, the governor of New York.

"I've been too busy to think about politics," the president replied.

MacArthur, knowing that the presidency *is* politics, laughed loudly.

Breaking into a wide grin, Roosevelt declared, "I'll beat that son of a bitch in Albany if it's the last thing I do!"

Roosevelt already had held the office of president of the United States longer than any other man, in spite of a strong tradition that no president should serve more than two terms. In 1940, with much of Europe in a bloody war and America threatened, Roosevelt had been elected to a third term, and now he was seeking yet another four years in the nation's highest office.

His latest bid for the White House received heavy criticism, mainly from the conservative media. Senator Burton K. Wheeler complained that Roosevelt would become a dictator and that his election to a fourth term would leave Congress with "no more authority than the German Reichstag [Adolf Hitler's rubber-stamp legislative branch]!"

Not all of Roosevelt's detractors were homegrown. A staunch foe was in far-off Berlin. Adolf Hitler told confidants that Roosevelt was the one man he did not want to see reelected because "he will ruin us." The führer ordered "all possible efforts" to be made to prevent the three-term U.S. president from winning at the polls.

Hitler had a long hatred for Roosevelt. In countless speeches, the führer had angrily blamed the president, "the Jews, and the millionaires" for igniting the war. The German leader's fury had intensified after Roosevelt and British Prime Minister Winston S. Churchill announced in early 1943 that the Allies would accept from Germany "only unconditional surrender."

If the hated American could be defeated at the polls in November, Thomas Dewey might adopt a more moderate stance toward the Third Reich, a hope for which there was no basis in fact.

Now, on the heels of Hitler's order, Foreign Minister Joachim von Ribbentrop, who had been the mastermind of several of the führer's bloodless "annexations" of countries prior to the eruption of a shooting war, organized a special group to pursue the mission. Its members were to launch a barrage of

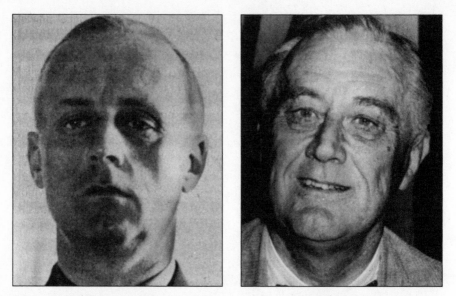

German Foreign Minister Joachim von Ribbentrop (left) orchestrated a global campaign to defeat President Roosevelt's bid for a fourth term. (National Archives)

vilifying personal attacks against Roosevelt in the neutral capitals of the world—a scoundrel, a deceiver, a drunk, a warmonger. The idea was that these abusive charges would be picked up by reporters and published in the American press.

This global machination was but one step in the plan to smear Roosevelt and send him back to his family estate at Hyde Park, up the Hudson River from New York City.

Two months after the anti-Roosevelt campaign began picking up steam, Ribbentrop sent a top-secret dispatch to German embassies in neutral capitals with orders to destroy the document immediately after it had been read. It stated that a "careful and energetic" effort had been in progress around the world to thwart Roosevelt's "grasp" for a fourth term. The foreign minister instructed the Nazi diplomats to send Berlin "precise information" on the impression that the endeavor was making in their respective locales.

Moreover, Ribbentrop wanted the diplomats to pump any prominent native who might have just returned from the United States about the mood of the American people and Roosevelt's prospects for being voted into office for the fourth time.

After a bitter campaign between Roosevelt and Dewey in which the Democrat's slogan was "don't change horses in midstream," the incumbent carried most of the big, heavily populated states and won handily. Hitler's global campaign had failed.

Franklin Roosevelt never lived to see the war's end. On April 12, 1945, just eighty-three days after he had been sworn into office for the fourth time, he died at his retreat in Warm Springs, Georgia. A few weeks later, Adolf Hitler, the man who had tried to defeat Roosevelt at the U.S. polls, was also dead, having killed himself in Berlin when the Soviets were only a few blocks from his bunker.[12]

Operation Ferdinand Bamboozles Germans

IN JULY 1944, six weeks after the Allies had stormed ashore in Normandy and carved a beachhead, frantic preparations were underway in Italy and elsewhere in the Mediterranean to launch an invasion of southern France, code-named Dragoon. It was the worst-kept secret of the war, maybe of any war.

The Allied high command could not conceal the one thousand vessels of all shapes and sizes assembled at ten Mediterranean ports. Nor could some three thousand warplanes collected at many airports be hidden. The looming operation was being discussed openly in the fashionable restaurants and sleazy bars in Rome and Naples.

Prime Minister Winston S. Churchill had vigorously opposed Dragoon and told confidants: "It may well be another bloody Anzio!"

If General Johannes Blaskowitz, leader of Army Group G and defender of southern France, were to learn or deduce the true Dragoon landing beaches along the Riviera, he could concentrate his forces and possibly drive the invaders back into the Mediterranean Sea. Consequently, invasion planners in Naples hatched an intricate sea-and-air scheme to hoodwink the Germans about the true landing beaches.

Preceded by a heavy airborne assault inland, the amphibious forces would go ashore along a forty-five-mile stretch of the Côte d'Azur (the Riviera), the targeted beaches being east of the German-held major port of Toulon. D-Day for Dragoon would be August 15, 1944, with the main amphibious assault to hit at 8:00 A.M.

The masquerade to deceive the Germans called for stirring up such a racket west of the actual landing beaches in the blackness of D-Day morning that General Blaskowitz would be confused about the true invasion site and hesitant to rush all of his reserves to confront the invaders.

Just before 2:00 A.M. on D-Day, U.S. Commander John D. Bulkeley was on the bridge of the destroyer *Endicott*, which was racing toward the bay at the small town of La Ciotat, a break in the rugged coast some sixty-five miles west of the nearest invasion beach. Bulkeley was in command of the deception operation, code-named Ferdinand.

Brash, cocky, and tough, the thirty-two-year-old Bulkeley had been a household name in the United States since the early weeks in the war in the

Pacific when he was a PT boat skipper and had rescued General Douglas MacArthur and his staff from Corregidor, a small rock island in Manila Bay that the Japanese had ringed. For his actions in those black days in the Pacific, Bulkeley had been awarded the Congressional Medal of Honor and every other decoration for valor the nation had to offer, some of them twice.

After two tours of duty in the Pacific, Bulkeley had led a flotilla of PT boats and minesweepers that spearheaded the assault on Utah Beach in Normandy, and now he was assigned a deception mission that might decide the outcome of Dragoon.

In the blackness of the Mediterranean, Bulkeley peered to both sides and to the stern, instinctively seeking a glimpse of the eight PT boats and seven motor launches in his tiny decoy flotilla. But he could not discern even dim silhouettes, because the vessels were spread over an area eight miles wide and twelve miles long. This small naval force was streaming reflector balloons to confuse German radar about its true size.

Since before midnight, the hazy night air in the La Ciotat region had been filled with the sounds of Allied engines as warplanes pounded ancient Marseilles, Toulon, and German installations around La Ciotat, being careful not to destroy the German radar station on a hill at the mouth of La Ciotat Bay. Four other Wehrmacht radar stations along the Marseilles-Toulon coastline had been knocked out, but this one was permitted to survive so it could pick up Commander Bulkeley's "fleet" as well as the swarms of Allied aircraft marauding about overhead in the darkness.

At 2:15 A.M., German technicians at the radar facility on the heights at Cap Sicie passed along an alarming report: a large Allied naval force had somehow infiltrated floating minefields in the mouth of La Ciotat Bay and was now steaming inside the harbor. This "large naval force" was Bulkeley's *Endicott* and fifteen small powerboats.

Adding to the ruse that convinced the Germans that Bulkeley's flotilla represented a formidable landing threat were three Corsica-based Wellington heavy bombers of the Royal Air Force. They had been circling over the little flotilla dropping "window," thin strips of a metallic substance that caused images to blur on enemy radar screens so that the precise number of vessels could not be counted.

Word of the looming landing at La Ciotat was flashed to German gun batteries along the coast between Marseilles and Toulon, and soon heavy concentrations of shells were splashing into the dark, placid waters of the bay. None of the projectiles hit Bulkeley's craft. After cavorting about in the harbor for nearly an hour, the phantom fleet dashed back to the open sea, its role in Ferdinand concluded.

At La Ciotat, a jubilant German commander promptly signaled a higher headquarters at Marseilles: "Attempted Allied landing beaten back!"

U.S. Navy Lieutenant Commander John D. Bulkeley (right),
with King George VI, before Bulkeley led Operation Ferdinand,
the machination that masked the true landing beaches in
southern France. (Courtesy Mrs. John D. Bulkeley)

Meanwhile, five C-47 transport planes flown by British pilots took off from an airfield outside Ajaccio, Corsica. The aircraft were loaded with parachutists in American garb. Flying due north toward Genoa, the flight suddenly altered its route and headed for La Ciotat, ninety miles to the west. In order to convey to German radar screens that the approaching flight was much larger, each C-47 flew at five-minute intervals, and air crews tossed out "window."

Flying at six hundred feet with a speed of 110 miles per hour, the lead C-47 knifed over the coastline near the La Ciotat radar station and was fired on by a German ack-ack battery. With other C-47s following on course, the aircraft headed for the drop zone between Rougiers and Signes, about fifteen miles north of Toulon.

At 3:49 A.M., the dark skies were awash with blossoming white parachutes as the fully equipped American parachutists drifted earthward. Immediately the cries echoed through the dark, rolling countryside: *"Fallschirmjaeger! Fallschirm-jaeger!"* (Paratroopers! Paratroopers!). Periodically, for twenty minutes, the invaders from the sky spilled out behind Hitler's South Wall until three hundred had landed.

German defenses were thrown into confusion by the airborne drop. Within minutes word was flashed up through the Wehrmacht chain of command. Hundreds of Allied paratroopers had landed north of Toulon. At each echelon the numbers were inflated, and by the time the report had filtered up to General Blaskowitz at Army Group G near Toulouse, *thousands* of enemy paratroopers had touched down.

A hodgepodge force of grenadiers had been rapidly thrown together in the Toulon region and dispatched inland at great speed with orders to wipe out the Allied paratrooper force that was a threat to Signes, where scores of collapsed white parachutes were strewn across the dark terrain. The Germans opened fire and were puzzled by the failure of the enemy airborne force to shoot back.

Charging the mass of white chutes, the Germans reached their quarry: three hundred lifelike rubber dummies dressed in precise replicas of helmets and other American paratrooper gear. Attached to each dummy were strings of firecrackers that had exploded on landing, conveying the impression to nervous Germans in the locale that an all-out firefight had erupted.

Curious to inspect the dummies, several German soldiers picked them up. There were sharp explosions followed by shrieks of pain from those whose hands had been blown off. The rubber figures had been booby-trapped.

The rubber-dummy hoax was the airborne component of Operation Ferdinand. As with Bulkeley's naval force in the La Ciotat Bay, the fake paratroopers were not expected to deceive the Wehrmacht for long, only to throw the Germans off-balance. Ferdinand was like a clever boxer who would feint a left hook to draw his opponent's attention in that direction before landing a haymaker with his right fist.

In the predawn period before H-Hour, a ghostly bank of mist hovered over the Riviera. Along these beaches of golden sand and tangled piles of rock, three of the U.S. Army's finest infantry divisions charged ashore on sectors unromantically labeled by Allied planners as Alpha, Delta, and Camel. Caught off-guard, the German defenders offered only spotty resistance. Operation Ferdinand had paid off big.[13]

Allies Ignore Battle
of the Bulge Warning

FRIENDS QUIPPED that Baron Hiroshi Oshima, the son of former Japanese war minister Kenichi Oshima, had been so closely associated with Germany throughout his career that he must be at least part German. In 1934, soon after Adolf Hitler had seized power, Lieutenant Oshima was sent to Berlin as an assistant military attaché. By 1938, he had reached the rank of lieutenant general and been appointed ambassador.

Cunning, intelligent, and affable, Oshima cultivated friendships with most of the top Nazis. Hitler trusted him to the point that over the years, he confided to his good friend the ambassador the most secret of German secrets. Each night,

Oshima transmitted to Tokyo over a radioteleprinter in a complex code, rambling dispatches that covered almost every word spoken to him by the führer and other Nazi leaders.

On September 4, 1944, Oshima had a long discussion with Hitler, who was quite upbeat even though the Allies had broken out of the Normandy beachhead and were racing eastward across France toward the border of the Third Reich. German forces, Hitler explained, were falling back behind the Siegfried Line, the concrete and steel fortification that stretched along the western frontier of Germany.

Hitler told Oshima that pulling back his armies behind the Siegfried Line would permit the battle situation to be "stabilized." Then he dropped a blockbuster. With most of the outside world—including the Allied high command headquarters in Paris—convinced that the Third Reich was on the brink of total defeat, Hitler said that he was organizing a new army of more than a million men, was reinforcing the Luftwaffe, and would combine these new forces with units to be withdrawn from "all possible areas." Then, he declared, he would open "a large-scale offensive in the West."

Hitler failed to tell his Japanese friend that a task force consisting of some of the Wehrmacht's most brilliant officers was already at work in Berlin, drawing up details of the offensive. It was code-named Wacht am Rein (Watch on the Rhine) to convey the impression that it was a strictly defensive plan to ward off looming catastrophe.

In reply to Oshima's question, the führer said he would have his mammoth attack ready to kick off in November (it would later be postponed until December 16, 1944).

Baron Oshima did not know that American cryptologists had broken the Japanese diplomatic code. When he began sending his lengthy report to Tokyo about Hitler's looming German offensive against the Allies (it would become known to the Allied world as the Battle of the Bulge), the ambassador had an eavesdropper. At about the same time that his copious coded messages reached Tokyo, they had been intercepted at a top-secret United States monitoring post in the unlikely locale of Asmara, Ethiopia.

After the Asmara post, staffed by three hundred technicians, acquired the raw intercepts from Oshima's radioteleprinter in Berlin, hundreds of miles to the north, the communication was enciphered and sent by radioteleprinter to two stations in the United States, one near Washington, D.C., and the other on a Virginia estate fifty miles outside the capital. After the intercepts from Asmara had been decoded, the secret reports were circulated to fewer than twenty government and military leaders, including the Allied supreme commander, General Dwight D. Eisenhower, at his headquarters in France.

By the time December rolled around, Eisenhower and his aides had apparently forgotten or discounted the first-person, play-by-play account by

General Oshima of Adolf Hitler's roll of the dice for victory or a negotiated peace in the West. When Wacht am Rein struck just before dawn on December 16, it achieved total surprise.[14]

Polish Underground Steals Hitler's Secret Weapon

IN LATE AUGUST and early September 1944, while Allied armies were racing eastward across France toward the German border after breaking out of the stagnant Normandy beachhead, near panic was gripping a handful of top British authorities and scientists. They knew that London was about to be struck by a rain of V-2 missiles, Adolf Hitler's terrifying new secret weapon.

One haunting specter dominated discussions by Prime Minister Winston S. Churchill and his staff: there was no defense against the missile barrage with which Hitler planned to smash London into a charred pile of rubble and force the Allies to seek a negotiated peace with Nazi Germany.

As a result of an epic espionage coup by the underground of Poland, British scientists knew that the V-2 was shaped like a fat cigar, was forty-seven feet long, weighed thirteen tons, and carried a one-ton warhead capable of leveling an entire block of buildings. Huge for the era, the projectile could attain a height of ninety miles and such enormous speed (990 miles per hour) that those on the receiving end would not hear it approaching.

As far back as November 1943, the Polish underground had been sending reports to London about mysterious activities taking place at the remote village of Blizna, which had been cleared of Polish civilians. German army men began arriving in droves. Ack-ack guns and powerful searchlights ringed the site.

Then a railroad spur connecting Blizna with the outside world was rapidly consructed, and tightly sealed freight cars carrying unknown cargoes arrived each day. The Germans named the facility the *Artillerie-Zielfeld Blizna* (Blizna Artillery Training Ground).

Early in 1944 Polish secret agents, who had been snooping around the fringes of the facility, suddenly heard a loud boom and looked up to see a strange sight in the sky—an enormous projectile trailing a fiery plume. A few days later an underground member, using a small, cheap camera, took a picture of another missile as it swooshed skyward from the center of the forest. The clandestine photo was rushed to London, where British intelligence officers greeted the image with deep concern.

A few days later, one daring Pole noticed a German freight train (whose cars were marked "dry goods") halted at a siding on the edge of the test center. At grave risk, he sneaked up to one open car and saw that it contained some sort of long object covered by tarpaulins. Glancing around nervously, he peeled back a corner of the tarp and saw a gigantic projectile shaped something like a torpedo. A sketch was drawn from his observation, and within hours it was being studied in London.

Then in May 1944, as Allied armies were preparing to assault Normandy from England, another Polish underground warrior pulled off a startling espionage bonanza. Somehow he had managed to draw a detailed and nearly perfect scaled map of the entire Blizna missile-testing grounds. This, too, was rushed to London.

Now an alarmed British intelligence sent an urgent request to the secret Polish underground headquarters in Warsaw: Could the Poles send key parts of a thirteen-ton V-2? It was an outrageous request. Blizna was so tightly guarded by SS troops that the British might as well have asked the Poles to smuggle out Adolf Hitler's desk from his battle command post behind the Eastern Front.

Only days later, a providential event occurred—a V-2 missile that had gone awry in flight plunged into the swampy bank of the Bug River and failed to explode. Its nose was buried deep in mud, and the projectile was largely intact. A farmer spotted the rocket and excitedly reported it to a member of the Polish underground.

News of the extraordinary event was flashed to the underground headquarters in Warsaw. A young engineer, Antoni Kocjan, and two other men rushed to the Bug River to photograph the V-2. It was risky business, for German patrols were already scouring the region in a frantic effort to locate the errant missile. Before departing, the partisans covered the projectile with brush and foilage.

On the following night, Kocjan and a few Polish scientists, masquerading as laborers, arrived at the site. Working feverishly for many hours and under the constant specter of discovery and execution by German patrols, the partisans used three teams of stout, snorting plow horses to pull the missile out of the sticky morass. The engines and steering mechanisms were removed by the scientists, piled onto farm carts, trundled across rough fields, and hidden in a nearby barn.

After dawn, the scientists took many photographs and measurements, made drawings, then dismantled the components into hundreds of pieces. These parts were put on the beds of two ancient trucks and covered with large loads of potatoes.

Driving toward Warsaw in the wheezing, coughing trucks was a frightening ordeal. Three times the vehicles were halted at roadblocks. While the partisans, hearts thumping, sat motionless, German soldiers studied the potato cargoes, poked bayonet-tipped rifles into the vegetables several times, then waved the trucks onward.

In London, British scientists were elated over the Bug River episode. In Warsaw the commander of the Home Army (Polish underground) set into motion Operation *Most* (Bridge) to smuggle the V-2 components out of Poland

A Polish underground warrior risked his life to snap this photo of a huge German V-2 at the Blizna testing grounds. (Author's collection)

and to London. A large bag containing the parts would be carried by Jerzy Chmielewski, who had spent a year in the notorious Auschwitz concentration camp before being released in March 1944—by a bribe of 150,000 zlotys secretly provided by the Home Army.

Chmielewski (code name Rafal) would be the leader of the traveling delegation that would include Tomasz Arciszewski (Tom), nominated by the underground Council of National Unity as the successor to the president of the Polish Republic, and Jozef Retinger (Salamander), a special emissary from British Prime Minister Churchill. Three months earlier, at age fifty-six, Retinger had parachuted into Poland on a secret political mission.

Just past 10:00 P.M. on July 25, 1944, a lumbering, unarmed C-47 transport plane (an American plane known to the British as a Dakota) lifted off from Brindisi in Italy and set a course for an abandoned airfield code-named Motyl (Butterfly), near the town of Tarnow in southern Poland.

The pilot was Flight Lieutenant Stanley G. Culliford, a New Zealander, and the copilot was a Pole, Flight Lieutenant Kazimierz Szrajer. The two officers and their British crew held no illusions that their mission would be routine. The C-47 would have to locate a tiny speck of ground in the darkness.

It was midnight at the pitch-black airstrip where a waiting band of partisans heard the faint hum of an approaching plane. The Poles had been notified by code phrases broadcast over BBC Radio in London that the C-47 was coming. The Eastern Front now ran through the middle of Poland, and the region was crowded with German army units.

Tension gripped the underground warriors. Only that morning, two German Storch reconnaissance planes had landed at Motyl. Soon the aircraft took off, but there was no certainty that they would not return at any moment.

Now the Dakota was circling overhead and the partisans watched the dim silhouette zooming in for a landing. Suddenly the dark locale burst into brightness; the pilot had turned on the powerful twin searchlights. The underground

*Polish underground leader
Jerzy Chmielewski smuggled
stolen V-2 rocket components
to London. (National
Archives)*

men cringed. If the roar of the engines had not alerted the nearby Germans, no doubt this glare of iridescence would grab their attention.

The plane rolled to a stop, and shadowy figures stole silently from the nearby woods. Haste was crucial. Jerzy Chmielewski tossed his cargo of V-2 components through the open door and the Poles clambered aboard. Lieutenant Culliford revved the engines for takeoff. No doubt the raucous roar could be heard for miles. Then the C-47 vibrated, edged forward a few inches, and refused to budge.

Culliford and Lieutenant Szrajer climbed out to inspect the undercarriage. It had been raining for several days, and the wheels had bogged down in sticky mud.

Culliford called out in a stage whisper for crew and passengers to get out to decrease the weight of the plane. The partisans began frantically shoveling mud away from the wheels. Then crew and passengers got back into the aircraft.

Again, the strident noise of revving engines. Again the C-47 refused to move. Everyone out!

It was found that the wheels had sunk even deeper into the mire. The tension was nearly unbearable.

Now the partisans dashed about collecting large sticks, which were placed under the wheels. Everyone back on board. Another roar of engines. The C-47 shuddered violently, straining to bolt forward, but remained stuck. For the third time, the wretched passengers and crewmen left the plane.

Following earlier instructions should the mission fail, Culliford and Szrajer prepared to set fire to the airplane. Meanwhile, the underground men, with heavy hearts, began digging feverishly into the mud with their bare hands. They clawed and scratched. Fingernails were torn out. Blood trickled down palms.

Now the Poles begged Culliford to give it one final try. Everyone climbed aboard. The engines were obstinate. They coughed and sputtered. But suddenly the plane pulled loose from its vise, surged down the runway, and lifted into the air. A flood of cheers from crewmen and Poles rocked the cabin of the C-47.

Glancing back, Culliford saw a string of headlights moving toward the airstrip, no doubt German trucks loaded with soldiers. But by now the partisans on the ground had hurried from the scene.

The flight back to Brindisi was without incident. After a night's rest while the C-47 was overhauled, the plane flew to Rabat, in North Africa. Chmielewski, with his bag of precious V-2 parts, and another Pole flew on to London, landing on July 28.

Minutes after the landing, a strident dispute erupted. Two British intelligence officers immediately tried to take possession of the bag of components, but the Pole refused, claiming that he had been authorized to hand it over to only authorized Polish officials. When the Britons tried to seize the bag, Chmielewski threatened them with a trench knife.

Then the British officers drove him to a remote farm, where they pulled pistols and said they would kill him if he did not hand over the bag. "Mr. Churchill has been waiting several days for this bag," the Britons exclaimed.

Chmielewski was unmoved, and he left the premises with his valuable V-2 components. That same day the bag was in the hands of the IInd Bureau (Polish intelligence) in London. Everything was promptly handed over to British intelligence, which passed the components along to British scientists, who began studying the V-2 components.

Earlier the scientists had theorized from available information that they could alter a missile's course by radio waves. But they soon learned that this technique would be impossible, because the steering mechanisms did not react to radio machinations. There would be no defense against the looming rain of German rockets, the first of which exploded in the London suburb of Chiswick on September 8.

In the months ahead, thousands of London civilians would be killed by the revolutionary V-2 onslaught. But thanks to the Polish underground, the British government was forewarned of Adolf Hitler's vengeance weapon and was able to evacuate large numbers of children and others to safety in the countryside.[15]

Grandma Was a Secret Agent

WHILE THE GLOBAL SPOTLIGHT had been shining largely on the battles in Europe and in the Pacific for three years in 1944, a war within a war had been raging in the Philippines. It was a covert conflict involving unsung heroes and heroines, mostly Americans and Filipinos. It was a vicious struggle against the brutal Japanese occupiers, and the penalty for detection and arrest was excruciating torture, then an agonizing death.

When the Japanese invaded the Philippines in December 1941, a few days after Pearl Harbor, a fifty-thousand-man American and Filipino force, greatly outnumbered and outgunned, was starved into submission a few months later. In Washington, President Franklin D. Roosevelt, knowing that the hopeless struggle in the Philippines was nearing its end, ordered his commander in the islands, General Douglas MacArthur, to escape to Australia, far to the south. There he was to organize an army to recapture the Philippines.

Knowing that it would be perhaps more than two and a half years before the woefully weak American armed forces could invade the Philippines, MacArthur had a top aide, his intelligence chief, Colonel Courtney Whitney, establish an underground network in the islands, mostly in and around Manila.

By August 1944, Manila, a city of one million people and the center of Japan's war efforts in that region of the Pacific, was infested with Allied spies. They came from all walks of life, and while going about their legitimate daily routines they collected pieces of information about the Japanese occupiers and their activities. Each lived under the constant threat of arrest and beheading by the Kempei Tai, Japan's dreaded secret police force.

An unlikely member of the Allied espionage apparatus was Mrs. Robert Yearsley, an elderly American grandmother who had lived alone in Manila for many years. Always cheerful and highly intelligent, she knew that it would be impossible to flee if the Kempei Tai discovered her clandestine activities.

At the risk of her life, Mrs. Yearsley served as a clearinghouse for messages going back and forth between leaders of the underground network, mostly Americans who had taken refuge in the mountains when the Philippines had fallen. Filipino boys, in the guise of doing household chores for the frail woman, acted as go-betweens, bringing and taking away messages.

Mrs. Yearsley also handled large sums of money, which had been smuggled to her by Colonel Whitney's organization. When an underground leader on Luzon, the main island, needed funds, he or she would telephone the "treasurer" and inquire about a certain cake recipe—just in case the Kempei Tai had tapped the telephone. That was the signal to send a certain amount of money by a Filipino boy to the caller.

In October 1944, General MacArthur fulfilled a pledge, "I shall return," made at the time he had arrived in Australia in March 1942. Now savage fighting was raging in Manila between American forces and die-hard Japanese defenders. Scores of Filipino men and women who had paved the way for MacArthur's return while serving in the underground did not witness the great day. They had been apprehended and executed by the Kempei Tai.

Despite the highly active espionage role Mrs. Yearsley had been playing for many months, she had never been suspected by the Japanese secret police.

When the Americans reached Manila, she was on hand to greet the liberators. But she could not see them, having been blind for many years.[16]

A Pregnant Spy Cuts a Deal

LATE IN NOVEMBER 1944, General Alexander M. Patch, the fifty-year-old leader of the U.S. Seventh Army, called in the head of his Office of Strategic Services (OSS) detachment, Major Henry Hyde, who had graduated from Harvard Law School seven years earlier at the age of twenty. Why, Patch wanted to know, was Seventh Army no longer getting the high-grade intelligence about the German units to its front that the OSS had been providing?

Three months earlier, in August, Patch's army had stormed ashore in southern France in Operation Dragoon, then rapidly driven to the northeast for more than two hundred and fifty miles to take up positions near the German border on the southern portion of the long Allied front. During that time period, Hyde had many agents behind German lines.

Now, he explained to Patch, the Frenchmen who had been such valuable secret agents in infiltrating their homeland in front of the advancing Seventh Army were largely unsuited for penetrating Germany. So Patch tacitly approved Hyde's suggestion that the OSS group launch an all-out effort to recruit selected German prisoners of war—in violation of strict rules laid down by SHAEF (Supreme Headquarters, Allied Expeditionary Force).

Using POWs as agents was also prohibited by the Geneva Convention, a pact drawn up many years earlier on how to conduct civilized warfare. Sandy Patch, a practical man, knew there was no such thing as civilized warfare. So he told Major Hyde that he could not permit such a project—while winking one eye.

Back at his headquarters not far from the front lines, Hyde promptly briefed one of his officers, twenty-five-year-old Marine Lieutenant Peter Viertel, on the need to step up the recruitment of spies to penetrate behind German lines. Viertel, the son of a Hollywood director, was brash, enthusiastic, and tireless. During the 1930s he had grown up in the movie capital, and his companions were mainly the female sex sirens of the era.

Now Lieutenant Viertel sprung an idea on Hyde, one that he had been mulling over in his mind for a week. Why not recruit German women as secret agents? Women had notable advantages over male spies. They would not have to explain to Gestapo agents and German police why they were not in the military service. Nor would they need the large number of passes and documents that male agents had to carry. There would always be risks, Viertel said, but the odds of being exposed were much less for female spies.

The prewar man-about-Hollywood spoke fluent German, and he soon recruited several women prospects, one of whom was given the code name

Maria. She was twenty years of age, blond, and sturdily built. Viertel had recruited her from a detention camp where she was being held as a Nazi collaborator. She had spent her entire life in Strasbourg, a large city near the German-French border. After the Franco-Prussian war of 1870, France ceded Strasbourg to Germany; the city became French again after World War I. German troops occupied it in 1940. So Maria, like many citizens of Strasbourg, was never sure if she was German or French.

Before selecting Maria to be a spy, Viertel looked over her record. She had worked in a German hospital and had been the mistress of a Gestapo officer. Confronted with these "charges," Maria explained that life had been exceedingly difficult for this child of poverty. So she had indeed bedded down with a few Germans. But now, she stressed to Viertel, she wanted to erase the collaborationist label, so the best way to do that was to aide the Americans.

Viertel found Maria to be highly intelligent, with street smarts, and she was not lacking in self-confidence. She pleaded for a chance, and Viertel accepted her, knowing that her background as an accused collaborator would be an ideal cover for snooping around inside the Third Reich.

Days later the female recruit was undergoing extensive training in parachuting, communications, and identifying various German military units and equipment.

On February 3, 1945, Viertel escorted Maria to a small airfield where she would take off for her designated drop zone. Her disguise would be as a German army nurse. Having worked in a German hospital during the Wehrmacht's occupation of Strasbourg, the masquerade would be a natural one.

After her parachute had been strapped on, Maria shocked Viertel by telling him that she was pregnant. Why wait until now? Because she would hold up her part of the agreement and hoped to be back to American lines in two weeks. Then she wanted an abortion to be arranged for her.

Now Viertel was faced with a quandary, the like of which he had never encountered in Hollywood, where there was always a simple answer on the silver screen to the most vexing of problems. Who was the father? the Marine asked. "My former Gestapo boyfriend," she replied.

A considerable investment in time and money had gone into getting Maria into Germany. Her pregnancy was not far along. She was eager to go. So she was put aboard an aircraft, and that night she jumped blind into the Third Reich.

After crashing to the ground, Maria hid her parachute and set out through the darkness to carry out her mission. Her masquerade as an army nurse was never challenged as she made her way past numerous police checkpoints while following the itinerary she had memorized.

Two weeks after jumping, she was back in American lines. As Viertel had anticipated, she proved to be a keen-witted agent, and she reported high-grade intelligence on various German headquarters, panzer parks, and troop bivouacs.

Maria told the Marine officer that she had fulfilled her mission, and now she expected her terms to be met. So she was driven to a Catholic hospital in Strasbourg, where her role as a collaborator was known. But, the OSS escort explained, Maria had performed an extraordinary act of heroism behind German lines, which was true. While fulfilling her mission of obtaining secret information, sacrifices had to be made, so she became pregnant, which was a lie.

The doctors were deeply impressed and said to leave the young woman with them. When the OSS officer returned a few days later to pick up Maria, he tried to pay the hospital for the abortion procedure, but the physicians would not take a franc. Maria, they declared, had risked everything, including her life, for *"la belle France."*[17]

"Faithful Heinrich" Betrays His Führer

IN THE LATE FALL OF 1944, powerful American, British, and French armies were arrayed along the western border of Germany, ready to launch a final mammoth offensive aimed at Berlin. On the homefront, the Herrenvolk (German people) had grown disillusioned after five years of carnage, and most were ready for any kind of peace settlement.

Reichsführer Heinrich Himmler, the most powerful man in Germany next to Adolf Hitler, was also secretly bent on seeking an end to the war—in a manner that would save his skin from postwar Allied justice.

Owl-faced and inscrutable, Himmler, through years of diligent pursuit of personal power, had made himself the leader of the Schutzstaffel (SS), the elite, black-uniformed army within the army, chief of the Geheime Staatspolizei (the dreaded Gestapo), commander of the Home Army (replacements), and the Minister of the Interior.

Himmler, a master of adroit intrigue, had for years professed his undying loyalty to his benefactor, Hitler. For his part, the führer called his long-time crony "Faithful Heinrich."

Now, with the handwriting on the wall for Hitler's proclaimed Thousand-Year Reich, "Faithful Heinrich" hatched a convoluted machination to seize power from Hitler and make peace with the Allies.

Centerpiece of the Himmler scheme was a prominent Swedish international banker, Jacob Wallenberg, whose business had taken him frequently to England and to Germany, even while the war was raging. During his London visits, he had established an acquaintance with Prime Minister Winston S. Churchill. It was Himmler's plan to coerce Wallenberg to convince the Briton that a negotiated settlement to end the war would be in Great Britain's best interest.

Nazi Germany's two most powerful men. Reichsführer Heinrich Himmler (left) beams in admiration for his benefactor Adolf Hitler. (National Archives)

Himmler would use Karl-Friederich Goerdeler, a former Oberburgermeister (mayor) of the major city of Leizpig, as a conduit to Wallenberg and to the Jewish leader Chaim Weizmann, both of whom might make contact with Churchill with the Reichsführer's "peace" proposal.

Goerdeler was certainly available. He was confined in one of the Gestapo chief's prisons, awaiting execution after having been implicated in a plot to murder Adolf Hitler on July 20, 1944. At that time, the führer had miraculously survived a bomb that had been planted by conspirators and exploded at his feet.

In the ensuing bloodbath unleashed by Hitler in Berlin, hundreds of "suspects" in the assassination attempt were executed without trial by Himmler's Gestapo and army officers loyal to the führer.

Goerdeler had been tipped off that the Gestapo had offered a reward of one million marks for information leading to his whereabouts, and he became a man on the run, going from one hideout to another. But he was located by the Gestapo on August 12 and charged with high treason. Curiously, the conspirator was not promptly executed.

No doubt Goerdeler was puzzled by the Gestapo's failure to kill him, but there was good reason for the situation. Himmler had quietly passed the word to Otto Ohlendorf, an official in the RHSA, the main Reich security office, to contrive excuses for keeping the prisoner from the hangman's noose, at least for the present time.

Ohlendorf, knowing of his prisoner's long record of high civic service, instructed Goerdeler to write long pieces on administrative matters—a topic about which absolutely no one in the Nazi heirarchy was interested—as an excuse for keeping the prisoner alive.

At Himmler's "request," Goerdeler wrote a letter to his friend Jacob Wallenberg in neutral Sweden. Gestapo agents dictated the wording. "Europe, the world, humanity, and civilization must be saved from Russia (Communism)" even if Great Britain had to endure the Nazi regime in Germany, Goerdeler wrote, as ordered.

Goerdeler's letter, which was taken to Stockholm by an official in the Swedish Embassy in Berlin, made no mention of Adolf Hitler, to whom Himmler owed his stature, rank, power, and wealth. The inference in the letter was that Great Britain and Germany could arrange a peace and that Nazism would remain in charge in the Third Reich, presumably with Himmler the new national leader in place of Hitler. That arrangement in Germany would be far better than permitting Josef Stalin's Red Army to overrun Germany and entrench Communism in the nation, it was implied.

Himmler had overlooked one key ingredient in his roundabout proposal to Winston Churchill: Germany was in disarray, hovering on the brink of destruction, and in no position to be dictating peace terms. Churchill responded to Himmler's secret appeal with silence.

Karl-Friedrich Goedeler was no longer of any value to Himmler. On February 2, 1945, the former Leipzig mayor was hanged.

After the failure of Churchill to respond to his peace plan, Himmler abandoned his efforts for a negotiated settlement for several months. Adolf Hitler had launched his final roll of the dice to snatch victory out of the jaws of defeat in a surprise offensive that became known as the Battle of the Bulge. But that last gasp had resulted in a crushing defeat for the Wehrmacht in early 1945.

Now, with the demise of the Third Reich a certainty, Himmler tried another peace approach. Through a Swede, Count Folke Bernadotte, a man of elegance and sophistication who traveled widely throughout Europe as head of the Swedish Red Cross, the Gestapo chief hoped to get the Allies to abolish their unconditional surrender policy, which had been announced by Franklin D. Roosevelt and Winston Churchill back in early 1943.

Bernadotte took Himmler's message to Churchill, who immediately called the new American president, Harry S Truman, on the tranatlantic scrambler telephone. "What's he got to surrender?" Truman snapped. "I don't know," the Briton replied.

That terse conversation concluded any hope Himmler might have to save Germany—and his own neck.

After calling on Hitler to celebrate the führer's birthday on April 20, 1945, Himmler slipped out of dark, bomb-battered Berlin, which was virtually surrounded by Soviet armies. A week later, with the Russians closing in on the bunker where the führer and his entourage were holed up, Hitler learned for the first time of efforts made by "Faithful Heinrich" to negotiate a separate peace with the Western Allies. Furious, Hitler ordered the immediate arrest of his long-time close crony, who had fled to Flensberg, in northern Germany.

On May 10, two days after Germany surrendered unconditionally, Himmler adopted an elaborate disguise, dressed as an average German soldier, wearing an eye patch, and minus the mustache he had sported during his entire adult life. Two weeks later he was halted at a British control post near Bremen. Chaim Weizmann, a future president of Israel, was the British officer who first was suspicious of the German "soldier."

Under interrogation, Himmler disclosed his true identity. After British officers left the room, he chomped down on a concealed cyanide capsule and was dead in a few minutes.[18]

Notes and Sources

Part One—Heading toward the Brink

1. **A British Mole in German Spy School**
   Author's archives.
   Ladislas Farago, *Burn After Reading* (New York: Walker, 1961), pp. 52–53.
   Wilhelm Hoetl, *The Secret Front* (New York: Praeger, 1954), p. 75.

2. **An Elderly German Casanova**
   Author's archives.
   Anthony Cave Brown, *Bodyguard of Lies* (New York: Harper & Row, 1975), pp. 181, 194.
   Ladislas Farago, *Burn After Reading* (New York: Walker, 1961), pp. 130–131.

3. **Return of a "Conquering Hero"**
   Author's archives.
   Details of Dr. Ignatz Griebl's and Kate Moog's 1937 visit to Germany came from interrogation files of the FBI.
   Leon Turrou, *The Nazi Conspiracy in America* (Freeport, NY: Books for Libraries Press, 1969), p. 9.

4. **The "Poor Little Rich Girl"**
   Harper's, July 1942.
   Ladislas Farago, *The Game of the Foxes* (New York: McKay, 1941), p. 346.
   FBI files (1938–1941) in possession of author.

5. **A Scheme to "Nazify" Thirty Million Americans**
   John Roy Carlson, *The Plotters* (Chicago: Regnery, 1943), p. 113.
   Leon G. Turrou, *The Nazi Spy Conspiracy in America* (Freeport, NY: Books for Libraries Press, 1969), p. 264.
   John Roy Carlson, *Undercover* (Chicago: Regnery, 1944), pp. 417–418.

6. **A Seminary Student Stalks Hitler**
   Peter S. Hoffman, *The History of the German Resistance* (Boston: Massachusetts Institute of Technology Press, 1976), pp. 117, 129.
   Author's archives.
   John W. Bennett-Wheeler, *Nememis of Power* (New York: Macmillan, 1964), p. 446.

7. **Standard Oil's Nazi Connection**
   Author's archives.

8. **Theft of Maginot Line Secrets**
   Ladislas Farago, *Burn After Reading* (New York: Walker, 1961), pp. 18–19.
   Author's archives.

9. **The Pope's Clandestine Peace Plan**
   Owen Chadwick, *Britain and the Vatican During the Second World War* (London: Cambridge, 1986), pp. 62–65.
   Foreign Relations of the United States, 1939, vol. 1 (Washington, D.C.: National Archives), pp. 372, 412.

10. **An American Forum to Promote Germany**
   Author's archives.
   New York Times, July 10, 1941.

11. **Roosevelt's Secret Scheme to Aid the British**
   U.S. Ambassador Joseph Kennedy memo to U.S. Secretary of State Cordell Hull, in *Foreign Relations of the United States, 1939* (Washington, D.C.: National Archives), p. 283.
   Donald C. Watt, *How War Came* (New York: Pantheon, 1989), p. 269.
   Author's archives.

12. **"Our Enemies Are Little Worms"**
   Alan Bullock, *Hitler: A Study in Tyranny* (New York: Harper & Row, 1963), p. 526.
   John Wheeler-Bennett, *Nemesis of Power* (New York: Macmillan, 1964), p. 446.
   Author's archives.

13. **Lulling Europe's Leaders to Sleep**
   Carl Burckhardt, *Meine Danziger Mission* (Munich: Südwest Verlag, 1969), pp. 336–337.
   Rüdiger Ruhnau, *Die Freie Stadt Danzig* (Warsaw: Interpress, 1979), pp. 172–173.
   Donald C. Watt, *How War Came* (New York: Pantheon, 1989), p. 535.
   Author's archives.

Part Two—A World Rocked by War

1. **A German Spymaster Plots against Hitler**
   International Military Tribunal, Document No. 3047 (Washington, D.C.: National Archives).
   American Historial Review, June 1956, p. 70.

2. **The Polish Assassin Wore Pigtails**
   Author's archives.
   Albert Marrin, *The Secret Armies* (New York: Antheneum, 1985), pp. 103–104.
   Robert Jackson, *Heroines of World War II* (London: Barker, 1976), p. 135.

3. **An American Celebrity Aids the Führer**
   New York Times, September 27, 1939.
   John Roy Carlson, *The Plotters* (Chicago: Regnery, 1943), p. 409.
   Michael Sayers and Albert E. Kahn, *Sabotage!* (New York: Harper, 1942), p. 214.

4. **A Civic-Minded Spy in Miami**
   Edwin P. Hoyt, *U-Boats Offshore* (New York: Stein & Day, 1978), pp. 70–71.
   Author's archives.
   "German Espionage and Sabotage Against the United States," U.S. Office of Naval Intelligence Review, January 1946.
   FBI interrogation reports, data on convictions for espionage (1937–1945).

5. **A Swedish Professor's Intelligence Coup**
   Author's archives.

6. **Greta Garbo: A Secret Agent**
   William Stevenson, *A Man Called Intrepid* (London: Harcourt Brace Jovanovich, 1975), p. 58.
   Author's archives.

7. **"You Will Spy for the Fatherland!"**
   Transcript of FBI interview of William G. Sebold, 1940.

Michael Sayers and Albert E. Kahn, *Sabotage!* (New York: McKay, 1971), pp. 24, 77. Author's archives.
Ladislas Farago, *The Game of the Foxes* (New York: McKay, 1971), p. 27.

8. **Hitler Finances an FBI Coup**
Michael Sayers and Albert E. Kahn, *Sabotage!* (New York: McKay, 1971), pp. 78–79.
Don Whitehead, *The FBI Story* (New York: Random House, 1956), pp. 168–169.
Transcripts of FBI interogations of subjects involved in undercover operation, 1946.

9. **Japanese Fishermen in the Caribbean**
Author's archives.

10. **Confiscating Nazis' Stolen Art Treasures**
Author's archives.

11. **A Propaganda Blitz against the United States**
Documents of German Foreign Policy (DGFP) (Washington, D.C.: National Archives), pp. 552–553, 558–559.
Page advertisement in the *New York Times*, June 25, 1940.
William L. Shirer, *The Rise and Fall of the Third Reich* (New York: Simon & Schuster, 1981), p. 748.

12. **The Secret Looting of Conquered Europe**
Author's archives.

13. **A Hollywood "Warrior" Is Knighted**
St. Louis Post-Dispatch, August 2, 1941.
Anthony Reed and David Fisher, *Colonel Z* (New York: Viking, 1985), pp. 176, 178.
H. Montgomery Hyde, *Secret Intelligence Agent* (New York: St. Martin's, 1982), p. 164.
Author's archives.

14. **Roosevelt: Conniver or Country Bumpkin?**
H. Montgomery Hyde, *Secret Intelligence Agent* (New York: St. Martin's, 1982), pp. 157, 158, 160.
Christian Science Monitor, August 22, 1941.
Cordell Hull, *Memoirs of Cordell Hull*, vol. 1 (New York: Macmillan, 1948), p. 828.
Author's archives.

15. **"Smuggling" Five Ships to England**
Ian Dear, *Sabotage and Subversion* (London: Arms and Armour, 1996), pp. 72–74.
Ralph Barker, *The Blockade Busters* (London: Collins, 1976), pp. 138, 140.
Author's archives.

16. **Plastic Surgery for a British Spy**
Author's archives.

Part Three—Nazi Germany on the March

1. **Nazi Diplomats Spy in the United States**
Ellis Zacharias, *Secret Missions* (New York: Putnam, 1946), pp. 219, 231.
Author's archives.

2. **Secret Trysts in Berlin Theaters**
Cordell Hull, *Memoirs of Cordell Hull*, vol. 1 (New York: Macmillan, 1948), pp. 104, 110.
Author's archives.

3. **J. Edgar Hoover: Rumormonger**
Author's archives.

4. **An Unlikely Counterfeit Traitor**
Max Lowenthal, *The Federal Bureau of Investigation* (New York: Sloane, 1950), pp. 425–426.
St. Louis Post-Dispatch, July 2, 1941.
Time, June 9, 1941.
Don Whitehead, *The FBI Story* (New York: Random House, 1956), p. 166.

5. **The Spy Who Fooled Both Sides**
Juan Pujol (with Nigel West), *Operation Garbo* (New York: Random House, 1985), pp. 77, 79.
J. C. Masterman, *The Double-Cross System* (New Haven: Yale University Press, 1972), pp. 114, 116.
Author's archives.

6. **Nine Germans Capture Belgrade**
Author's archives.
Alan Bullock, *Hitler* (New York: Harper & Row, 1963), p. 635.
Janusz Piekalkiewicz, *Krieg auf dem Balkan* (Munich: Südwest Verlag, 1984), pp. 132, 136.

7. **The "Directress of Masquerades"**
M. R. D. Foot, *SOE in France* (London: Her Majesty's Stationery Office, 1966), pp. 11, 12.
Author's archives.
E. H. Cookridge, *Inside SOE* (London: Barker, 1966), p. 116.

8. **Ruses to Aid Trapped British Force**
John Strawson, *The Battle for North Africa* (New York: Bonanza, 1969), pp. 56–57.
Geoffrey Barkas, *The Camouflage Story* (London: Cassell, 1952), pp. 123, 125.
David Irving, *The Trail of the Fox* (New York: Dutton, 1977), p. 102.

9. **"We Stand behind Every Camel!"**
Author's archives.
David Fisher, *The War Magician* (New York: Coward-McCann, 1983), pp. 55, 58, 60.
Anthony Cave Brown, *Bodyguard of Lies* (New York: Harper & Row, 1975), pp. 51, 54.

10. **An Enemy Agent in the Spymaster's Family**
Author's archives.
Anthony Cave Brown, *Bodyguard of Lies* (New York: Harper & Row, 1975), p. 57.
Ladislas Farago, *Burn After Reading* (New York: Walker, 1961), pp. 158, 159.

11. **Mission: Hide Alexandria Harbor**
Desmond Young, *Rommel the Desert Fox* (New York: Harper, 1950), p. 79.
Seymour Reit, *Masquerade* (New York: Hawthorn, 1978), pp. 134, 138.
Author's archives.
Jasper Maskelyne, *Magic* (London: Stanley Paul, 1949), pp. 47, 59.

12. **Nazi Spies Visit the White House**
Harper's, June 1942.
Transcript of Kurt Ludwig testimony at his espionage trial, February 1942.

13. **Escaping in Disguise from a Death Camp**
Author's archives.

14. **The World's Strangest Business**
L. Bell, *Sabotage* (London: Laurie, 1957), pp. 112, 117, 123.
Author's archives.
E. H. Cookridge, *Inside SOE* (London: Barker, 1966), pp. 90, 92.

15. **French Gold Cache Kept from Hitler**
   Author's archives.
   William Stevenson, *A Man Called Intrepid* (New York: Walker, 1975), pp. 322, 325.
   New York Times, September 4, 1941.

16. **The German "Butcher's" Gardener**
   Henri Michel, *Shadow War* (New York: Harper, 1972), p. 352.
   Author's archives.
   Anthony Cave Brown, *Bodyguard of Lies* (New York: Harper & Row, 1975), p. 249.

Part Four—A Sleeping America Awakens

1. **A Plot to Coerce the United States into War**
   William Stevenson, *A Man Called Intrepid* (New York: Walker, 1975), pp. 298–299.
   Chicago Tribune, December 12, 1941.
   Messages of Dr. Hans Thomsen, diplomat in German Embassy in Washington, *DGFP*,
      IX (Washington, D.C.: National Archives), pp. 976–981.

2. **American Postcards Aid Pearl Harbor Attack**
   Author's archives.

3. **Urgent Mission: Disguise California**
   Viscount Alanbrooke, *Diaries*, vol. 1 (London: Collins, 1957), pp. 292–293.
   Stetson Conn, Rose C. Engelman, and Byron Fairchild, *Guarding the U.S. and Its Out-
      posts* (Washington, D.C.: Office of the Chief of Military History, 1964), pp. 82,
      87, 92.
   New York Times, March 16, 1973.
   Author's archives.
   "Camouflage in Wartime," *Lockheed-Vega Aircraftsman*, June 1943.

4. **The Mysterious Camp X**
   Allan Clark, *Barbarossa* (New York: Morrow, 1985), p. 25.
   Roger Manvell and Heinrich Fraenkel, *The Canaris Conspiracy* (New York: McKay,
      1969), p. 80.
   William Stevenson, *A Man Called Intrepid* (New York: Walker, 1975), p. 190.
   Author's archives.

5. **Probing Secrets of the Atlantikwall**
   Author's archives.

6. **Contrivances to Save Jewish Children**
   Author's archives.
   Lucy Dawidowicz, *The War Against the Jews* (New York: Holt, Rinehart and Winston,
      1975), pp. 124, 137.
   Gerald Reitlinger, *The Final Solution* (New York: Barnes, 1953), p. 107.

7. **Sneaking a Danish Leader to London**
   Anthony Cave Brown, *Bodyguard of Lies* (New York: Harper & Row, 1975), pp. 510,
      513.
   E. H. Cookridge, *Inside SOE* (London: Barker, 1966), p. 565.
   Author's archives.

8. **An "Insane" Man in U.S. Navy Post**
   Author's archives.
   Ladislas Farago, *Burn After Reading* (New York: Walker, 1961), pp. 278, 283.

9. **A German Deception Masterpiece**
   Author's archives.
   Benno Zieser, *The Road to Stalingrad* (New York: Ballantine, 1956), pp. 87–88.
   Erich von Manstein, *Lost Victories* (Chicago: Regnery, 1958), pp. 138, 145.

10. **A Deluge of Phony Food Coupons**
    Charles Cruickshank, *The Fourth Arm* (London: Oxford, 1981), p. 147.

11. **Impersonating a Submarine Fleet**
    Jasper Maskelyne, *Magic* (London: Stanley Paul, 1949), p. 47.
    Illustrated Story of World War II (Pleasantville, NY: Reader's Digest Association, 1969),
       p. 45.
    Author's archives.

12. **The "Phantom Field Marshal"**
    John Keegan, *The Mask of Command* (New York: Viking, 1987), pp. 264, 287.
    Walter Goerlitz, *History of the German General Staff* (New York: Praeger, 1954),
       p. 399.
    Author's archives.

13. **German Soldiers Help a Woman "Terrorist"**
    Author's archives.
    Maurice Buckmaster, *They Fought Alone* (New York: Norton, 1958), pp. 139, 140.

14. **Escaping Captivity by a Ruse**
    Ladislas Farago, *War of Wits* (London: Hutchinson, 1956), pp. 168, 172.
    E. H. Cookridge, *Inside SOE* (London: Barker, 1966), p. 588.
    W. S. Moss, *War of Shadows* (London: Bordman, 1952), p. 205.

15. **The Grand Mufti's Rejected Report**
    Roger Manvell and Heinrich Fraenkel, *The Canaris Conspiracy* (New York: McKay,
       1969), pp. 91–92.
    Author's archives.
    André Brissaud, *Canaris* (New York: Grosset & Dunlap, 1974), pp. 281, 283.

16. **British Magicians Hoodwink Rommel**
    Winston S. Churchill, *The Second World War*, vol. 4 (Boston: Houghton Mifflin,
       1948), pp. 464, 467.
    Geoffrey Barkas, *The Camouflage Story* (London: Cassell, 1952), pp. 198, 202.
    Anthony Cave Brown, *Bodyguard of Lies* (New York: Harper & Row, 1975), p. 112.
    Author's archives.

Part Five—Turning of the Tide

1. **A Danish Spy Preaches to the Germans**
   Author's archives.
   E. H. Cookridge, *Inside SOE* (London: Barker, 1966), p. 567.

2. **Japan Wants Lethal Gas on England**
   SRS files, September 19, 26, 28, 1942. Washington, D.C.: National Archives.
   Author's archives.
   Bruce Lee, *Marching Orders* (New York: Crown, 1995), p. 11.

3. **General Eisenhower's Furious Wife**
   Author's archives.

4. **The Gestapo Tricks British Spymaster**
   Author's archives.

E. H. Cookridge, *Inside SOE* (London: Barker, 1966), p. 210.

M. R. D. Foot, *SOE in France* (London: Her Majesty's Stationery Office, 1966), p. 198.

5. **London's Devious "Shadow Warrior"**
   Author's archives.

6. **Jim, the Talented Forger**
   Author's archives.
   Stanley W. Lovell, *Of Spies and Stratagems* (Englewood Cliffs, NJ: Prentice-Hall, 1963), pp. 104–105.

7. **The Lady Journalist Was a Spy**
   R. Harris Smith, *OSS* (Berkeley: University of California Press, 1972), pp. 25–26.
   Eliose Engle and Lauri Paananen, *The Winter War* (New York: St. Martin's Press, 1962), p. 67.

8. **America's Black Propaganda Experts**
   Author's archives.

9. **A "Water Donkey" Subterfuge**
   Author's archives.
   Ian V. Hogg and J. B. King, *German Secret Weapons in World War II* (New York: Chartwell, 1976), pp. 53–54.

10. **Strange Role for a Copenhagen Hotel**
    Author's archives.
    E. H. Cookridge, *Inside SOE* (London: Barker, 1966), pp. 571, 574.
    J. Haestrup, *Kontakt med England* (Copenhagen: Thanning, 1959), pp. 134, 168.

11. **War among London's Spy Chiefs**
    R. Harris Smith, *OSS* (Berkeley: University of California Press, 1972), p. 165.
    Author's archives.
    Henri Michel, *The Shadow War* (New York: Harper, 1972), p. 306.

12. **A Cat Bombardier**
    Author's archives.
    Stanley P. Lovell, *Of Spies and Stratagems* (Englewood Cliffs, NJ: Prentice-Hall, 1963), p. 63.

13. **A Plot to Kidnap the Pope**
    André Brissaud, *Canaris* (New York: Grosset & Dunlap, 1973), pp. 308–309.
    Wilhelm Hoettl, *The Secret Front* (New York: Praeger, 1954), pp. 221, 222.
    Author's archives.
    K. H. Abshagen, *Canaris* (London: Hutchinson, 1956), p. 221.

14. **Capturing an Island by Deceit**
    Author interviews with Ivan F. Woods, 1984, and General Matthew B. Ridgway, 1988.
    Forrest Dawson, ed., *Saga of the All American*, privately printed, 1946.

15. **"Fishermen" Blow Up Key Canal**
    Maurice Buckmaster, *They Fought Alone* (New York: Norton, 1958), p. 218.
    Author's archives.

Part Six—The Allies' Road to Victory

1. **Cat-and-Mouse Duel with the Gestapo**
   J. Kramarz, *Stauffenberg* (London: Deutsch, 1967), p. 122.
   Eberhard Bethge, *Dietrich Bonhoeffer* (London: Collins, 1969), pp. 713, 815.
   K. Bartz, *The Downfall of the German Secret Service* (London: Kimber, 1956), p. 125.

234 Notes and Sources

2. Hedy Lamarr Creates Panic
Author's archives.
Stanley P. Lovell, *Of Spies and Stratagems* (Englewood Cliffs, NJ: Prentice-Hall, 1963), p. 34.

3. A Bluff Saves an Underground Chief
Author's archives.
Maurice Buckmaster, *They Fought Alone* (New York: Norton, 1958), pp. 232–234.

4. A Stowaway Lands on a Hostile Beach
Episode told to the author by four-star General Mark W. Clark (Ret.), 1983.

5. Sardine Treats for U-Boat Crews
Author's archives.

6. Heists by the "Oslo Gang"
Anthony Cave Brown, *Bodyguard of Lies* (New York: Harper & Row, 1975), pp. 413, 675.
Author's archives.
E. H. Cookridge, *Inside SOE* (London: Barker, 1966), p. 548.

7. Fashion Model Unmasks German Spy
Aline, Countess of Romanones, *The Spy Wore Red* (New York: Random House, 1987), pp. 17, 258, 269.
Author's archives.

8. A Trojan Horse Ploy
Author's archives.

9. A Cherbourg Priest Plays Kickball
Author's archives.

10. History's Most Incredible Impersonation
Author's archives.
Arthur Bryant, *The Turn of the Tide* (New York: Doubleday, 1957), p. 205.
Viscount Alanbrooke, *Diaries* (London: Collins, 1957), p. 397.
Dwight Eisenhower letter to General George C. Marshall, dated May 21, 1944. Eisenhower Library, Abilene, Kansas.

11. "Black Radio" Blackmails Germans
Charles Cruickshank, *The Fourth Arm* (London: Cassel, 1977), pp. 132, 141.
Sefton Delmer, *Black Boomerang* (New York: Viking, 1962), pp. 97, 108, 204.

12. A Nazi Campaign to Defeat Roosevelt
Charles Hamilton, *Leaders and Personalities in the Third Reich* (San Jose, CA: Bender, 1984), p. 234.
Bruce Lee, *Marching Orders* (New York: Crown, 1995), p. 189.

13. Operation Ferdinand Bamboozles Germans
Author interviews with Vice Admiral John D. Bulkeley (Ret.), 1992, 1994.
Interview with Lieutenant General William P. Yarborough (Ret.), 1993.
Interview with Lieutenant General Richard J. Seitz (Ret.), 1991.
Interview with Captain Douglas Fairbanks, Jr., USNR (Ret.), 1994.

14. Allies Ignore Battle of the Bulge Warning
Robert F. Merriam, *Dark December* (Chicago: Ziff-Davis, 1947), pp. 36–37.
Author's archives.
SRS 1419, September 8, 1944. Records Branch, U.S. Army, Washington, D.C.

15. **Polish Underground Steals Hitler's Secret Weapon**
    Jozef Garlinski, *Hitler's Last Weapons* (New York: Times Books, 1978), pp. 156, 158.
    Author's archives.
    Bohdan Arct, *Poles Against the "V" Weapons* (Warsaw: Interpress, 1972), p. 134.

16. **Grandma Was a Secret Agent**
    Author's archives.

17. **A Pregnant Spy Cuts a Deal**
    U.S. Seventh Army History (privately printed, 1946), pp. 178–179.
    Author's archives.
    Joseph E. Persico, *Piercing the Reich* (New York: Viking, 1979), p. 263.

18. **"Faithful Heinrich" Betrays His Führer**
    John Toland, *Last 100 Days* (New York: Random House, 1966), p. 163.
    Anthony Cave Brown, *Bodyguard of Lies* (New York: Harper & Row, 1975), p. 265.
    Allen W. Dulles, *Germany's Underground* (New York: Macmillan, 1947), p. 145.
    Author's archives.

Index